D1599328

577825

ROBERT HERRICK'S "HESPERIDES"
AND THE EPIGRAM BOOK TRADITION

Pieter Brueghel the Elder, "Land of Cockaigne"
(courtesy of the Bavarian State Collection, Munich)

ANN BAYNES COIRO

Robert Herrick's *Hesperides* and the Epigram Book Tradition

THE JOHNS HOPKINS UNIVERSITY PRESS
BALTIMORE AND LONDON

For Annabel Patterson

This book has been brought to publication with the generous assistance of the Andrew W. Mellon Foundation.

The Johns Hopkins University Press, 701 West 40th Street, Baltimore, Maryland 21211
The Johns Hopkins Press Ltd., London

The paper used in this publication meets the minimum requirements of American National Standard for Information Sciences–Permanence of Paper for Printed Library Materials, ANSI Z39.48-1984.

LIBRARY OF CONGRESS CATALOGING-IN-PUBLICATION DATA
Coiro, Ann Baynes, 1951–
    Robert Herrick's Hesperides and the epigram book tradition.
    Bibliography: p.
    Includes index.
    1. Herrick, Robert, 1591–1674. Hesperides. 2. Epigram. I. Title.
PR3512.H43C6 1988   821'.4   87-22827
ISBN 0-8018-3571-2 (alk. paper)

Contents

Preface and Acknowledgments

୬ଈ୰. This study places Robert Herrick in a new and largely unfamiliar context. The epigram and the epigram book have been set aside by modern criticism as unyielding to postromantic strategies of reading. Because isolated epigrams are often simply scurrilous, flatly definitive, abjectly flattering, or merely clever, they seem to offer no latitude for critical response. But the Renaissance valued epigrams and epigram collections highly, and it is profitable to look at both Herrick and this genre again and together.

The reading of an epigram book is a complicated game of allusion, irony, and qualification, and, therefore, the epigram book requires readers who "read it well," that is, not as small poems in isolation, but as a sequence of poems that together create a work of art. Poems that, alone, are "simple" and "obvious" together expand exponentially. In the collections of Martial and Catullus, where the Renaissance found the classical precedents for the epigram book, lyric and epigram, private and public placed side by side are infected by each other, so that the private voice is spoken on a public stage and in the public voice we hear the individual.

Looking at *Hesperides* from this perspective removes some of the apparent difficulties that have traditionally diminished Herrick's reputation. *Hesperides* has seemed a cumbersome vehicle for a few perfect lyrics. But if we examine the vehicle more closely, we find that the canonical poems become even richer when placed within their ironic and qualifying context.

The first part of the book is devoted to the cultural, political, and generic implications of the title and to "The Argument of his Book," the poem with which Herrick introduces his volume. The second part tells very briefly the epigram book's intricate and little-known history. Although Herrick will sometimes figure only tangentially in this section, a recognition of the genre within which he works is essential for an understanding of *Hesperides*. Finally, in the third part I trace several threads throughout *Hesperides:* the epigrams of praise, those of mockery, those of advice, and the opening and closing poems that frame the volume. I am deeply indebted to previous readings of *Hesperides;* my reading is not intended to deny but to enrich the ways Herrick has been read before.

This study had its beginning in a Folger Institute seminar, and I am grateful to the Institute for the several fellowships that have helped me proceed toward its end. The staff and readers of the Folger have always been an astonishing source of learning and good will upon which I have drawn with gratitude. Peter W. M. Blayney and Laetitia Yeandle, in particular, have been generous with their uncanny knowledge of Renaissance publishing and Renaissance manuscripts. I am also grateful for permission to reprint portions of this work that have appeared elsewhere: part of Chapter 1 appeared, in an earlier version, in *ELH* 52 (1985); an abbreviated version of Chapter 8 appeared in *Renaissance Papers 1986.*

I have been very fortunate in my careful and perceptive readers. Roger Rollin and Claude Summers both gave generously of their extensive knowledge of Herrick and helped clarify the shape of my argument. At the University of Maryland, Morris Friedman, Gary Hamilton, and Joseph Wittreich pointed me in several suggestive directions; Judith Hallett encouraged me to explore Catullus and Martial more extensively; and Joyce Irene Middleton's friendship has meant a great deal. This book took its final form during one exciting year at Hamilton College, and I shall always be grateful to my students and colleagues there. Nancy Sorkin Rabinowitz and Patricia Cholakian, in particular, have been acute readers and friends. Peter J. Rabinowitz read carefully, offered several invaluable suggestions, and helped with all kinds of practical details. Arnetta Correa, Mary Conley, and Debra Layland have understudied for me at home to critical acclaim. I also really want to thank those who, in the words of the eldest, made this all practically impossible—my children Alec, Rhys, and Claire. I shall never be able to repay my husband, David, for all he has done.

Finally, I wish to thank Annabel Patterson. She stood by with firm hand and kind voice through the genesis and development of the dissertation that became the present study. She is a great scholar, a great teacher, and a great friend. It is to her that I dedicate this book.

Part One

LEMMA

HESPERIDES:

OR,

THE WORKS

BOTH

HUMANE & DIVINE

OF

ROBERT HERRICK *Esq.*

OVID.

Effugient avidos Carmina nostra Rogos.

LONDON,

Printed for *John Williams,* and *Francis Eglesfield,*
and are to be sold at the Crown and Marygold
in Saint *Pauls* Church-yard. 1648.

The title page of Robert Herrick's *Hesperides,* 1648
(courtesy of the Folger Shakespeare Library)

CHAPTER ONE

"Read'st my Booke unto the end": The Integrity of *Hesperides*

✣ In 1935 F. R. Leavis characterized Robert Herrick with words that have marked him ever since, that have, in fact, achieved the weight of authority and apparent inevitability in determining Herrick's place in the canon of seventeenth-century literature. Herrick's poetry, according to Leavis, is "trivial." "Herrick's game, Herrick's indulgence . . . does not refer us outside itself . . . we are to be absorbed in . . . the 'solemn' rite."[1] Leavis went on to compare Herrick very briefly, and to Herrick's distinct disadvantage, with Marvell and Carew. A few years later T. S. Eliot constructed a similarly cursory comparison between Herrick and George Herbert, making Herrick, in the process, his paradigmatic "minor" poet.[2]

Herrick's reputation has improved since his service as a whipping boy for the New Criticism. Nevertheless, Leavis's and Eliot's basic assumptions still determine to a surprising degree the way Herrick is perceived today. Illuminating readings have emerged from serious consideration of Leavis's suggestion of ritual (or "ceremony") in Herrick's poetry, but other major features of Herrick's poetry, especially its literary and historical context, have until very recently remained unexamined.[3] Eliot's dismissal in "What Is Minor Poetry?" of the notion that there could be any "continuous purpose" in *Hesperides* authorized the selection and isolation of critically approved poems in anthologies. *Hesperides* itself has been set aside as simply the accidental vehicle for the few poems that criticism has selected out as worthy of sustained attention. The best-known criticism of any of Herrick's poetry, for example, is Cleanth Brooks's close reading of "Corinna's going a Maying," a reading that must, of necessity, ignore the poem's context within *Hesperides*.[4]

I propose that *Hesperides* should be read in its entirety. Indeed, following John L. Kimmey's seminal argument in 1971 that Herrick assembled *Hesperides* "with a firm plan and purpose in mind," the general consensus

of recent criticism is that there is some cohesive pattern to *Hesperides*.[5]
The nature of that integrating structure has not, however, been established.

Robert Herrick is the only Renaissance poet who gathered together
the work of his lifetime into one polished, self-presented and self-present-
ing volume. Surely his poetry should be read upon the terms he himself
makes explicit. Surely, too, the place of *Hesperides* in the Stuart literary
tradition should be weighed more carefully than it has been. Even the
conventional alignment of Herrick with his contemporaries as a member
of a group, a Cavalier poet or a son of Ben, can acquire new resonance if
we stop to consider what Jonson really meant as a model to Herrick, and
whether that model was compatible with Cavalier irresponsibility.

I believe, however, that in order to discover Herrick's larger intentions
in *Hesperides* and to place it properly in its own historical context, we
must recognize the generic tradition within which Herrick wrote. I shall
argue that *Hesperides* is best understood as an epigram book, a genre that
allows lyric and epigram to stand side by side in complicating proximity
and that was open in the Renaissance to an astonishing variety of intentions and interpretations. More than a hundred years ago, Edmund Gosse
observed that "no one carefully reading the *Hesperides* can fail to be
struck with the extraordinary similarity they bear to the epigrams of
Martial, and the parallel will be found to run throughout the writings of
the two poets."[6] Modern scholarship, however, remains remarkably unin-
formed on the structure and function of the epigram book as a distinctive
genre, with the result that, all too often, *Hesperides* has been seen as simply a random and "trivial" collection.

As a point of entry into the density and profusion of Herrick's secular
poetry, it is illuminating to look first at the title Herrick chose for his
volume and at the circumstances of its publication in the critical year of
1648, at the moment of the final collapse of the Stuart regime. Both the
title and the publication date have traditionally been integrated into a
purely lyrical reading of Herrick's poetry in which "Hesperides" is taken
to be simply a classical adornment and 1648 a particularly unfortunate
moment to publish a volume inappropriate to a nation at war. On both
of these specific points I would like to take issue with the traditional critical stance as a way of anticipating a reading of *Hesperides* that proposes a
high degree of contemporary relevance and structural complexity.

꧁꧂. The Stationers' Register records that in 1640 Andrew Crooke applied to publish "the seuerall Poems" of Robert Herrick, but apparently that volume never appeared. Herrick's poetry was published eight years later, not by Andrew Crooke, but by Francis Eglesfield and John Williams in London and Thomas Hunt in Oxford. During the interim between the initial entry in the Stationers' Register and the publication of Herrick's poetry, the civil war began and ended, the king's cause was lost, and Herrick—expelled in 1647 for his royalism from his living in Dean Prior—went to London. There he saw a carefully arranged selection of his poems through the press (a significant number of which appear to have been written after 1640), changing his title from "Poems" to *Hesperides*.

Hesperides is a curious, beautiful, and allusive title.[7] It creates the overarching structure that the 1,130 poems inhabit and remains a hermeneutical device against which each individual poem can be read. The readings we now have of the title, however, are characteristic of an earlier stage of Herrick criticism, when only his lyric poems were selected out of the body of *Hesperides* and praised for their delicacy and miniature precision but faulted for a lack of moral force or breadth of vision. "Hesperides" has been taken to indicate, for example, that the poems are flowers or golden apples in a garden of poetry set in the western lands of Devonshire, or that they are Daughters of Evening and thus poems of later life, or that they are little stars, the daughters of Hesperus, the evening star.[8] But limiting the title to any of these essentially decorative functions trivializes the poetry and minimizes any sense of underlying unity of intention in the volume. When in 1944 T. S. Eliot, for example, compared the literary status of Herrick and Herbert, he found *The Temple* to be "something more than a number of religious poems by one author: it was *as the title is meant to imply*, a book constructed according to a plan" (italics added), but in Herrick Eliot found no significant authorial intention in the title or the volume.

It is clear, however, that there are "continuous purposes" and conscious patterns structuring *Hesperides*. "The Argument of his Book" is, for one thing, a succinct statement of intent. Herrick also frames the volume with eight introductory and eight concluding poems, and he addresses the book throughout, speculating about its fate in the world. Kimmey has discovered a clear narrative thread in *Hesperides* as the persona grows old, leaves the country to return to the city, and finally dies.[9] Herrick also teases us to puzzle out underlying patterns by embedding smaller sequences of cross-reference in *Hesperides*, such as the "Julia" poems, the burial epitaphs, and the series of self-conscious and self-mocking pairs of lyric and epigrammatic poems which are dotted throughout the volume.[10]

One would therefore expect that the title naming this complex volume of jokes and dreams and miniature subversions would have a larger potential meaning than a decorative one can bear. If *Hesperides* is read as an epigram book, the title carries even greater weight, for the lemma, or title of an epigram, is intrinsic to the poem. A true epigram cannot be fully understood without the key that the lemma provides. Title and work are intricately bound.[11]

In the choice of *Hesperides* as his title Herrick does more than signify golden fruit or flowers; he alerts the reader to the classical image of the earthly paradise. The Hesperides were a mythical place associated by both classical writers and the authors of Renaissance mythological dictionaries with death and immortality. They were thus frequently conflated with the Fortunate Isles, the Islands of the Blest, and eventually with Elysium. Most commentary on Herrick's title has seen *Hesperides* as an enclosed garden, but it is a significant aspect of the myth that the Hesperides are, not a walled garden, but two islands separated by a narrow body of water and surrounded by a protecting ocean.[12]

On these islands at the western edge of the world live the daughters of Hesperus (or of Atlas, in some versions), who guard Juno's tree with its freight of golden apples, aided by a dragon who is sometimes read as a metaphor for the surrounding sea. It was the eleventh labor of Hercules to seize the golden apples of immortality and to return safely from the edge of the world. Thus, the myth of the Hesperides has connotations of death confronted and defeated. Since the Hesperides are associated with the Elysian Fields, it is also a place where dead heroes are rewarded in an earthly paradise.

On the other hand, and especially in the seventeenth century, it has associations with the Land of Cockaigne, where all pleasures are gratified without moral strictures. Only twice is the word "Hesperides" itself used in poems by Herrick or attributed to Herrick. In "The Description: Of a Woman," for example, a poem in the manner of Carew's "Rapture" that was not published in *Hesperides* but was attributed to Herrick in the seventeenth century, the Hesperides are the female genitalia:

> But now my Muse hath spied a dark descent
> From this so peerless, precious prominent—
> A milky high way that direction yields

Unto the port mouth of th'Elysian fields—
A place desir'd of all, but got by these,
Whom Love admits to this Hesperides.
Here's golden fruit, that far exceeds all price,
Growing in this love-guarded paradise.
Above the entrance, there is written this:
This is the portal to the bower of bliss.

("The Description: Of a Woman,"
s-6, ll. 65–74)[13]

If "The Description" is Herrick's, he nevertheless did not include it in *Hesperides*. Ominously, the only poem that refers to "Hesperides" within *Hesperides* is a warning "To Virgins" of the rape implicit in the myth:

Heare ye Virgins, and Ile teach,
What the times of old did preach.
Rosamond was in a Bower
Kept, as *Danae* in a Tower:
But yet Love (who subtile is)
Crept to that, and came to this.
Be ye lockt up like to these,
Or the rich *Hesperides;*
Or those Babies in your eyes,
In their Christall Nunneries;
Notwithstanding Love will win,
Or else force a passage in:
And as coy be, as you can,
Gifts will get ye, or the man.

(H-297)

In fact, within the context of *Hesperides* itself, the pleasures (or dangers) of sexual consummation are nowhere to be found.[14] If in *Hesperides* Herrick circles sexual consummation with attraction and fear, however, he offers abundant varieties of other sensual pleasures, especially those of rich odors, beautiful sights, and reeling drunkenness.

Abraham Cowley's "A Dream of Elysium" (1633) provides a neat synopsis of each of these three possible interpretations of the earthly paradise. Here are "Trees with golden Apples loaded down" surrounded by all the world's great poets who have earned "A large reward for their past deeds, and gaine / A life, as everlasting as their Fame":

By these, the valiant heroes take their place,
All who sterne Death and perils did imbrace,
For Vertues cause . . .

. . . .

Next them, beneath a Mirtle Bowre, where Doves,
And gall-lesse Pidgeons build their nests, all Loves
Faithful perseverers, with amorous kisses,
And soft imbraces taste their greediest wishes.[15]

Each of these aspects of the earthly paradise—poetic immortality, a "rich Plantation" of heroes, and sensual indulgence—figures centrally in Herrick's *Hesperides*.

Finally, in Elizabethan and early Stuart England, the myth of a garden island on the western edge of the world had potent national significance. The Hesperides, or the Fortunate Isles, became a Renaissance commonplace for England itself. Both ancient geography and classical mythology linked Hesperides with England and lent authority to an identification that exactly suited England's self-image under Elizabeth, an island set apart and blessed with another Golden Age under another Astraea.[16] From Spenser's *Faerie Queene* to Drayton's *Muses' Elisium* and *Poly-Olbion*, from John of Gaunt's plea to Richard II for "this other Eden, demi-paradise" to Ben Jonson's Stuart masques, her poets identified England with the Fortunate Isles. One of Jonson's goals in his masques was to transfer successfully to James the powerful image of Elizabeth's blessed island. In *The Fortunate Isles and their Union*, for example, Jonson builds the entire masque upon the association of England with Hesperides in order to praise James, first king of all Britain.

If Herrick were an Elizabethan poet, or if he had published the volume earlier in his life, a modern reader would make the connection immediately between *Hesperides* and England itself. But by the end of the Caroline reign, just months before the execution of Charles I, the imagery of a golden age on an edenic island had faltered and failed. It is the tenuous, decaying nature of the image that becomes part of its evocative force as the title of Herrick's poetry. The titular myth is an extended metaphor both for a disintegrating national dream and for the role of the artist in a revolutionary society, especially since each of the key elements of the Hesperides myth—the island and the nymphs, the golden apples, the tree, and Hercules—appears recurrently throughout the volume, with the result that the myth gradually acquires thematic status.

It is clear from Herrick's poetry that he had invested heavily in the Stuart myths. Poems written earlier in his career are lyric encomia to the idea of kingship, and these poems are clear evidence of Herrick's strong attraction to order and ceremony. But as he arranged his volume for publication in 1648, all of the individual poems are complicated and sometimes undercut by their context in the whole volume. Indeed, it is the high finish of the royalist iconography and its clear importance to Herrick's poetic that makes the force of its questioning in *Hesperides* powerful and disturbing. The lyrics of royal praise, for example, become more and more hedged in by frank epigrams critical of Stuart policy. The lyric poems diminish in number and are replaced by sententious epigrams. The *carpe diem* poems become more deeply poignant next to the late poems on the civil war, poems that Herrick places throughout the volume, including its pastoral opening, as warnings that this island paradise exists in time. *Hesperides*, as a whole, goes beyond royalist propaganda, using its recognized forms, symbols, and allusions to question the efficacy of that cultural program. Each element of the Hesperidean myth appears in the volume first as a conventional compliment to the Stuarts but then as an ironic questioning of Stuart ideals and perhaps of panegyric poetry itself. By tracing the images of the garden, the apples, the tree, and Hercules through the volume, it is possible to see the ambiguity of Herrick's *Hesperides*. If we grant Herrick the capacity for irony, for self-mockery, and for deliberate resonance in the presentation of his volume, then I believe we can read the volume itself with new eyes.

꧁꧂ Renaissance mythological dictionaries organized classical literature and humanist learning under proper and place names and were useful reference tools for Renaissance poets, including Spenser, Jonson, and Milton.[17] D. J. Gordon has called these dictionaries "the common property of Europe, the everyday authorities on classical mythology."[18] For modern readers, the dictionaries are an invaluable guide to the poetic shorthand available to Renaissance writers. The entry for the "Atlanticae Insulae" in Charles Stephanus's *Dictionarium*, for example, shows how felicitous was the ancient identification of England with the western islands. Stephanus describes

two islands which they call the Blessed and the Fortunate. These, separated from each other by a small space of sea, are a thousand miles distant from

Africa. . . . There, as Homer and other poets say, are the Elysian fields and the homes of the Blest. Pliny seems to call these islands the Hesperides.

For further information, Stephanus directs the reader to the entry for "De Campiis Elysiis" in Natale Conti's *Mythologiae,* where Conti describes a place strongly reminiscent of Herrick's Hesperides:

There the winds, most sweet and fragrant, blow gently, as if crossing over an incredible variety and sweetness of flowers. For, as is the perfume of many roses, violets, hyacinths, narcissi, myrtles, laurel, cypress, such is the sweetness of the breathing breezes. . . . Here it is always spring.

Conti then includes a passage of Tibullus which lends classical authority to his description:

But me, because I am always affable to tender love, Venus herself leads into the Elysian fields. Here are dancing and singing, and the ranging birds echoing the sweet song in their throat. The untilled land brings the odors of casia and the benign earth blooms with fragrant roses. A train of youths plays in the company of maids, and assiduously Love embroils the battle.[19]

This world of flowers suggests the hundreds of floral poems in *Hesperides* and the "train of youths" which "plays in the company of maids," while "Love embroils the battle" suggests "Corinna's going a Maying." More specifically, one of Herrick's longest poems—and one in which imagery and resolution are characteristic of his poetry in general—begins with extended borrowings from the same passage of Tibullus that Conti had used to describe the "Atlanticae Insulae." In "The Apparition of his Mistresse calling him to Elizium" (H-575), she cajoles:

> Let our soules flie to'th'shades, where ever springs
> Sit smiling in the Meads; where Balme and Oile,
> Roses and Cassia crown the untill'd soyle.
> . . . .
> Where ev'ry tree a wealthy issue beares
> Of fragrant Apples, blushing Plums, or Peares:
> And all the shrubs, with sparkling spangles, shew
> Like Morning-Sun-shine tinsilling the dew.
> Here in green Meddowes sits eternall May,
> Purfling the Margents, while perpetuall Day
> So double gilds the Aire, as that no night
> Can ever rust th'Enamel of the light.

Here, naked Younglings, handsome Striplings run
Their Goales for Virgins kisses; which when done,
Then unto Dancing forth the learned Round
Commixt they meet, with endlesse Roses crown'd.
And here we'l sit on Primrose-banks, and see
Love's *Chorus* led by *Cupid;* and we'l be
Two loving followers too unto the Grove.

Herrick's mistress draws both the poet and the reader into this extended fantasy of a "Grove" where there is always spring and always daylight, where the great poets live as demigods; but at the end of the poem, the fantasy is revealed to be a dream. What appears to be daylight is only "double gilded"; in reality, this is a place where "Night determines."

The movement from dreaming fantasy to disillusioning reality which "The Apparition" creates is a paradigm for the entire volume. Many of Herrick's poems are a duplication of this mythic land of eternal spring, especially those in the first half of *Hesperides*. But the death that is implicit in the *carpe diem* poems becomes more and more frequently explicit in *Hesperides*, and the poetry of eternal beauty is counterpointed by burial epitaphs and by sententious or mocking epigrams that shatter the vision of Eden.

The placement of "The Apparition" in *Hesperides* is, I would argue, intentional and highly significant. At the center of *Hesperides*, Herrick explicitly acknowledges the seductive power of the pastoral shade and ceremonial game, and he simultaneously acknowledges that poetry is a fragile illusion. The epigraph of "The Apparition" is "Desunt nonulla . . ." [Some things are lacking . . .]. The poem is incomplete on a literal level because the cock has crowed and driven away the charming specter of the poet's Muse. But beyond that, the lovely place and the lovely poem are both fantasies and both incomplete because they are at odds with reality. This "Elizium" and the larger "Hesperides" at whose center the poem lies are visions of an earthly paradise created by poetry but proven insubstantial by the cold light of day.

Indeed, there is a clear turning point in the development of tone, imagery, and form in *Hesperides*. Many critics have noted the change in the course of the volume to shorter and more pessimistic poems. Kimmey has identified the century of poems from H-600 to H-700, the center of the volume, as the phase in which the poet's attitude and technique begin to change from lyric celebration of beauty to serious moral advice or crude mockery, with fewer and fewer "mistress" poems.[20] In other words, the tension between the lyric and the epigrammatic vision, which the poet portrays in little throughout, is writ large in the volume itself. Among these hundred poems are clear laments for England's position in the late 1630s and 1640s: "Upon the troublesome times" (H-596), "The bad season makes the Poet sad" (H-612), "The Poet hath lost his pipe" (H-573). It is here, at almost the precise, mathematical center of *Hesperides,* that Herrick placed "The Apparition of his Mistresse calling him to Elizium," first published in 1640 but probably written before 1637. "The Apparition" is one of Herrick's longest poems, but it stands at the threshold of that phase of the volume where the two- and four-line epigram becomes the dominant form. The iambic pentameter of "The Apparition" is itself cut off by one clipped, tetrameter couplet:

> I vanish; more I had to say;
> But Night determines here, Away.

Both thematically and formally, then, "The Apparition" is a key transition, a pivot in *Hesperides.*

There is no way to draw exact conclusions about the distribution of optimism and pessimism in Herrick's poetry, although there are recognizable moods and patterns in the volume. Similarly, although generally poems that we know were written earlier are in the first half of the volume and later poems in the second half, the poems are arranged skillfully enough to keep the reader from making complacent assumptions about chronology.[21] Nevertheless, it can be said that most of the poems in praise of Cupid, the flower poems, and the poems of mythic happiness occur in the first half of *Hesperides* and that in this first half the mythic land is closely linked to the actual island of England, transmuted into an ideal country.[22] Herrick does not rely solely on the commonplace identification of Hesperides with England but makes the connection explicit by introducing the Stuart monarchy into his island from the start. The title page is stamped with a richly decorated crown; the prefatory poem dedicates the volume to Charles, Prince of Wales; and the whole book is divided by poems to the royal family placed in key, privileged positions. Near the beginning of *Hesperides,* for example, there is an important triad of poems addressed to the royal family in mythological terms. Henrietta Maria becomes a goddess who is invited to rest in *"This Sacred Grove"* (H-265); James, duke of York, is the "Soveraigne of [the Muses'] Spring" and the "Prince of *Hellicon*" (H-266); Charles I rules "This *great Realme of*

Poetry" (H-264); and Charles, Prince of Wales, becomes Hesperus himself in the prefatory poem. By using the imagery of the Hesperides myth, Herrick elevates the Stuarts to a position as dual rulers of both a poetic and a political kingdom. *Hesperides* is not only a garden of flowers, but England itself.

It is only in the first half of *Hesperides*, however, that this vision of England and its monarchy holds a central artistic place. A series of poems addressed or referring to Charles I and his son Charles clarify the changing sense of place in *Hesperides*. The first in time of composition, "A Pastorall upon the birth of Prince Charles" (H-213A), is an eclogue celebrating the birth of Prince Charles on May 29, 1630, and was probably sung before the king at court. Amintas and Amarillis, two shepherds who have remained with their flocks, welcome back a friend, Mirtillo, who has been at court. He tells of the birth of the heir and how it was marked by the appearance "At Noone of Day" of "a silver Star." The star is used further to reinforce the Christic symbolism imposed on Charles's birth, but what is not made explicit is that it was Hesperus, the evening star, and therefore a rather inauspicious omen, that made its unusual appearance on that day.[23] In light of this poem and of the prefatory poem, where the "star-led" birth is also central, then, the title of *Hesperides* itself becomes part of an extended compliment to the Prince of Wales, whose star, however, was both something of a prodigy and associated with endings, rather than beginnings.

In a second pastoral poem ("A Pastorall sung to the King," H-421), again spoken by three shepherds, the similarity of genre and procedure serves to mark the change of tone. Again it is Mirtillo who has been to court and who returns to the pastoral world, but this time the subject is Amarillis and her departure from the shepherds' paradise, which leaves not only Mirtillo bereft but the pastoral world disordered:

> Mon. Bad are the times. Sil. And wors then they are we.
> Mon. Troth, bad are both; worse fruit, and ill the tree:
> The feast of Shepheards fails. . . .

J. Max Patrick suggests a probable date of composition for this pastoral of either 1642, when Henrietta Maria temporarily went abroad, or 1644, when she left England permanently.[24] Amarillis is, thus, the queen, and her absence from the world of *Hesperides* has the same effect on the seasons as the rape of Proserpina. This poem is, therefore, implicitly connected with another, which, though addressed to the poet's self rather than to any members of the royal family, further articulates the seasonal myth. Tellingly, Herrick placed "The bad season makes the Poet sad" (H-612) at almost the precise midpoint of *Hesperides:*

> Dull to my selfe, and almost dead to these
> My many fresh and fragrant Mistresses:
> Lost to all Musick now; since every thing
> Puts on the semblance here of sorrowing.
> Sick is the Land to'th'heart. . . .

Whereas the image of a garden of eternal spring is at first a vehicle for praise, it becomes ultimately laden with regret—regret not only for a lost ideal but, more dramatically, for the poet's loss of power. There is an increasing sense of desperation as the poet is exiled from the pastoral world that enabled him to sing. The powerful threat of time comes to bear another weight of meaning for the poet; in these "untuneable Times" (H-210), these "troublesome times,"

> Where shall I goe,
> Or whither run
>   To shun
> This publique overthrow?
>   (H-596)

The golden apples, the second element of the Hesperides myth, have usually been taken to represent Herrick's poems. Within the context of the myth, the Herculean apples of immortality are an appropriate emblem for a volume governed by the ideal of poetic immortality. Early in the volume, in his exuberant poem "To live merrily, and to trust to Good Verses" (H-201), Herrick presented the golden apples as a composite image of inspiration and intoxication:

> Now is the time for mirth,
>   Nor cheek, or tongue be dumbe:
> For with the flowrie earth,
>   The golden pomp is come.
>
> The golden Pomp is come;
>   For now each tree do's weare
> (Made of her Pap and Gum)
>   Rich beades of *Amber* here.

. . . .

Trust to good Verses then;
   They onely will aspire,
When Pyramids, as men,
   Are lost, i'th'funerall fire.

And when all Bodies meet
   In *Lethe* to be drown'd;
Then onely Numbers sweet,
   With endless life are crown'd.

Just as the veiled rose, the "Christal'd Lillie," and the fly within the amber bead are more beautiful for being artfully embedded and metamorphosed, so too the diurnal world is only beautiful forever in the metamorphosis of poetry.

But since the immortality of poetry is arguably the most important principle of Herrick's aesthetic, its source of immortality has to be more complicated. In the prefatory poem, Herrick had constructed a witty compliment to Prince Charles as Hesperus, proposing him as the instrument of the poet's immortality. Patrick feels that Herrick "almost certainly" wrote this poem for the volume he intended to publish in 1640, since in that year Charles was to be formally presented as Prince of Wales.[25] There is no specific mention in the poem of Hesperus, and this poem is, in general, an adult version of the compliment Herrick paid Charles in "A Pastorall upon the birth of Prince Charles" (H-213A).

In 1648 the fortunes of the royal family had altered still further for the worse, and Prince Charles could no longer serve as a guarantee of the poet's or even poetry's survival. The last poem addressed to Prince Charles in *Hesperides* is on the occasion of "his coming to Exeter" (H-756) on August 29, 1645. This poem is spoken in the voice of the latter half of the volume, one of qualified praise strongly tempered by advice. Charles has triumphed in Exeter, but "Something there yet remaines for Thee to do":

Meane time thy Prophets Watch by Watch shall pray;
While young Charles fights, and fighting wins the day.
That done, our smooth-pac't Poems all shall be
Sung in the high Doxologie of Thee.

                           (italics added)

15

It is now Charles who may receive immortality from his poets, on the condition that he succeed. This is a radical shift from the prefatory poem and one that is consistent with the most moving and final royal poem in *Hesperides*, "TO THE KING, Upon his welcome to Hampton-Court" (H-961). By August 1647, Charles was in the custody of the army and under virtual house arrest at Hampton Court. Herrick's poem celebrates Charles's return to his "long'd-for home" and bids him

> Enter and prosper, *while our eyes doe waite*
> For an Ascendent throughly Auspicate:
> Under which signe we may the former stone
> Lay of our safeties new foundation:
> *That done;* O Cesar, live, and be to us,
> Our Fate, our Fortune, and our Genius;
> To whose free knees we may our temples tye
> As to a still protecting Deitie.
>
> (italics added)

The king's prophets now stand in a different relationship to him. It is they who have the power to bequeath divinity on him through their art. The poem implies that even if Charles were to be freed in a compromise with the military, he would be little more than a figurehead, set up and regarded by his poets "*as to* a still protecting Deitie." Indeed, the poem hints at an even darker possibility—that the king's very life may be in danger.[26]

It is therefore clear that at least by the 1640s Herrick believes that the golden apples of immortality are earned by poets and not bequeathed by rulers. When Herrick praises Denham's "Cooper's Hill" in 1642, for example, he concludes:

> . . . yet live Princes under thee:
> The while their wreaths and Purple Robes do shine,
> Lesse by their own jemms, then those beams of thine.
>
> (H-673)

And at the very end of the volume he returns, not surprisingly, to this central theme. The first poem of *Hesperides* invoked the immortality bestowed by divine-right monarchy, but the final poem reflects the political situation of England in 1648:

Fames pillar here, at last, we set,
Out-during *Marble, Brasse,* or *Jet,*
Charm'd and enchanted so,
As to withstand the blow
Of   overthrow:
Nor shall the seas,
Or O U T R A G E S
Of storms orebear
What we up-rear,
Tho Kingdoms fal,
This pillar never shall
Decline or waste at all;
But stand for ever by his owne
Firme and well fixt foundation.

(H-1129)

Just as the dedicatory poem to Prince Charles is conventional, so too is this final shaped poem on the immortalizing power of poetry. The conventional nature of "The pillar of Fame" does not, however, lessen its force at the end of *Hesperides.* Closing the frame of the volume that opened with a page defiantly (and ominously) stamped both with a crown and the date 1648, the "pillar"'s conventional stance that poetry will survive fallen kingdoms takes on vivid force. Surely Herrick and his contemporary readers recognized the significance of this pillar, with its terrible, dizzying turn on the last dimeter line, "Tho Kingdoms fal."

It is significant, too, that by the end of this process of poetic and political maturation the symbol of permanence has had to be changed. While the golden apples were an adequate symbol of magical powers, capable of transmission from kings to poets, what Herrick needed for his later vision of that relationship was something man-made, solidly and patiently constructed against adversity.

The third element of the myth, the tree, becomes a central metaphor in Herrick's garden, functioning in one sense as the protective, pastoral shade under which so many of the idyllic poems in *Hesperides* are written. At the same time, it is a standard Stuart metaphor for Charles I, the pastoral king, the metaphor that Charles himself chose as an emblem for his reign.[27] As the Prince of Wales, Charles was to have been presented to the court in Jonson's masque *Neptune's Triumph for the Return of Albion* as embowered in a *"Tree of Harmonie,"* and almost without exception

17

Lemma

Charles was shown in his great state paintings under his signature oak.[28]
Perhaps the most magnificent icon of Charles's reign is Van Dyck's vast
painting, circa 1635, of *Charles I on Horseback*, where the king sits under
a spreading oak to which is tied the inscription in Latin, "Charles, King
of Great Britain."[29] In James Howell's royalist allegory, *Dodona's Grove,
or the Vocall Forest* (1640), Charles becomes an oak and England a talking
forest: "Under the Branches of the Stately Caledonian Oke . . . the Lillies
and Roses White and Red, did bourgeon round about him, the Muses and
Graces made Festivals, the Fauns, Satyrs, and Nymphs did dance their
Roundelays, all the Trees of the field did clap their hands; and never was
seen such Halcyonian dayes."[30] Howell's description of England demonstrates how intrinsic to Stuart propaganda was the idea of a new golden
age under Charles.

   In his poetry, Herrick uses the same symbol of the royal tree to praise
Charles, but he also uses it to warn him. In one of the important royalist
poems in *Hesperides,* "TO THE KING, to cure the Evill" (H-161), the poet
praises the divine nature of the king with fabulous passion as "that Tree
of Life, whose Fruits did feed, / And Leaves did heale, all sick of humane
seed." Charles's hand is a *"Magick Bough"* and a "high Enchantment." The
king's touch will cure both the poet and the garden of all evil.[31] Claude
Summers has demonstrated how this poem is both an encomium to the
king and "a serious comment on national affairs," a warning to England
to submit "to the healing ritual of kingship."[32] That the idea of a king is
a "high Enchantment" to Herrick is certainly demonstrated in "The bad
season" as well. When the Hesperidean spring has ended and the poet is
rendered almost mute by winter, the thought of Charles again in his
rightful place so exhilarates the poet that his voice lifts in the end to an
excited crescendo; it is important to note, however, that the poet's tri-
umphal vision is thickly hedged by qualifiers and shadowed by the poet's
obsessive awareness of his own imminent death:

> But *if* that golden Age *wo'd* come again,
> And Charles here Rule, as he before did Raign;
> *If* smooth and unperplext the Seasons were,
> As when the Sweet Maria lived here:
> I *sho'd* delight to have my Curles halfe drown'd
> In Tyrian Dewes, and Head with Roses crown'd.
> And once more yet (ere I am laid out dead)
> Knock at a Starre with my exalted Head.
>
> (H-612; italics added)

18

The emphatic distinction that Herrick makes between the former "Raign" of Charles and the possibility of a future "Rule" points to the argument that Herrick makes in epigrams throughout *Hesperides:* that a king must actively rule his people rather than rely only upon the panoply of his ceremonial kingship.

As the volume progresses, it becomes more and more difficult for the poet to believe that the "smooth and unperplext" season will return. His last attempt to cling to the English Hesperides is an allegorical vision of England after the civil war, "Farwell Frost, or welcome the Spring" (H-642), placed past the midpoint of the volume. Herrick's allegory, like Howell's, portrays England as a forest and the king as an oak, but here the oak is torn by savage storms. "Farwell Frost" predicts that the oak will survive and offer the "Branch of Peace." By the end of *Hesperides*, however, the title becomes at best nostalgic. Just as all the flowers in the garden will die, so too will the royal oak. In an early epigram as hard-edged and clear in its message as some of the royal lyrics are euphoric, Herrick prophesies:

> *All things decay with Time:* The Forrest sees
> The growth, and down-fall of her aged trees:
> That Timber tall, which three-score *lusters* stood
> The proud *Dictator* of the State-like wood:
> I meane (the Soveraigne of all Plants) the Oke
> Droops, dies, and falls without the cleavers stroke.
>
> (H-69)

Although Herrick is traditionally seen as an unquestioning royalist like Howell, his metaphor of the oak felled by its own weakness is closer to the worm-eaten royal oak in Marvell's Nunappleton poem.[33]

The final element of the Hesperides myth is, of course, Hercules himself, the male principle violating the feminine garden. Herrick occasionally puns with his own name and plays with the idea of himself as Hercules among his nymphs, but, as Gorden Braden has pointed out, in spite of all the nymphs that the poet inveigles, there is not a single consummation in *Hesperides*.[34] The Herrick / Herakles pun is characteristic of the self-mockery that makes Herrick's prettiness more than it seems.

Politically, the symbolism of Hercules, like so much else in *Hesperides*, is ambiguous. On the one hand, Hercules is traditionally a moral hero, a champion of virtue, and a dedicated opponent of tyrants. In *Mystagogus Poeticus, or the Muses Interpreter* (1647), Alexander Ross described Hercules as "the type of a good King, who ought to subdue all monsters,

Lemma

cruelty, disorder, and oppression in his Kingdom, who should support the Heaven of the Church with the Shoulders of Authority"; and Earl Miner explains the imagery of Hercules as "traditional and the distinctions exact. . . . Hercules, the active and princely hero, is the prototype of the 'Warlike Prince.'"[35] Henrietta Maria's warrior father, Henry IV, based an elaborate state propaganda campaign on the identification of himself as the "Gallic Hercules," the military hero who would usher a new golden age into France.[36]

As Stuart rhetoric, however, the introduction of a myth associated with Hercules seems to be a strange complication. The "Warrior Prince" was not the mythological emblem that the Stuarts chose for themselves. Hercules appears in his warrior guise on a side panel of the Whitehall Banqueting House ceiling, fiercely clubbing a snaky-headed woman, but this panel is balanced by the rest of the ceiling's iconography, which insistently stresses peace over strife. Hercules himself is counterbalanced by Wisdom.[37]

When Hercules' Hesperidean labor does enter the vocabulary of Stuart masques, it is rewritten. In Thomas Carew's *Coelum Britannicum* (1634), for example, all the heavens are rearranged, and the Olympian gods give up their time-honored vices before Charles can appear at the end of the masque in a new kind of Hesperides:

> These are th'Hesperian bowers, whose faire trees beare
> Rich golden fruit, and yet no Dragon near.
>
> . . . .
>
> Pace forth thou mighty British HERCULES,
> With thy choyce band, for onely thou, and these,
> May revell here, in Loves Hesperides.[38]

The British Hercules is Charles I, and his "choyce band" consists of all the ancient British heroes, but they enter an easy garden, with no protecting dragon. This ceremonial Hercules created by his court poets should be read in the extraordinarily ironic context of Carew's "In answer to an Elegiacall Letter upon the death of the King of Sweden," written in indirect praise of Gustavus Adolphus, killed in 1632.[39] Carew argues that such a noble hero is above the pitch of the British muse; instead:

> . . . these are subjects proper to our clyme.
> Tourneyes, Masques, Theaters, better become
> Our *Halcyon* dayes; what though the German Drum

Bellow for freedome and revenge, the noyse
Concernes not us, nor should divert our joyes.

(ll. 94–98)

Instead of avenging the Protestant hero, the British will sit "Vnder secure shades" (l. 46) in what appears to be a rather decadent peace, just as the British Hercules will relax in "a delicious garden" rather than defeat tyrants as he would have done before Charles's poets rewrote the myth.

The fact that Hercules was himself an imperfect hero further complicates the image. It has been argued, for example, that James I was displeased with Jonson's masque *Pleasure Reconciled to Virtue*, since Comus, the "belly-god" parody of Hercules in the antimasque, struck him as uncomfortably close to the gluttonous excesses of his own court.[40]

Hercules was also the Renaissance emblem of a warrior emasculated by feminine dominion. In the *Defence of Poesy*, Sidney says of the image of Hercules "in a womans attyre, spinning, at *Omphales* commaundement" that "it breedes both delight and laughter: for the representing of so straunge a power in Love, procures delight, and the scornefulnesse of the action, stirreth laughter."[41] The strange power of love was represented to Stuart England in the influence Queen Henrietta Maria was known to have over her king, which was resented by royalists and parliamentarians alike. From the first, Charles had been associated with a softer Hercules in the mythology of the Stuart masques; Jonson had welcomed Charles to manhood in a masque about Hercules and his famous choice made at the crossroads between two beautiful women, Pleasure and Virtue.[42] Traditionally, Hercules chose Virtue, abjuring a life of ease forever. In the main masque of *Pleasure Reconciled to Virtue*, however, Charles is to be trusted with pleasure, as his father, styled in the masque "HESPERUS, ye glory of ye WEST, the brightest star, y^t from his burning Crest / lights all on this side y^e *Atlantick seas*," and Hercules watch.[43] Virtue gives Charles "an entraunce to the *Hesperides*, / faire *Beuties garden*," where she will stand watch that he not "grow soft, or wax effeminat here," the danger traditionally inherent in any island of unearned peace and prosperity.

In 1648, in light of Charles's ineffectual reign and failed military effort against the parliamentarians, the implied presence of the Herculean hero in the softly feminine garden of the *Hesperides* is a way of suggesting the tensions and failures in Stuart idealism.

Hesperides as a name, then, belongs to the special vocabulary of the Stuart masque. Jonson draws frequently upon the western paradise in his masques, as does Carew in *Coelum Britannicum*.[44] Even in Milton's atypical masque, *Comus*, the Hesperides shimmer at the edge of the forest where the "mansion" of the Attendant Spirit lies:

> All amidst the Gardens fair
> Of *Hesperus*, and his daughters three
> That sing about the golden tree.
> . . . .
>   [where] eternal Summer dwells[45]

and stands in airy contrast to the grosser attractions of Comus.

Herrick bows to the memory of Ben Jonson throughout *Hesperides*. His title can certainly be read as his personal variation on Jonson's *Forrest* or *Under-wood*, but it also suggests the titles of Jonson's masques like *The Fortunate Isles* or *The Golden Age Restored*, and it may even be revealing to consider *Hesperides* as a poetic masque, the quintessential Stuart art form.[46] Not only did the Stuarts use the masque to express and vindicate their belief in kingship by divine right, but, ironically, they allowed the masques to blind them to the reality of their situation. Year after year during the eleven years of personal rule, Charles and Henrietta Maria gave each other extravagantly expensive compliments in which Charles became the sun, or in which he rearranged the heavens, or "repastoralized" England into a verdant Eden, and all that time the monarchy fell deeper and deeper into debt and deeper out of favor with the people they ruled.[47] The masque became both the apotheosis of the Stuart monarchy and its hollow mockery.

In part, the mockery we may hear in any masque is retrospective (and, of course, by 1648 Herrick's recall of the masque form would also be retrospective). But even during the height of the power and influence of the Stuarts and their masques the masque was, as a genre, deeply and inherently problematic. It may be naive to believe, for example, that the masque can be read as simply as Jonson would have it in the address "To make the Spectators vnderstanders" prefacing *Loves Triumph through Callipolis* (1630):

Whereas all Repraesentations, especially those of this nature in court, publique Spectacles, eyther haue bene, or ought to be the mirrors of mans life, whose ends, for the excellence of their exhibiters (as being the donatiues of great Princes, to their people) ought alwayes to carry a mixture of profit, with them, no lesse then delight.[48]

Stephen Orgel and Roy Strong choose this as "a very precise statement of how Jonson conceived the masque to work." The court was to see "not an imitation of itself, but its true self," an affirmation of "the identity of fictive and real."[49] Even within this "precise" statement, however, is audible Jonson's discomfort with such "publique Spectacles," which he wrote "commanded from the King." The "mixture of profit," the "ought to be," sound more like hints of Jonsonian satire than pure panegyric delivered on command.[50]

The structure of the Stuart masque from 1616 onward was invariable. It opened with an antimasque that, as Stephen Orgel describes it, "presented a world of disorder or vice, everything that the ideal world of the second, the courtly main masque, was to overcome and supersede" and progresses to a final pastoral resolution, which embodies "the ultimate ideal that the masque asserts."[51] The antimasques in Jonson's plays, for example, occasionally employ crude humor or lower-class figures who speak in broad dialects. At times the antimasque goes beyond offending decorum to become positively menacing, such as the antimasque of murderous hags in *The Masque of Queens*. Jonson's main masques are extravagantly complimentary, as in *Chloridia*, written for Henrietta Maria, in which the queen's presence showers the whole world and even Hell itself with the flowers of spring.

It is important to remember that Jonson's "mirrors of mans life" do reflect *both* the ideal of the main masque and the coarse and sometimes threatening reality of the antimasque. By 1640, the final year in which masques were performed for royalty, they held up a mirror that clearly reflected not the softened edges of royalist affirmation but carnival images of disorder. Davenant's *Salmacida Spolia*, for example, the last Stuart masque, is explicitly "foreboding."[52] The power of the king as a symbolic ideal, capable of spreading order and fertility—the central conceit of every masque written up until this historical moment—fails in *Salmacida Spolia*. "Philogenes," the "Lover of his People," can only endure the malignant power of Discord, not defeat it: "'tis his fate to rule in adverse times / When wisdom must awhile give place to crimes." The chorus can only "grieve" that the blessings of the king and queen "are too great to last." Finally, the people's wrath and ingratitude will not be calmed, but will rise up. The king becomes not a magical, mythological deity, but an image of the suffering Christ.

The title of Davenant's masque is itself double-edged. Davenant carefully explains that the "spoils of Salmacis" is the peace that resulted when barbarous invaders drank from the stream and were "reduced . . . to the sweetness of the Grecian customs" (2:730). But the fountain of Salmacis was a mythic code that, in spite of Davenant's elaborate explanation, carried an extraordinarily ambivalent meaning. (And some explanation was certainly needed, since the fountain of Salmacis never figures in the masque itself. The title functions, finally, as an elaborate gloss upon the text.) The fountain of Salmacis created Hermaphrodite, a figure that CARLOMARIA attempted to make a triumphant emblem of their reign but that in high Renaissance culture symbolized "luxury, idleness, and effeminate pleasures."[53] *Salmacida Spolia* can be read, therefore, as a deeply pessimistic and saddened prediction of the fate of the absolute monarch, an apotheosis of the king into a figure of Christlike suffering and, at the same time, a murmured reminder of the conditions of the Stuart court that contributed to the triumph of Discord.

Similarly, the *Hesperides* of Robert Herrick opens on a scene of pastoral beauty decorated with flowers and cupids. One of the earliest poems in the volume is a graceful "Song to the Maskers" (H-15), and all the way through to the middle of the volume are charming poems about Mab and Oberon and the English country fairies of cream bowls and innocent pinches. It is the "merrie England" that Leah Marcus has described, a place of country festivals, hockcarts, and Maypoles, where the king and queen are given central roles as rulers in "This *great Realme of Poetry.*"

But *Hesperides* is a masque turned upside down, with the antimasque voices of mockery, disorder, and warning raised very strongly at the end and never returned to their marginalized position. Here are Grudgings, Loach, and Zelot; here is poverty and old age. Here, too, are the realistic poems of advice to the king. Running through the second half of the volume is a series of "Hag" poems, borrowed directly from the antimasque of Jonson's *Masque of Queens* and standing in direct contrast to the benign fairy poems of the first half of the volume.[54] A comparison of two framing poems from the beginning and end of the volume, one a masque and one an antimasque song, shows the powerful and disturbing difference. "A Song to the Maskers" lies fifteen poems from the beginning of *Hesperides* and is based upon a conceit, typical of Herrick, that the dancers' sweat is "oyle of Roses," delighting the spectators:

> As Goddesse *Isis* (when she went,
>   Or glided through the street)

Made all that touch't her with her scent,
And whom she touch't, turne sweet.

(H-15)

At the other end of the volume, eight poems from the end of *Hesperides*, Herrick placed the final "Hag" poem (H-1122), which stands in grotesque contrast to the masquing song:

The staffe is now greas'd,
And very well pleas'd,
She cockes out her Arse at the parting,
To an old Ram Goat,
That rattles i'th'throat,
Halfe choakt with the stink of her farting.

The violent disgust of this poem is part of the sense of farewell at the end of *Hesperides*. It is clear at this point that the theatrical and decorative garden has become impossible to maintain as an enclosed space from which such shocking realism can be excluded.

Eight years after the appearance of *Hesperides*, Robert Fletcher published *Ex otio Negotium. Or Martiall His Epigrams Translated* (1656). One of the original poems Fletcher contributed to the volume, "Another [Epigram on the people of England]," demonstrates a contemporary use of the metaphor of Hesperides from a political perspective different from Herrick's:

Brittain a lovely Orchard seem'd to be
Furnished with nature's choise varietie,
Temptatious golden fruit of every sort,
Th' Hesperian Garden fann'd from fein'd report,
Great boyes and smal together in we brake,
No matter what disdain'd Priapus spake,
Up, up we lift the great Boyes in the trees,
Hoping a common share to sympathize:
But they no sooner there neglected streight
The shoulders that so rais'd them to this height;
And fell to stuffing of their own bags first,
And as their treasures grew, so did their thirst.
Whiles we in lean expectance gaping stand
For one shake from their charitable hand.

> But all in vain the dropsie of desire
> So scortch'ed them, three Realms could not quench the fire.
> Be wise then in your Ale bold youths: for fear
> The Gardner catch us as Moss caught his Mare.[55]

This epigram, with its clear assumption that the Garden of the Hesperides was a public symbol of the privilege, wealth, and pleasure enjoyed by the Stuart court, and now ripe for the picking by the revolutionaries, is a strong demonstration—in reverse, as it were—of the cultural and political force of Herrick's governing metaphor.

The title of Herrick's poetry, then, both knits the volume together and places his poetry in its contemporary context. *Hesperides* not only makes an affecting political statement but also makes a significant statement about the role and predicament of the artist in a revolutionary society. *Hesperides,* Herrick's "Sacred Grove," is a paradise at the edge of the world, the garden of death and immortality. It is also a complex admission that the Stuart dream of a golden age on an edenic island was a self-deception.

꧁꧂ Finally, we must ask before we enter *Hesperides* what we are to make of the presence and the placing of *His Noble Numbers*—standing clearly apart from the secular poetry, divided by their own title page and by opening poems that abjure the "unbaptized Rhimes" that precede them. Yet the first title page includes both books: *Hesperides: / or, / The Works / Both / Humane & Divine / of Robert Herrick Esq.;* and the Greek epigram from Hesiod's *Theogony* on *Noble Numbers'* title page, which translates, "We know how to say many things that bear the guise of truth, and we also know when we intend to state the truth," seems to look both forward to the divine poems and backward to *Hesperides.*

His Noble Numbers offers an alternative to the world of *Hesperides.* In Horace's epode 16, "The Woes of Civil Strife. A Remedy," he pleads with good men to escape from Rome, since it is being ground to destruction by civil war:

> You who have manliness in you, desist from your womanish
> wailing
> And set your sails for flight from these Etruscan shores.
> Still the circúmfluent Ocean remains; let us go, then, and look
> for

The blessèd fields of plenty in the Happy Isles,
Where there is never-plowed earth that brings Ceres to annual
  harvest,
Where never-grafted vines bear grapes the year around,
Where there is never a failure of fruit on the boughs of the olive
  And where the darkly ripened figs adorn their trees,
Where from the hollows of oaks trickles honey, and where
  from the mountains
The limpid waters downward dance with splashing feet.
. . . .
Jupiter set all those islands apart for a race of good people
  When he debased the Golden Age with bronze alloy;
Ages he hardened with bronze, then with iron, and forth from
  the latter
My poet's vision now foretells good men's escape.[56]

Herrick's *Noble Numbers* are, in many ways, a call for the same escape of
the good man from an impossible situation, but it is *Hesperides* itself from
which the poet must flee. *Noble Numbers* is made up almost entirely of
very brief, literal epigrams. Bone-dry, prosaic, stripped of metaphor, Herrick's divine poems seem at times designed to alienate the reader from
poetry itself. Only by sacrificing the tension that plays throughout *Hesperides* between lyric and epigram, and between fantasy and reality, can
Herrick obtain the spare, univocal quality of *Noble Numbers*. In the
Noble Numbers epigram "His Petition" (N-39), for example:

If warre, or want shall make me grow so poore
As for to beg my bread from doore to doore;
Lord! let me never act that beggars part,
Who hath thee in his mouth, not in his heart.
He who asks almes in that so sacred Name,
Without due reverence, playes the cheaters game,

Herrick touches on his deepest fears—fear of the civil war, of his own
destitution and social degradation, and of the degradation of his poetic
voice—fears that have been played out across the complex texture of
Hesperides, but that here are simply stated.

Perhaps the most compelling alternative to *Hesperides* in *Noble Numbers* is "The white Island: or place of the Blest" (N-128), central both
textually and thematically, which begins:

Lemma

> In this world (the *Isle of Dreames*)
> While we sit by sorrowes streames,
> Teares and terrors are our theames
> > Reciting.

It is startling, disturbing, and moving to remember that it is Hesperides that is the isle of dreams. It is one of the children of Night enumerated by Hesiod in the *Theogony:*

> But Night bore horrible Moros, and black Ker,
> > End and Fate,
> and Death, and Sleep, and she bore also
> > the brood of Dreams,
> she, dark Night, by herself,
> > and had not been loved by any god,
> · · · · · · · · · · · · ·
> and the Hesperides, who across
> > the fabulous stream of the Ocean
> keep the golden apples
> > and the fruit-bearing orchards,
> · · · · · · · · · · ·
> And she, destructive Night, bore Nemesis,
> > who gives much pain
> to mortals; and afterward cheating Deception
> > and loving Affection
> and then malignant Old Age
> > and overbearing Discord.
> > > Hateful Discord in turn
> > > bore painful Hardship,
> and Forgetfulness, and Starvation,
> > and the Pains, full of weeping,
> the Battles and the Quarrels, the Murders
> > and the Manslaughters
> the Grievances, the lying Stories,
> > the Disputations,
> and Lawlessness and Ruin.[57]

Herrick's *Hesperides* does seem, in the end, to belong among this night-marish brood of age, betrayal, and war.

There are more dream poems in Herrick than in any other seventeenth-century poet, and the many poems that call for an escape from reality through drunkenness act out the same kind of retreat from reality.[58] Perhaps it is only in sleep and in dreams that the "teares and terrors" become bearable. But on this other Hesperides, "the place of the Blest,"

> In that *whiter Island*, where
> Things are evermore sincere;
> Candor here, and lustre there
>   Delighting:
>
> There no monstrous fancies shall
> Out of hell an horrour call,
> To create (or cause at all)
>   Affrighting.
>
> There in calm and cooling sleep
> We our eyes shall never steep;
> But eternall watch shall keep,
>   Attending.

Here is a world stripped of insincerity, devoid of dreams and the "monstrous fancies" they call up from hell; here the light of candor and simplicity shines on everything. Here the truth is stated and never veiled; here eyes are never closed to conjure "apparitions." "The white Island" is Herrick's calm rejection of Hesperides, of Elizium—of poetry itself and the terrifying undercurrents of language. Only by stripping his poetry of the dreams that have supplied its power can Herrick achieve equilibrium in *Noble Numbers*.

Hesperides, then, is a book intricately bound to its own historical circumstances. For too long Herrick has been read as an artist only of the small, the perfect miniature. The brilliant import of *Hesperides* is its weaving of so many brief moments into one greater whole that reflects both the poet's private world and the public world that inevitably surrounded and invaded it. The very perfection of Herrick's individual poems makes the wrenching polarities of the volume as a whole more powerful and moving.

CHAPTER TWO

"The Argument of his Book"

🙢 We usually read Robert Herrick forward or backward: backward into the context of the classical tradition which he knew well and echoed extensively, or forward into a romantic context of the lyric poet singing timeless songs. He has, however, infrequently been read within the context of his own generation and the literary ambitions and assumptions peculiar to it. It is conventional, for example, to compare Herrick with Jonson, since Herrick is preeminent among the "sons of Ben," yet their literary relationship has never been explored in detail. And there is no convention in Herrick criticism for comparing Herrick with any Renaissance poet other than Jonson. Although *Hesperides* is intensely personal and original in its presentation as an entirety, in order to understand Herrick's innovations and the disturbing brilliance of the literary structure he created it is necessary to read his poems against the literary background in which he was writing. It is my contention that *Hesperides* is, and would have been perceived as, both a book of epigrams and *more* than a book of epigrams, an innovative mix of pastoral lyric and epigram that complicates both genres. Furthermore, I believe that it is revealing to read all of *Hesperides*, lyric and epigram, within the context of the models and evolving conventions of the Renaissance epigram book.

Any reader of Herrick logically starts with "The Argument of his Book," where Herrick introduces *Hesperides* by listing some of the subjects of his poetry and by alerting us to the generic traditions within which he is working:

> I Sing of *Brooks*, of *Blossomes*, *Birds*, and *Bowers*:
> Of *April*, *May*, of *June*, and *July*-Flowers.
> I sing of *May-poles*, *Hock-carts*, *Wassails*, *Wakes*,
> Of *Bride-grooms*, *Brides*, and of their *Bridall-cakes*.

I write of *Youth,* of *Love,* and have Accesse
By these, to sing of cleanly-*Wantonnesse.*
I sing of *Dewes,* of *Raines,* and piece by piece
Of *Balme,* of *Oyle,* of *Spice,* and *Amber-Greece.*
I sing of *Times trans-shifting;* and I write
How *Roses* first came *Red,* and *Lillies White.*
I write of *Groves,* of *Twilights,* and I sing
The Court of *Mab,* and of the *Fairie-King.*
I write of *Hell;* I sing (and ever shall)
Of *Heaven,* and hope to have it after all.

(H-I)

The first generic signal that Herrick offers has been picked up by his critics from the beginning—his repetitive insistence on the verb "sing." From the seventeenth century when Herrick's songs appeared in commonplace books and anthologies both before and after the publication of *Hesperides,* through the revival of interest in Herrick in the nineteenth century when Swinburne called Herrick "the greatest song-writer—as surely as Shakespeare is the greatest dramatist—ever born of English race," until the present when the image of Herrick as an exclusively lyric poet has been qualified but remains predominant, the singing voice of the persona has been the element of the "Argument" on which readers have concentrated, especially since the litany of subjects which the poem iterates seems so appropriate for song.[1]

The second generic signal that Herrick offers has proven less accessible to twentieth-century readers. One of the few people to realize that Herrick's opening had epigrammatic connections was Rosalie Colie. In *The Resources of Kind,* Colie arrived at the epigrammatic nature of the "Argument" by working backward from the poems, where the epigrams far outnumber the lyrics. Colie pointed out that the "Argument," beginning with the epic *propositio* "I sing," introduces an epic in miniature, where pastoral, georgic, epithalamion, historical allegory, and sacred poetry were to be encapsulated in epigrams. "By choosing the epigram as his major poetic form," Colie argued, "Herrick has reduced the pretentions of genres 'large' in scope or theme or size—has mocked them, treated them as metaphors, even as he exploits their official topics."[2]

The sonnet form itself is also a generic marker, since in Renaissance critical theory "the equivalence of the sonnet and the ancient epigram is constantly asserted" as a way of giving the sonnet a classical precedent.[3]

In 1548 Sébillet declared, for example, that the sonnet "suit l'épigramme de bien près, et de matière, et de mesure: Et quant tout est dit, Sonnet n'est autre chose que le parfait épigramme de l'Italien, comme le dizain du Françoys."[4] Colie explains that the epigram and the sonnet were seen as "'like' one another," were sometimes taken "almost as twins, sometimes as brother and sister."[5] The complex relationship between the epigram and the sonnet can be seen, for example, in Sir John Davies's "Gulling Sonnets," as well as in his epigrams written in sonnet form. Alastair Fowler has pointed out that "Sidney's spoken diction and sharp wit, Shakespeare's couplet closures, Herrick's fourteen-line love epigrams" are all examples of how the "epigrammatic modulation" began to blend with the sonnet after 1590.[6] In *The Scourge of Folly* (1611), another book of epigrams, John Davies of Hereford writes his epigrams of praise in sonnet form, whereas his corrective epigrams are in more typical epigram form.[7]

Such a distinction in content was characteristic of the twinned purposes of the sonnet and the epigram, the sonnet being seen as more appropriate for "sweet" or sugared themes and the epigram for the "sal" or salt of satire. Sir John Harington's "Comparison of the Sonnet, and the Epigram" dramatizes this polarity:

> Once, by mishap, two Poets fell a-squaring,
> The Sonnet, and our Epigram comparing;
> And *Faustus*, hauing long demurd vpon it,
> Yet, at the last, gaue sentence for the Sonnet.
> Now, for such censure, this his chiefe defence is,
> Their sugred taste best likes his likresse senses.
>   Well, though I grant Sugar may please the taste,
>   Yet let my verse haue salt to make it last.
>   (1.37; McClure 38)[8]

But while the two forms might have different purposes, "few epigrammatists made strict *formal* distinctions between the sonnet and the quatorzain epigram."[9] Even in its briefest, two-line form, the epigram shared with the sonnet a reliance upon a crucial "turn." Just as a sonnet sets up a situation in the beginning and develops it, comments upon it, or reverses it in the octave or the final quatrain and couplet, so also the epigram attempts to produce the same effect of surprise, enlightenment, or amusement, but in the briefest possible space. Epigrams were highly prized in the Renaissance for their brevity but especially for their "point," or "turn." The English epigram standing alone might be said to be relatively static, where the sonnet is dramatic, but formally they are so closely related that most epigram writers routinely used the sonnet form for their more complex epigrams.

But another important epigrammatic signal that the "Argument" offers is the poem that Herrick used as a model. "The Argument of his Book" is closely patterned on "de subiecto operis sui," the sonnet with which Thomas Bastard, a well-known epigrammatist, opened his 1598 volume, *Chrestoleros. Seuen Bookes of Epigrames:*

> I Speake of wants, of frauds, of policies,
> Of manners, and of vertues and of times,
> Of vnthrifts and of friends, and enemies,
> Poets, Physitions, Lawyers, and Diuines,
> Of vsurers, buyers, borowers, ritch and poore,
> Of theeues, and murtherers, by sea and land,
> Of pickthankes, lyers, flatterers lesse and more,
> Of good and bad, and all that comes to hand;
> I speake of hidden and of open things:
> Of strange euents, of countries farre and wide,
> Of warres, of captaynes, Nobles, Princes, kings,
> *Asia, Europe,* and all the world beside.
> This is my subiect, reader, I confesse,
> From which I thinke seldom I doe digresse.[10]

The similarity of Herrick's poem to Bastard's has been noted before, but the only significance that has been drawn from Herrick's imitation has been his borrowing of the pattern.[11] An important point that should be stressed, however, is that Herrick turned to an epigrammatist for a model opening. That he did so further privileges the importance of the epigram in Herrick's poetics.

Herrick's borrowing of Bastard's poem was not an idiosyncratic return to an obscure poet. Within the ongoing critical dialogue in the Renaissance about what the English epigram could and should do, Bastard held a significant position. In the dedication of *Chrestoleros,* Bastard puts forward what he felt was innovative about his epigrams: "I haue taught Epigrams to speake chastlie; besides, I haue acquainted them with more grauitie of sence, and barring them of their olde libertie, not onely forbidden them to be personall, but turned all their bitternesse rather into sharpnesse" (p. 5). Bastard thus precedes Jonson in his plea for the moral seriousness of the epigram. He consciously places himself in the satiric tradition of epigram writers: "Such are my Epigrams well vnderstood, / As salt which bites the wound, but doth it good" (2.16).

Indeed they are; *Chrestoleros* is full of a sometimes shrill attack on the "times"—on enclosure, gunpowder, and contempt for learning, for exam-ple.[12] It is only when he writes of "Nobles, Princes, kings" that he becomes cautious. A married clergyman, Bastard lived with his family a marginal existence, which he laments repeatedly in his poems, and he obviously dared not make important enemies. His poems to Elizabeth, for example, seem adulatory. It is only after approaching the queen with effusive and conventional praise that he offers careful advice and criticism. In a charac-teristic pair of epigrams, he first gives Elizabeth a standard compliment on the fortieth anniversary of her coronation:

> Now fourty solemn feasts, thine english nation.
> Fedd with sweet peace & plentie all the while.
> Hath yeelded to thy happy coronation.
> O fayrer keeper of the fayrest yle.
>
> (7.13)

but he follows this with an epigram-sonnet that slips council in after flattery:

> *Eliza,* thou has spread a goolden peace,
> Ouer thy land thrise blessed be thy raigne.
> And were it that some ciuill wars did cease,
> Which in our selues deuided we sustaine:
> Betweene the patron and poore minister,
> Landlordes and Tenants, raigning more and more.
> Betweene the borrower and the vsurer.
> Betweene so fewe rich, and so many poore:
> Ours were the golden age, but these home iarres,
> Houses, and fields and states haue ouerthrowne.
> And spoyled vs no lesse then foreyne wars.
> Thanke we this idle mischefe of our owne.
> But who did heare, or who did euer read,
> Peace without wars, or something else in stead.
>
> (7.14)

Bastard is caught in the classic dilemma of the public poet, who has set himself the task of speaking "of hidden and of open things" but who must live in fear of the consequences. What he devises as a result is the curious amalgam of outspoken praise and stage-whispered criticism that, for different reasons, Herrick would use as well. Although he has promised to draw a "mappe of men" (1.3) and to speak of "Nobles, Princes, kings" in his book of epigrams, Bastard ultimately excuses himself from an impossible situation. Another compliment to the queen is followed by the apology "I doe digresse, / Presuming thus to talke of Maiesty." An epigram is only to "dandle little meanings pretily"; when the poet attempts something larger, the restrictions of the form, both spatial and conceptual, prevent him:

> I attempting those things to recyte,
> Which come not in the compasse of my verse,
> . . . cannot make matter saye.
> Where so much matter must be cast away.
>
> (2.31)

Bastard's fellow epigrammatists, who were in less precarious social straits, put a different construction on his reticence and on the political role of the epigram. Sir John Harington, Elizabeth's godson and court epigrammatist, who walked the witty and dangerous line between criticism of Elizabeth and treason, praised Bastard's "pleasant Booke of English Epigrams," telling Bastard that "A Poet is one step vnto a Prophet" (2.64; McClure 160). But Harington later attacks Bastard for his cowardice in stopping short of the epigram's full range:

> It was a saying vs'd a great while since,
> The subiects euer imitate the Prince,
> A vertuous Master, makes a good Disciple,
> Religious Prelates breede a godly people.
> And euermore the Rulers inclination,
> Workes in the time the chawnge and alteration.
> Then what's the reason, *Bastard*, why thy Rimes
> Magnifie Magistrates, yet taunt the times?
>   I thinke that he, to taunt the time that spares not,
>   Would touch the Magistrate, saue that he dares not.
>
> (2.84; McClure 180)

In another epigram, this one in the form of a sonnet like Bastard's tempered praise of Elizabeth, Harington turns Bastard's own poem savagely against him and argues for the true role of a minister and of an epigrammatist:

You that extoll the bliss of this our nation,
And lade our ears with stale and lothsom praise
Of forty yeares sweet peace and restfull dayes,
Which you advance with fayned admiration,
Much better would it sewt your high vocation
To beat down that your flattring tongues do raise,
And rather seeke som words of commination
For tymes abounding with abhomination.
Say that Gods wrath against vs is provoked,
And tell vs tis to vs the scripture saies,
"I forty yeers have brookt this generation."
And said, "Theis people have not known my wayes."
   For law with lust, and rule with rape is yoked,
   And zeall with schisme and Symony is choked.
                    (McClure 367)

Harington raises the crucial dilemma of the epigrammatist or any pub-lic poet—the difficulty of being a poet who speaks the truth in a danger-ous world and the temptation to be blinded by money and position.

How then would a reading of Herrick's "Argument" in the context of the Renaissance epigram book alter and deepen a reading of *Hesperides?* As a first stage in providing an answer, we need a closer look at the struc-ture of the catalogue sonnet, which, in Herrick and his model Bastard, serves to indicate the structure of the book that follows: that is to say, the catalogue sonnet does not merely catalogue the subjects to be introduced, but in its own formal arrangement suggests certain crucial distinctions between them.

Bastard's poem is not simply a list of subjects; it takes advantage of the dramatic structure of the sonnet by introducing a crucial "turn" at the beginning of the sestet. After collecting a miscellaneous list of subjects in the octave, all dangling from the initial "I Speake . . . ," Bastard interrupts the list at the sestet to reiterate his presence and to add a new level of com-plexity: "I speake of hidden and of open things." Bastard's declaration colors all the subjects that have come before it by suggesting another level of meaning. Even more pointedly, it colors what follows in the remainder of the sestet, the most obviously political section of the poem. In the final couplet, too, the epigrammatist points to himself with a self-deprecatory joke. The epigrammatic poet-persona is traditionally in the foreground of his work, both as the memorializer of his society and as its conscience;

at the same time he mocks himself and his own importance, perhaps as a safeguard against close scrutiny.

That Bastard's poem had both generic and structural significance is further demonstrated by another imitation of "de subiecto operis sui" nearly contemporary with Herrick's "Argument." Samuel Sheppard opens his 1651 *Epigrams Theological, Philosophical, and Romantick* with a catalogue poem that he explicitly models on Bastard's:

> I write of Feare, of Love, of Harme, of Hate,
> Of Honour, Magnanimity, of Fate,
> Of Courtezans, of Chastity, of Charmes,
> Of Policie, Of Perfection, and of Arms,
> Of Heaven, Earth, and Hell, of Temperance
> Of Prodigality, of Choice, of Chance,
> Of Knaves, of Poets, Cowards, and Valliant men,
> Of Art, and Eloquence, and now and then,
> Of Kings, and Captaines, Queenes, and Queans, of Schism,
> Of Theeves and Panders, sometimes Aphorism,
> Drops from my quill; thus Proteus-like I've dealt,
> To please thee (Reader) be thou what thou wilt.[13]

Sheppard, a former minister, had been highly critical of the king in the early 1640s, but when it became clear that Charles was in actual danger, Sheppard became a key figure in the dangerous guerrilla warfare waged by the royalist weeklies in 1647 and 1648.[14] After the king was executed, Sheppard made a realistic accommodation with the Protectorate and wrote poetry that he was careful to see did not go too far. The poem introducing his *Epigrams* is a truncated and awkward imitation of Bastard's, but it echoes the same structure in its swing from the octave into the concluding quatrain, where Sheppard makes explicit that he will be writing not only of society and social ethics but of the political situation that overarches and influences that society. Where Bastard says he will write "Of warres, of captaynes, Nobles, Princes, kings," there Sheppard declares that he too will write "Of Kings, and Captaines, Queenes, and Queanes, of Schism."

In both Bastard's and Sheppard's poems there is a crucial phrase at the turning point of the poem—Bastard's "hidden and open things" and Sheppard's "now and then"—which requires special interpretive attention. Both phrases prompt the reader to ask "where" and to scrutinize the poems that follow with special care, since the poet's intentions are not to be explicit but will be woven subtly throughout. In each case the phrase in the ninth line invites a hermeneutic response to the poems that will follow and indicates that the poems may be interpreted as comments on the political situation of their times.

When Herrick constructs his catalogue sonnet, he uses the pivotal movement of the ninth line in exactly the same way but to far greater advantage. After the moment of suspended spring and cherished ceremonial which the "octave" creates—the "April, May," the "June and July-Flowers," and the "May-poles, Hock-carts, Wassails, Wakes"—the pivotal statement of the "sestet," "I sing of Times trans-shifting," is powerful in its sense of change. Although "Times trans-shifting" has the potential of manifold readings, one thing that it certainly signifies is the disintegrating political situation of England in the 1640s. These are the "untuneable times," the "troublesome Times," "the bad season" of *Hesperides* (H-210, -596, -612): not just Old Time in his immutable rounds, but the "Times" of a generation which was dissolving everything that Herrick saw as precious in England. In the epigram "On himselfe" (H-592), Herrick uses "trans-shift" in a way that serves as a significant gloss on the "Argument":

> Live by thy Muse thou shalt; when others die
> Leaving no Fame to long Posterity:
> When Monarchies trans-shifted are, and gone;
> Here shall endure thy vast Dominion.

The epigram conveys the same sense of two kingdoms, poetic and political, that threads throughout *Hesperides* and draws in miniature the same conclusion. When Herrick pulled together his book of epigrams and modeled his introductory poem on Bastard's, he was writing in a political context much richer than one of simple Cavalier propaganda. Like Bastard and like Jonson, he is aware of the slender line that the epigrammatist walks between counsel and danger and between flattery and self-abasement.

A further, telling gloss is provided by the next epigram "On himselfe" at midvolume. This epigram recalls even more explicitly the subjects proposed by the "Argument" and rejects them:

> Ile sing no more, nor will I longer write
> Of that sweet Lady, or that gallant Knight:
> Ile sing no more of Frosts, Snowes, Dews and Showers;
> No more of Groves, Meades, Springs, and wreaths of Flowers:
> Ile write no more, nor will I tell or sing

Of *Cupid,* and his wittie coozning:
Ile sing no more of death, or shall the grave
No more my Dirges, and my Trentalls have.

(H-658)

Herrick certainly does not exclude lyric poems, graceful songs of love, or celebrations of perfect small moments from the second half of *Hesperides,* although their number is radically diminished. Nevertheless, there is a sense in these poems on political and personal crisis, which are clustered at midvolume and which occur frequently from that point on in *Hesperides,* that the lyric poems must be sadly modulated by their context and by the persona's consciousness of and doubt about his own characteristic procedures. The last two lines of "Ile sing no more . . . ," for example, reveal how closely we should read Herrick:

Ile sing no more of death, or shall the grave
No more my Dirges, and my Trentalls have.

Although a cursory reading suggests that the poet *rejects* dirges and trentalls, death and the grave, a second reading hears the ambivalence, the question that the poem raises in the end. In fact, dirges and death increasingly occupy him. Furthermore, the epigram "Ile sing no more . . ." is followed immediately by a little song that sings an epigrammatic tune, deliberately reversing the conventional topics of lyric and epigram. It is a rollicking ditty on a whore who gives off a divine odor and a "sweet Lady" who stinks.

A. Leigh DeNeef has posited that in the "Argument" Herrick "achieves a complete reversal of [Bastard's] tone and overall effect." The contrast, according to DeNeef, is between a "realm of light, joy, and celebration and one of darkness, moral squalor and implicit condemnation" where "evil is rampant and in which order is surely threatened, if not already overthrown."[15] But such a sharp polarization misses the bipartite structure of Herrick's poem as well as the debt Herrick was acknowledging to the epigram tradition. When DeNeef concludes that Herrick's "Argument" provides us with a "sense of order, integration, and completeness," he is stating the present consensus about the poem (and, by implication, about the book it introduces).[16] However, while the uniform delicacy and beauty of Herrick's images and the ascending order of existence which the poem builds do serve to unify the poem, the elusive metamorphosis of the "sestet" introduces doubt, change, twilight, and death and certainly subverts any sense of fixed order or absolute moral goodness. Even the overall structure of the poem militates against a sense of integration. Whereas Bastard's poem, for example, is a true sonnet with three quatrains and a concluding couplet, Herrick's "Argument" is already "sprung" from the sonnet form, broken into a series of seven epigramlike couplets.

Herrick is, as we shall see, the slipperiest of poets; through the myriad epigrams of *Hesperides* he leads the reader through constantly shifting tones and assumptions. Even in the rhythm of the "Argument"'s "sestet" he signals the fluidity of the world of which he will write:

> I sing of *Times trans-shifting;* and I write
> How *Roses* first came *Red,* and *Lillies White.*
> I write of *Groves,* of *Twilights,* and I sing
> The Court of *Mab,* and of the *Fairie-King.*
> I write of *Hell;* I sing (and ever shall)
> Of *Heaven,* and hope to have it after all.

After the problematic sentence, "I sing of Times trans-shifting," nothing is certain. The long, flowing lines of the "octave" give way to the chopped, fragmentary lines of the conclusion. Flowers are not now what they once were; the poet enters shadowy groves and deceptive twilights. In place of Bastard's joke that "all the world beside" is his "subject," Herrick adds new worlds altogether—fairyland, hell (whatever it may be in the garden of *Hesperides*), and heaven. Rather than "integration and completeness," the "Argument" ends on a note of mystery and change. Under the surface of Herrick's poetry, change is always lurking; next to lovely Julia is ugly Joan, and under the surface of the "Argument" the same fluid currents, the same deliberate uncertainties also flow.

From the "sestet" on, also, the "I" becomes more and more insistently present, no longer announcing his intentions only at the beginning of every other line, but making himself doubly present at the end of the line as well. The poet's role as artificer is pushed more sharply into the foreground—I sing, I write—so that the presence of the persona serves to fragment the lines. Like Bastard's self-reflexive joke, which ends "de subiecto," and like Sheppard's self-conscious declaration that he will become all things to all readers, Herrick's "Argument" points in the end to the persona himself.

The active presence of the poet here is not, however, a sign of subjectivity in the postromantic sense, but a mark of the special kind of self-consciousness that derives from identifying oneself in the social and political order. The imagery of the last six lines, for example, is all drawn from the lexicon of poetic tributes to the monarchy. Sir Thomas More, for one, used the metamorphosis of roses in his celebrated epigram on the Union of York and Lancaster:

> The White Rose was dy'd purple, by hot Jars:
> The Red grew pale, as let Blood, by fierce wars;
> But now the Roses, mutually make One;
> The Strife was quenched, by this Knack alone.
> Both Roses bud, and flourish, lively still;
> Although Subjected, to a single Will.
> One Species includes both; and both agree
> Copartnership, in Beauty; Majesty.
> They who were Parties unto either side;
> Shall need no more, well-wishes to divide,
> And He who Envies, in the Quag-mire Sticks:
> Astonish'd when he feels, the Rose hath pricks.[17]

In Caroline England the roses took on an even more particular meaning, since it was an instantly recognizable trope that Charles I was the red rose of England and Henrietta Maria the lily of France, imagery that was reliably brought out by any court poet.[18] Furthermore, Joan Ozark Holmer has shown how the "Court of Mab, and of the Fairie-King" in the poetry of Herrick, Browne, Drayton, and Sir Simeon Steward was gentle satire of the luxurious court created by Henrietta Maria and presided over by Charles I.[19]

Finally, the last couplet of the "Argument" begins with four words that bring the already slowed meter of the poem to a complete halt—"I write of Hell." In *Hesperides* there are no poems literally about hell; that is, unless we are to assume that the painfully recorded collapse of the monarchy and the end of "merrie England" can be so construed.[20] If the "Argument" is indeed to be read as a paradigm for the movement and tone of *Hesperides* as a whole, then England in 1648 must be so construed, for the grinding half of the paradigmatic catalogue proleptically corresponds to the poems that occur with increasing frequency toward the end of *Hesperides*, where the poet cries that he can no longer write, that he is dead to his mistresses and his Muse, and that the poetry of blossoms and birds is no longer possible. Interspersed throughout the pastoral beauties of *Hesperides* and becoming much more frequent toward the end of the volume are cynical epigrams on policies, manners, physicians, lawyers, usurers, liars, flatterers, nobles, princes, kings—everything on Thomas Bastard's list and more. "The Argument of his Book" captures in little the unique combination of pastoral (I sing) and epigram (I write) which makes *Hesperides* a generic innovation. By beginning with the epic formula, Herrick initiates as well the pattern of mockery, self-mockery, and miniaturization that characterizes the wry, deflected wit of the epigram book. Together, the pastoral lyrics and the myriad epigrams—political, coarse, sententious, and celebratory—create a complex and multivalent work.

Part Two

THE EPIGRAM BOOK TRADITION

The frontispiece of *Hesperides*, 1648
(courtesy of the Folger Shakespeare Library)

CHAPTER THREE

The Classical Models

꧁꧂ *Hesperides* seems to the twentieth-century reader to be a self-contradictory mix of beauty and ugliness, of idealized love and bitter cynicism, of elaborate literary poses and stark self-revelation, of whimsy, ambition, humor, and despair. Herrick's poetry is not, however, a random list of poems but a remarkably complex arrangement of brief poems into a larger whole. Herrick took the genre of the epigram book, which Ben Jonson had elevated to its highest achievement in English, and refashioned it. The result is in many ways the most accomplished example of the epigram book in the English Renaissance, drawing upon the example of Jonson but also reinterpreting Martial, "Anacreon," and the English tradition that preceded and followed Jonson.[1]

The epigram has been relatively neglected by literary historians, perhaps because its essential brevity and economy make it sound unambiguous and therefore uninteresting to postromantic readers. The English Renaissance, however, prized the vigorous compression and the incisive point of the epigram. Thomas Pecke, for example, a seventeenth-century anthologist, called the epigram "the very Nerves of this exquisite Art" of poetry, and Ben Jonson argued that "even one alone verse sometimes makes a perfect *Poeme*."[2] Whereas most poetry could be accused of storytelling and therefore of a kind of falsehood, the epigram came very close to plain statement of universal truth.[3] "Truth" is the key word in Jonson's dedication of his *Epigrammes* to Pembroke; indeed, it was because of the "truth, and libertie" of his epigrams that they required Pembroke's protection.

The epigram is the oldest form of written poetry, composed originally to be chiseled onto statuary or monuments as an epitaph or epithet. Virtually every attempt at a definition of the epigram has been based on its origins carved in stone; the word *epigram* itself derives from the Greek word for inscription. Even Lessing, for example, in a curious exception to his aesthetic of poetry as dramatic rather than static or pictorial, defined the epigram by returning to its origins as an inscription. In *Zerstreute Anmerkungen über das Epigramm* (1771), he argued that the first part of the epigram is analogous to the monument or statue, the second to the inscription that elucidates it: "The true inscription is not to be thought of apart from that whereon it stands, or might stand. Both together make the whole from which arises the impression which, speaking generally, we ascribe to the inscription alone. First, some object of sense which arouses our curiousity; and then the account of this same object, which satisfies that curiousity."[4]

Renaissance theorists defined the epigram as an all-inclusive form, limited only by a formal brevity. In 1545, Robortello declared that the epigram could be a species of Aristotelian tragedy or comedy or even epic poetry when it praised heroes. In 1559 Minturno reiterated Robortello's blanket definition: "Whatever can be *elegantly, acutely, and briefly expressed,* whether concerning persons or things, and whether in praise or blame, the serious as well as the jocose, comes within its limits" (italics added).[5] But Minturno goes on to argue that the epigram's pointedness is not something easily achieved, since it is not attributable simply to cleverness and brevity: "It is remembered because of the feelings it arouses, and is not explicable in the normal way."[6]

Julius Caesar Scaliger, the foremost literary lawgiver and systematizer of the Renaissance, was as comprehensive in his discussion of the epigram as Robortello and Minturno had been before him: "For there are as many kinds of epigrams as of things. . . . They are expressed in as many kinds of verses as there are. They are composed in as many words and kinds of words, forms, shapes, figures, and modes as there are kinds, species, forms, figures, and sorts of words in the entire range of languages, nations, peoples, and races."[7] Theoretically, therefore, any brief poem could be termed an epigram. Scaliger did, however, divide the epigram into types, which he characterized by culinary terminology. First he excoriated "foeditas" (filth and vileness) epigrams as beyond the pale of good poetry. Within the limits of acceptability were those epigrams that were "mel" (honey), "fel" (gall), "acetum" (vinegar), and "sal" (salt).[8] Scaliger's theoretical terminology was later subsumed into the vocabulary of the epigram itself. An epigram of Herrick's, for example (H-1084),

> Love's of it self, too sweet; the best of all
> Is, when loves hony has a dash of gall

summarizes the structure of *Hesperides* by using the traditional epigrammatic terminology.

During the Renaissance, epigrams were enormously popular; they were used as models for schoolboy compositions and were included in most commonplace books—indeed, entirely taking over many of them.[9] Epigrams were gathered up in collections ranging from the purely scurrilous to the serious and ambitious, like Jonson's. Thomas Pecke, who in 1659 had called the epigram the "Nerves" of poetry, went on to say that "if a Poem be good, it consists of nothing else, but various Epigrams; cemented by a dextrous sagacity."[10] Modern critics of the seventeenth century have agreed. Mario Praz suggested in *The Flaming Heart* that "the epigrammatic tendency is discernible in all the literary works of the seventeenth century."[11] And Fowler goes even farther: "The great epigrammatic transformation that took place [in the seventeenth century] profoundly affected a large part of literature, and even altered the literary model in an irreversible way. By making for concision, it changed the usual scale, texture, and standard of finish. . . . it gave the couplet—as much the epigrammatic distich as the heroic couplet—its Augustan primacy."[12] In 1683, Dryden and Sir William Soames translated Boileau's reaction in *L'Art Poetique* (1674) to the supremacy of the epigram in all literary forms by the end of the seventeenth century:

> The *Epigram,* with little art composed,
> Is one good sentence in a Distich closed.
> These points, that by Italians first were prized,
> Our ancient Authors knew not, or despised:
> The vulgar, dazzled with their glaring light,
> To their false pleasures quickly they invite;
> But public favour so increased their pride,
> They overwhelmed Parnassus with their tide.
> The *Madrigal* at first was overcome,
> And the proud *Sonnet* fell by the same doom;
> With these grave *Tragedy* adorned her flights,
> And mournful *Elegy* her funeral rites:
> A hero never failed 'em on the stage,
> Without his point a lover durst not rage;
> The amorous shepherds took more care to prove

> True to their point, than faithful to their love.
> Each word, like *Janus,* had a double face:
> And prose, as well as verse allowed it place.[13]

By 1712 Addison could declare that "our general Taste in *England* is for Epigrams," a taste that he deplored: "A Reader of plain common sense . . . would neither relish nor comprehend an Epigram of Martial."[14] Addison endeavored in several *Spectator* essays to lead his readers away from this "Gothick Taste." Geoffrey Hartman has demonstrated, however, that the formal origin of romantic lyric poetry is the inscriptional epigram, especially those in the Greek Anthology.[15]

Yet despite these suggestive comments, both early and late, a typical brief summary of the current critical history of the Renaissance epigram mentions the creditable work of Sir John Davies, laments the popular epigram collections of the 1590s, and ends with the unmatched excellence of Jonson.[16] Certainly Jonson is usually seen as both crowning and virtually ending the history of the epigram in the English Renaissance. Such a sketchy view is, of necessity, a distortion. Both John Heywood and Sir John Harington hold a place at least as important as that of Davies in the history of the epigram, although both have been largely neglected. From the 1580s on, there was, as we have seen, an ongoing critical dialogue about the form and purpose of the epigram. Nor did the epigram end with Jonson; instead, it took on a new vigor and direction that culminated in Herrick's *Hesperides* and *Noble Numbers,* the sacred epigrams of Herbert and Crashaw, and, as Judith Scherer Herz has recently suggested, Milton's sonnets.[17] Since Herrick is the heir of this rich and controversial history, an understanding of the complicated development of the English epigram is a necessary prelude to a reading of *Hesperides.*

When Jonson told his "meere English Censurer" that he was attempting a reformation of English poetry by writing his epigrams "in the old way and true," he was making a distinction between the two epigram traditions available to him—the classical models of Greek and Roman literature and the vigorous and sometimes tasteless English epigram from which he wished to disassociate himself (*Epigrammes,* 18). Both the classical and the native tradition did influence Jonson, however, and from them both Herrick drew as well.

The two primary classical sources for the epigram—the epigrams of

Martial and the Planudean and Palatine Greek Anthology—gave rise to
two distinctly different epigram traditions that nevertheless existed side by
side in many Renaissance collections of poetry, nowhere more intricately
than in *Hesperides*. Although the Greek Anthology, which includes some
of the earliest written poems, far predated Martial, it was not brought to
light until the Renaissance, and its influence on the English epigram was
gradual. Italian humanists like Robortello and Minturno had favored the
simplicity and muted point of the Greek Anthology model. But the
theorist who had the most profound impact on the literature of Northern Europe was Scaliger, who pronounced firmly for Martial as the supreme classical model.[18]

MARTIAL

In order to understand the rich and multifaceted nature of the epigram
book tradition, it is important to recognize at once the primary influence
on Martial's "witty little books of Epigrams" (1.1) of Catullus's "little
book so carefully polished" (1).[19] Martial identified both the language and
the structure of his books with the "liber Catulli" and used this identification both as an excuse for lewd language and subjects and as a form of
protection against Caesar's wrath.[20] That Catullus, traditionally regarded
as Rome's definitive lyric poet, can be read as an epigrammatist has been
reaffirmed by the surge of brilliant readings that have emerged in the last
few years, readings that argue more and more persuasively that Catullus
arranged his book in a complex and suggestive pattern of lyric and epigram, love and politics, private desire and social ties. Kenneth Quinn has
proposed, for example, "thematic recall as a principle of poetic structure
in Catullus."[21] And T. P. Wiseman has recently suggested that Catullus arranged the "Lesbia" poems, the occasional poems, the political epigrams,
and the long mythological poems in such a way as to create a poetic
"world" based upon his own society.[22] Catullus's desperate passion for
"Lesbia" should, therefore, not be excerpted from the body of the poet's
work, but read as it is placed, woven between myth, politics, and scatology.

Catullus's book falls into three major divisions: short poems in poly-
metrics (1–60), the long and difficult poems at the center of the work (61–
68), and fifty epigrams in elegiacs (69–116).[23] Wiseman has pointed out
crucial "programme poems" throughout the three groups which signal
changes in the poems to come, a concept of key importance to the epigram book tradition. One of these "programme poems," for example, is
an epigram addressed to Caesar (93),

> Nil nimium studeo, Caesar, tibi velle placere,
>   nec scire utrum sis albus an ater homo.

[Utter indifference to your welfare, Caesar, is matched only by ignorance of who you are.]

which announces a change in theme for the conclusion of the book, a series of attacks on Caesar's political partisans. Catullus's penultimate poem, for instance, is an obscene ribbing of one of Caesar's closest political allies.[24]

When Martial points to Catullus as his predecessor, he points not so much to individual poems as to a body of work, a book that because it is both lyric and epigrammatic can create, in a series of brief poems, a whole world.

Almost from the beginning of Herrick scholarship, Catullus has been identified as Herrick's primary classical model. An impression that somehow Herrick is "the most Catullian of poets" has significantly influenced a great deal of thinking about Herrick's poetry.[25] Actually, however, as James McPeek has carefully demonstrated, Herrick shows almost no direct influence from Catullus.[26] The Catullan poem most often cited in connection with Herrick, "vivamus, mea Lesbia," enunciates universal classical sentiments. For the last stanza of "Corinna's going a Maying," Herrick's preeminent "Catullan" poem according to most critics, Herrick appears to have turned to *The Anatomy of Melancholy*, one of his favorite sources, where Burton summarized in one neat passage the classical wisdom on *carpe diem*, including, among many other references, the famous tag from Catullus.[27] The clearest discernible parallel between Catullus and Herrick is the shape of their books. The beginning of both books is dominated by love poetry; the end of each is dominated by political epigrams. Because there is so little other evidence for Catullus as a direct influence on Herrick, it seems unlikely that the arrangement of his book is deliberately Catullan. The shared narrative and generic parabola is, nevertheless, intriguing.

In fact, however, almost every particular instance of Catullan influence on Herrick that McPeek was able to find he traced through Martial. As an epigrammatist, Herrick can be recognized as "Catullan," but this similarity is probably due more to a common generic tradition than to any direct influence. It is Martial, Catullus's literary successor, who carried the epigram book to the Renaissance, and it is chiefly to Martial that Renaissance writers turned.

Martial took the ancient form of the epigram and molded it to his own individual genius. The stamp of his personality is so strong that when we think of the epigram today we generally think of it as Martial wrote it. But to speak of "the epigram" in this context is misleading, since Martial's most important contribution to the epigram tradition was structural, the creation of a sequence of loosely connected epigrams that together are more than the sum of their parts.[28] One of Martial's most effective means for establishing a book of epigrams is his unifying persona, who enjoys observing the society of men and women and who carries on a sardonic dialogue with his reader. As seductions are planned and then consummated in adjacent epigrams, or as he makes dinner appointments and later sends a thank-you note, the persona hints at an autobiography, thereby giving to each volume a vague sense of time passing.

"Martial" is urbane, detached, witty. He has a keen eye for hypocrisy and foolishness in first-century Rome, but his epigrams capture these vignettes of folly or greed in order to amuse himself and his reader, not in order to correct the faults he sees. Martial is not a satirist in the sense that his aim is to remedy the ills of society. Rather, he simply takes pleasure in catching people out and then freezing their folly with mocking irony. Indeed, the city, with its juxtaposition of poverty and wealth, its anonymity, its crowds, odors, and noise, is the essential milieu of the Martialian epigram.[29]

But complicating Martial's persona of the sophisticated city-dweller are his poems in praise of country life where the pretense and sophistication of urban life can be left behind. He congratulates his friend Licinianus, for example, for his decision to leave Rome and return to Spain, their shared homeland (1.49). Martial not only praises the pleasure intrinsic to the mountains of Spain but also disparages the Roman life Licinianus will leave behind:

> lunata nusquam pellis et nusquam toga
>   olidaeque vestes murice;
> procul horridus Liburnus et querulus cliens,
>   imperia viduarum procul;
> non rumpet altum pallidus somnum reus,
>   sed mane totum dormies.
> mereatur alius grande et insanum sophos:
>   miserere tu felicium
> veroque fruere non superbus gaudio,

dum Sura laudatur tuus.
   non inpudenter vita quod relicum est petit,
      cum fama quod satis est habet.

(ll. 31–42)

[Nowhere will be seen the crescent shoe, nowhere the toga, and clothes smelling strong of purple dye; far off will be the odious Liburnian messenger, and
querulous client; the haughty commands of widows will be far off; your deep
slumber the pale defendant will not break, but all through the morning will
you dream. Let another win the loud and frantic "bravo"; do you pity the
"fortunate," and without pride enjoy true happiness, while your Sura earns
applause. Not presumptuously doth life seek what remains to it when fame
hath its sufficiency.]

Martial himself returned to Spain in about A.D. 98 when he was fifty-
eight years old. Book 10 is full of Martial's plans to return home, although
by book 12 he has already become bored with the country life and com-
plains in his epigrams of missing Rome. Thus Martial's plans, decisions,
and indecisions become part of his epigram centuries; gathered together,
they form a kind of fragmented autobiography.

In the dedicatory epistle to the first book, Martial states that "the un-
disguised freedom of my expressions" [lascivam verborum veritatem] is
simply "the language of epigram" [epigrammaton linguam]. He would
apologize for such language, except that "in this style writes Catullus, in
this style Marsus, in this style Pedo, in this style Gaetulicus, in this style
every one who is read through" [sic scribit Catullus, sic Marsus, sic Pedo,
sic Gaetulicus, sic quicumque perlegitur]. Because Martial's epigrams are
for our pleasure and his, lewdness and coarse language are permissible,
even expected, since Martial intends both to appeal to and mock our baser
humor, a subversive double purpose typical of Martial's many-layered art.

That Martial's strategy has been a long-term success is evidenced by the
way we remember him today. It is the sexual rudeness, the frank appraisal
of human appetite that we associate with Martial, proof that he was right
about what people will read when no one is looking. But it is important
to remember that Martial was Catullus's heir in more than one sense.
There is also a strain of "lyricism" in every book of Martial's epigrams.
Approximately a third of the epigrams in each of Martial's centuries are
"sweet"—epitaphs, love poems, epigrams of praise. These poems, which
might be termed exquisitely brief lyrics if they were read outside the
frame of the epigram book, are an essential part of the epigram book's
sophisticated and endlessly surprising dynamic.

In the introduction to his first book of epigrams, Martial specifies the time and the audience for his poems:

> Epigrammata illis scribuntur qui solent spectare Florales. Non intret Cato theatrum meum aut, si intraverit, spectet. Videor mihi meo iure facturus si epistulam versibus clusero:
> Nosses iocosae dulce cum sacrum Florae
> festosque lusus et licentiam volgi,
> cur in theatrum, Cato severe, venisti?
> an ideo tantum veneras, ut exires?

[Epigrams are written for those who are accustomed to watch the Ludi Florales. Let Cato not enter my theatre, or, if he does enter it, let him watch the show. I imagine I shall be acting within my rights if I close this epistle with some verses:
When you were familiar with the pleasant solemnity of Flora and the ritual festivals and the license of the crowd, why, stern Cato, did you come into the theatre? Or had you only come in order that you might go out?][30]

His epigrams are to be Martial's "theatrum meum," the structural fiction that Ben Jonson was to imitate in *Epigrammes,* written in "the old way and true." More specifically, Jean Humez has demonstrated that Martial's epigrams are carefully arranged around the Saturnalia, and even more particularly, around the *ludi Florales,* lewd mime shows that were performed during this period of license and social reversal.[31] Prostitutes were the central and honored performers in the *ludi Florales;* slaves became masters, and a mock king was appointed for the day in the Saturnalia. Since the poems convey a sense of the chronology of the festival, they make even more explicit Martial's intention that his epigrams are to be read in a state of inebriation and during a time of ritual abandon, and they serve to reinforce the suggestion of fictional time structuring the volume. At the same time, Martial's festival framework incorporates into the structure of his book the essentially anarchistic nature of the epigram.

The delimiting principle of Martial's books of epigrams is absurdly and intentionally mechanical; Martial published his epigrams in groups of about one hundred because

> Cui legisse satis non est epigrammata centum,
>   nil illi satis est, Caediciane, mali.

(1.118)

[He who is not glutted with the reading of a hundred epigrams is not glutted, Caedicianus, with any amount of badness.]

It is worth noting here that Martial makes this comment in his epigram 118. He is probably mocking himself, but it is also true that neither Martial nor later epigrammatists felt constrained by the exact number one hundred (Jonson's *Epigrammes*, for example, number 133). Each "hundred" epigrams is constructed as a unified volume with an introduction, a conclusion, and thematically related poems arranged throughout. Martial required variety in a book of epigrams; his poems therefore vary in length from one to fifty lines and vary in subject matter from epitaphs for young children to obscene twittings of sexual foibles. Holding this diversity together in Martial's epigram books, however, is always a loose net of formal structure, of recognizable symmetries and asymmetries, enough to give the reader an intuition of patterning, but not so much as to regiment the essential randomness of the epigram's observations on life. In a poem whose seriousness about the epigram book structure is in characteristic counterpoint to the flippancy of the epigram to Caedicianus, Martial advised a would-be writer of epigrams:

> Quod non insulse scribis tetrasticha quaedam,
>   disticha quod belle pauca, Sabelle, facis,
> laudo nec admiror. facile est epigrammata belle
>   scribere, sed librum scribere difficile est.
>
> (7.85)

[Your writing, not without wit, certain quatrains, your composing nicely a few distichs, Sabellus, I applaud, yet am not surprised. 'Tis easy to write epigrams nicely, but to write a book is hard.]

Martial makes the point very firmly in his prefatory remarks that there is a strict limit to the epigram's range. He will never attack anyone by name, but shield them behind a general title:

> Spero me secutum in libellis meis tale temperamentum ut de illis queri non possit quisquis de se bene senserit, cum salva infimarum quoque personarum reverentia ludant.

[I hope that I have in my books pursued a course of such moderation that no-one who thinks well of himself may be able to complain about them, since they have their fun without infringing the respect due even to the lowest class of persons.]

The subtle irony of Martial's discretion, of course, is that all readers suspect that they see themselves in the unnamed fool; and, indeed, Martial addresses several poems to specific readers who had been foolish enough to complain about Martial's mockery of them. His epigrams are a multilayered game, like Hamlet's play to catch the king, in which Martial can plead innocence while his victims, intended or not, expose their own guilty consciences. Who, after all, always "thinks well of himself"?

These poems to self-exposing fools serve to remind us, as well, of the intrinsic timeliness of Martial's epigrams. Whereas the epigrams of the Greek Anthology are ahistorical, Martial's epigrams are rooted in first-century Rome. Like Catullus's poems, they are a slice of life, a generation raised to an art form.

There is one infamous exception to Martial's mocking humor, however. Since life in first-century Rome was mortally dangerous to anyone who criticized Caesar, the worldly and pragmatic Martial took the wiser course of profuse, almost unctuous flattery of Domitian. Martial's poems to Domitian are not merely incidental to his epigram books but intrinsically bound with Martial's conception of each of his books of one hundred poems. Martial not only addressed poems to Domitian within the centuries but used poems to Caesar to signal the introduction of each book and to act as a frame for the epigrams that follow. There is, however, clear potential for subversion in this procedure; for the contrast between these groveling poems, surrounded as they are by the rest of Martial's frank, realistic epigrams, invites a skeptical reading.

It has been traditional to take Martial at his word in these epigrams, however, and thus to condemn him for the sickening praise of a tyrant. Since Martial, along with Statius and other Silver Age artists, has been classified by modern criticism as a "mannered" writer, his poems of imperial praise are assumed to be empty convention (a critical assumption that parallels the reading of Herrick current until recently).[32] Certainly it was dangerous even to whisper criticism. All of the principal sources available—Tacitus, Pliny, Suetonius, Dio Cassius—agree that under Domitian's rule there was no latitude at all for political criticism in literature and that Domitian punished even an imagined slight ruthlessly.[33] Under the Roman principates of Tiberius, Claudius, and Nero, government censorship became increasingly harsh until finally Domitian declared himself both "Dominus et Deus" and imperial censor in perpetuity, making explicit his absolute control over all matters secular and religious.[34] But government censorship, rather than eradicating political criticism, "gave rise, paradoxically, to a new kind of dissent, a literature of pretense in which criticism of the regime was directed into more subtle and furtive modes of expression. Writers developed the art of criticizing by innuendo and double entendre, of communicating to the perceptive reader a sense of irony and ambiguity in apparently innocent and even eulogistic remarks."[35]

Quintilian, Martial's contemporary and fellow countryman, makes explicit not only the possibility of political criticism but the rich literary value of speaking in a double voice:

> Quamlibet enim apertum, quo modo et aliter intellegi possit, in . . . tyrannos bene dixens, quia periculum tantum, non etiam offensa vitatur. Quod si ambiguitate sententiae possit eludi, nemo non illi furto favet.

[You can speak as openly as you like against . . . tyrants, as long as you can be understood differently, because you are not trying to avoid giving offence, only its dangerous repercussions. If danger can be avoided by some ambiguity of expression, everyone will admire its cunning.][36]

Indeed, John Garthwaite has demonstrated a number of Martial's strategies of subtle criticism, all of which involve reading the poems to Caesar in the context of their surrounding epigrams.[37] Since Martial and Statius were virtually the only poets willing to praise Domitian at all, both Frederick Ahl and Garthwaite argue that Domitian could not afford to silence them.[38] Even if he read the satire between the lines, to punish it would mean exposing what might otherwise appear to be enthusiastic eulogy. Poet and emperor coexisted, therefore, in what Ahl calls an "uneasy truce."

Martial's poems to Domitian develop the premise, for example (and it was probably more fact than fiction), that the poet is only allowed to write and amuse by the whim of Caesar. The image Martial used most frequently in his poems to Domitian is that of the imperial pet rabbit who can hop in and out of the jaws of the Colosseum lions with impunity because he is under the emperor's protection, as in the following epigram, one of eight on the lion and the rabbit in book 1:[39]

> Delicias, Caesar, lususque iocosque leonum
> vidimus (hoc etiam praestat harena tibi)
> cum prensus blando totiens a dente rediret
> et per aperta vagus curreret ora lepus.
> unde potest avidus captae leo parcere praedae?
> sed tamen esse tuus dicitur: ergo potest.
>
> (1.14)

[The tricks, Caesar, the play and pranks of the lions we have seen—this tribute, too, the Arena pays thee—when the hare was seized, and yet so oft was
let loose from the fondling fangs, and ran here and there through the open
jaws. Whence inspired can a ravaging lion spare his captured prey? But he is
called thine; therefore can he spare.]

Martial chose to disarm Domitian's potential displeasure by explicitly
recognizing the threat of his anger while disparaging the importance of
the epigrammatist:

> Contigeris nostros, Caesar, si forte libellos,
>   terrarum dominum pone supercilium.
> consuevere iocos vestri quoque ferre triumphi,
>   materiam dictis nec pudet esse ducem.
> qua Thymelen spectas derisoremque Latinum,
>   illa fronte precor carmina nostra legas.
> innocuos censura potest permittere lusus:
>   lasciva est nobis pagina, vita proba.
>
>   (1.4)

[If perchance, Caesar, you shall come upon my books, lay aside the frown
that rules the world. Your triumphs too have been wont to endure jests, and
no shame is it to a commander to be matter for wit. With the air that views
Thymele and the mime Latinus, therewith I pray you to read my verses. A
censor can permit harmless trifling: wanton is my page; my life is good.][40]

Martial's complicated and probably dangerous game allowed him to place
his adulatory, or apparently adulatory, poems to Domitian in the incongruous and rather compromising context of his lewd and mocking epigrams. Telling, for example, is a sly, self-mocking epigram on Martial's
own procedures:

> Lascivos leporum cursus lususque leonum
>   quod maior nobis charta minorque gerit
> et bis idem facimus, nimium si, Stella, videtur
>   hoc tibi, bis leporem tu quoque pone mihi.
>
>   (1.44)

[Because a larger and lesser page of mine presents the airy gambols of hares,
and the lions' play, and twice I do the same thing—if this seem to you excessive, Stella, do you in turn serve up to me twice a dish of hare!]

57

But, however they were intended by Martial, the poems to Domitian became the classical precedent for the use of the epigram as the vehicle for
praising rulers effusively.

Renaissance poets, then, could draw upon Martial's example to fashion
an epigram book spoken by a strong, sharply etched persona, capable at
once of royal flattery and of the frankest sarcasm; and they were familiar
with a structure of many short poems held together by a sufficient number of formal conventions to make the entire book a complicated game
of interpretation. The Martialian epigram book can be read sequentially
like a sonnet cycle; yet it calls attention to its own artificiality and views
itself as sardonically as it does its victims. It provided classical precedent
for a book of poetry which, while based upon and critical of characters
and events of a specific time, aspired as well to timeless art.

Herrick's debt to Martial is extraordinary, although it is the Roman,
Martialian aspects of Herrick's poetry that have been downplayed in
most readings of his poetry. The urbane, sardonic voice of many of Herrick's brief epigrams, for example, is strongly reminiscent of Martial.
Martial's persona is located initially in the city and then returns home to
the provinces—with nostalgia, regret, and, finally, impatience—at the end
of the cycle of epigram books. Throughout the beginning of *Hesperides*,
Herrick's persona speaks from Devonshire, sometimes with urbane an-
noyance and sometimes with celebration, but toward the end of *Hesperides* he returns home to the city, reassuming his rights as a "free-born
Roman citizen." Herrick thus takes the narrative pattern of Martial's
twelve books and reverses it to suit his own life and the historical circumstances of late Caroline England. Even the number of Herrick's poems
(1,130) suggests the 1,172 epigrams that are divided among Martial's twelve
books.

Like Martial, and unlike Jonson, Herrick is not a satirist. He takes and
shares with us a sometimes perverse pleasure in the oddities of human
nature, but he does not write to change them. Like Martial, and in direct
contrast with Jonson's practice, Herrick employs the "epigrammaton linguam," pointedly including within the eight poems that introduce *Hesperides* a translation of Martial (11.16):

> To read my Booke the Virgin shie
> May blush, (while *Brutus* standeth by:)
> But when He's gone, read through what's writ,
> And never staine a cheeke for it.
>
> (H-4)[41]

Like Martial, and like Jonson, Herrick carries on a dialogue with his reader and with himself. Herrick takes the teasing suggestion of auto-biography implicit in all epigram books in imitation of Martial and uses it to shape his book with patterns of spring and winter, of youth, age, and death, of king and no king.

Martial's epigrams of praise to Domitian establish the structural importance, the self-consciousness, and the ironic possibilities of this problematic genre. Herrick's carefully placed epigrams of royal praise are among his most successful poems—aureate, ceremonial, and yet, at times, resonant with foreboding and doubt.[42] I will argue that like Martial's and like Jonson's epigrams of praise, their complexity increases when placed in the context of their book.

Finally, the importance of festival as structure and subject in Martial's epigrams brings us back to the ceremonial nature of *Hesperides*. Martial's Saturnalian frame is mirrored by the masquing structure suggested by *Hesperides*. The Roman Saturnalia reverses social order: master waits on slave, the mock king rules a licentious court.[43] The Stuart masque, in contrast, praises, asserts, indeed *creates* a social and moral order that radiates from the presence and power of the king. Nevertheless, in every masque the Saturnalian antimasque is an insistent subtext, mocking and sometimes frightening. Renaissance antiquarians believed that the Saturnalia was the historical original of English Mayday rites. Leah Marcus has argued, therefore, that in Herrick's Mayday poems, most notably, "Corinna's going a Maying," he makes a direct and conscious connection with the pagan Saturnalia.[44] While the connection of Mayday and Saturnalia is clear, in fact, the English tradition that most closely resembles Saturnalia is Twelfth Night, when a mock king is crowned in a carnival atmosphere of class reversal. Critics have stressed the aspect of Herrick's ceremonial poetry that affirms the hegemony; tellingly, however, the final ceremony Herrick celebrates in *Hesperides* is "Twelfe night, or KING and QUEENE" (H-1035).

THE GREEK ANTHOLOGY

The Greek Anthology was one of the great rediscoveries of Renaissance humanists.[45] The Planudean Anthology, thoroughly expurgated by a fourteenth-century monk, Maximus Planudes, and first printed in Florence in 1494, was the only version known in the early Renaissance. The German scholars Joannes Soter and Janus Cornarius published selections from the Greek Anthology that also included Renaissance epigrams in the Greek tradition by Thomas More and others. Estienne's edition of 1556, based on those of Soter and Cornarius, was particularly influential. In the early seventeenth century, Salmasius discovered a complete manuscript in the library of the counts of Palatine; this and Grotius's Latin translation of the Planudean abridgement revealed more fully the epigram's possible range.[46] The Anthology had an immediate effect on the continent but reached England much more gradually.[47]

The Greek Anthology is a collection of poems that spans hundreds of years from the earliest Greek literature to late medieval additions. Modern editions usually follow the format of the Palatine Anthology, which divided the poems by subject matter into fifteen books, among them Dedicatory, Sepulchral, Erotic, Hortatory and Admonitory, and Convivial and Satirical epigrams; proems to various anthologies; and epigrams upon sculpture.

Although it includes the epigrams of at least three hundred authors, there is a remarkable degree of homogeneity among the poems. The overriding theme of the Anthology is death—not surprising in light of the epigram's origin as an epitaph. There are, for example, the many tombstone epitaphs, many poems on sailors lost at sea, many poems on that subject which Poe recommended as the most affective for poetry, the death of young women. Complementing the poems on death are *carpe diem* poems, poems on the fleeting nature of woman's beauty and the cruelties of love. One poet can be singled out as preeminent among the writers of the Anthology, however. "Anacreon"'s poems became the prototypical model for later contributions to the Anthology. Indeed, there are several epitaphs for his grave in the Anthology. "Anacreon" himself is a synthetic character, the creation of later readers who lumped the poems of a number of authors under this name.[48]

A gentle melancholy pervades the Greek Anthology and, even in the "Convivial and Satirical" section, it is almost entirely free from pointed satire. Although the Greek epigram is not tightly constructed around a "point" like the Roman epigram, the poems are generally brief, and this formal brevity reinforces the idea of transiency and the tone of regret which many of the Anthology epigrams convey. The Amatory epigrams collected in book 5 lack the coarse ribaldry of Roman epigram and dwell instead on the beauty of women and boys.[49] Since our present definition of the epigram is so strongly influenced by the example of Martial, we tend to classify the poems inspired by the Greek Anthology as lyric.[50] The Renaissance, however, included under the rubric of the epigram, along with the wit and satiric point of Martial, the elegiac sadness, the prettiness, and the erotic flirtatiousness of the Anthology.

Herrick's poetry can serve as an example of the nature of the Anthology's influence.[51] Herrick's poems to his household lars, his poems on offering sacrifices to the gods, his many little epigrams on his burial and the epitaphs he suggests for himself, his series of poems on Venus and Cupid, are borrowed specifically from the epigram tradition of the Greek Anthology. H. H. Hudson has suggested, for example, that "To the Virgins, to make much of Time" may be modeled on an epigram in the Greek Anthology by Ausonius or on a Renaissance translation of the Anthology epigram.[52] Many of the poems of praise in *Hesperides* are written as inscriptions on statues which may be drawn from the Anthology's inscriptional verses on sculpture, and the "Argument" might be placed in the tradition of proems to poetry volumes which the Anthology collected.

But more far-reaching than its specific influences was the range the Anthology opened for the epigram to more traditionally lyric subjects. It is the Greek epigram, for example, that Italian and French poets and theorists claimed as the classical forerunner of the sonnet, a brief poem that can be amatory, satirical, dedicatory, or laudatory.[53] Clearly, it is a misleading anachronism to insist upon a strict distinction between Renaissance "lyric" and "epigrammatic" poems. Martial himself had assumed the role of the heir of Catullus, the classical poet who had revolutionized the concept of lyric poetry. In the Renaissance, lyric and epigram are closely related, not only by common subject matter, but by their brevity, their simplicity, their lucidity, and their polished formality. Nowhere in the Renaissance are the two branches of epigram, Roman and Greek, more pervasively and successfully intermingled than in Herrick's *Hesperides*.

BETWEEN TWO WORLDS: SIR THOMAS MORE AS EPIGRAMMATIST

The epigrams of Thomas More form a natural bridge between the classical and the native English traditions. More wrote his epigrams in Latin, translating or modeling many of them on poems in the Planudean Anthology. On the other hand, he borrowed proverbs and fabliaux from the medieval tradition and injected a political dimension into his epigrams that is never apparent in the Greek Anthology.

Virtually every sixteenth- and seventeenth-century collection of poems from the Anthology includes More's epigrams from the Greek.[54] Translations of his poems were included as well in collections of English epigrams from, for example, Timothe Kendall's *Flowers of epigrammes* (1577) to Pecke's *Parnassi Puerperium* (1659). Because of their wide circulation and because they were held up to schoolboys for emulation, they had considerable influence on English epigrammatists. Sir John Harington, for example, probably studied them while a student at Eton College. And since More's epigrams mix pious sentences with scurrilous jokes, they were mined not only by schoolmasters but by jestbook collectors.

More's vigorous versions of the Greek epigram prune away mythological decorations and aim instead for the Anthology's aphoristic style. Typical of the poems in More's *Epigrammata* are the numerous epigrams mocking women for their vanity, such as "On an Old Woman who uses Dye in Vain" (no. 58), a poem More translated from the Greek Anthology:

> Saepe caput tinguis, nunquam tinctura senectam,
> Aut tensura genis quae tibi ruga tuis.
> Desine iam faciem stibio perfundere totam,
> Ne persona tibi haec sit modo, non facies.
> Quum nihil assequeris fuco stibioque, quid amens
> Vis tibi? nunquam Hecuben haec facient, Helenen.

[You keep dyeing your hair, but you will never dye old age or smooth the wrinkles of your cheeks. Now stop sprinkling your whole face with powder, lest you end up a mask, not a face. Since you will get nowhere with paint and powder, madwoman, what are you about? These devices will never make a Helen of a Hecuba.][55]

On the other hand, there are epigrams mocking men for their shallow valuation of women for beauty alone. There are a number of epigrams that mock the predictions of astrologers; that point out the faults of bad paintings; that explain the truth to cuckolded husbands; that revile drunkards. There are cutting epigrams on the value of wives, such as epigram no. 86, again a translation from the Greek Anthology:

> Res uxor grauis est, poterit tamen utilis esse,
> Si propere moriens det sua cuncta tibi.

[A wife is a burden, but she could be useful—if she dies betimes and leaves you all she owns.]

But these are balanced by More's long and original epigram to "Candidus" on "How to Choose a Wife" (no. 143) and by the astonishing epitaph on his first wife, expressing his love for her but also his love for his second wife; the epigram concludes with the wish that they all three could have lived together on earth, as they certainly will in heaven (no. 258). Yet these poems too are just slightly mocked by a Greek Anthology epigram that More translated on men who marry again (no. 138):

> Qui capit uxorem defuncta uxore secundam,
> Naufragus in tumido bis natat ille freto.

[The widower who marries again is a shipwrecked sailor who a second time sails the stormy sea.]

The epigrams that seem most characteristically More's, however, are those on the brevity of life. The Greek Anthology does play endlessly upon the theme of inevitable death. But More's epigrams are peculiarly Renaissance meditations on death. "On Scorning this Life" (no. 69), for example, counsels against worldly ambition.[56] "Life Itself is a Journey toward Death" (no. 75) anatomizes the course of a man's life:

> Nugamur, mortemque procul, procul esse putamus.
> At medijs latet haec abdita uisceribus.
> Scilicet ex illa, qua primum nascimur hora,
> Prorepunt iuncto uitaque morsque pede.
> Partem aliquam furtim qua se metitur, et ipsam
> Surripit e uita quaelibet hora tua.
> Paulatim morimur, momento extinguimur uno,
> Sic oleo lampas deficiente perit.
> Vt nihil interimat, tamen ipso in tempore mors est.
> Quin nunc, interea dum loquimur, morimur.

[We waste our time and think that death is far, far away. But it lies hidden deep in our entrails. In fact, from the very hour of our birth, life and death steal forward together, step by step. An hour, in the process of measuring itself out, secretly steals that very measure from your life. Little by little we die, but in a single instant we cease to exist; thus a lamp goes out when its oil is gone. Even when it does not kill, death is present in time itself. Why, even now, while we are talking, we are dying.]

There are only two epigrams addressed by More "to himself" in the *Epigrammata*. One, written on his escape from a storm at sea (no. 259), is nevertheless a chilling and relentless reminder to himself that death is inescapable:

Quam te plura manent optata tristia terra,
In rapido fuerant quam subeundo freto?
. . . .
Quin eadem tumidas frustra uitata per undas
Te premet in plumis insidiosa tamen.

(ll. 7–12)

[How many more troubles await you on the land you yearned for than you would have had to endure on the rushing turmoil of the sea. . . . Yes, that same death which you escaped to no purpose on the swelling sea will overwhelm you on your pillow, only more treacherously.]

One would expect, therefore, that the Anacreontic element in the Greek Anthology would be ill-suited to More's temperament. Indeed, the only epigram of this sort that More translates, "Choriambics on the Pleasant Life. From the Greek" (no. 89), has implications beyond its message of decadent enjoyment:

Non est cura mihi Gygis,
Qui rex Sardibus imperat.
Aurum non ego persequor,
Reges non miser aemulor.
Curae est, barba suauibus
Vnguentis mihi perfluat.
Curae est, ut redolentibus
Cingam tempora floribus.
Curae sunt hodierna mi,
Nam quis Crastina nouerit?
Tornato bene Mulciber
Argento mihi poculum
Iam nunc effice concauum,
Et quantum potes imbibum.
Et fac illud ut ambiant
Non curras, neque sydera,
Orion neque flebilis.
Vites fac uirides mihi,
Botri fac mihi rideant
Pulchro cum Dionysio.

[I care nothing about Gyges, king of Sardis. My search is not for gold; I do not make myself miserable by competing with kings. My ambition is to have my beard well annointed with agreeable perfumes, my brow wreathed with fragrant blossoms. I am content with today, for who can know tomorrow? Now, Vulcan, make me a well-rounded silver cup, make it deep and as inexhaustible as you can. And have it decorated round about, not with chariots, constellations, or doleful Orion—instead make green vines and grapes to charm me, and add a handsome figure of Dionysus.]

More's choice of this poem from among all of the Anacreontea is revealing. Its dismissal of kings and their concerns is a key to an important and original contribution of More's *Epigrammata*. For although More uses the *Epigrammata* as a vehicle of royal praise, more significantly it is an abstract on the art of ruling; indeed, More devises his epigrams of praise to act as mediating buffers between the poet's corrections and the king's potential displeasure.

Since the way in which More's epigrams are arranged constitutes part of their force, it is important to establish that this arrangement was authorial. In the first edition of 1518 and in subsequent editions, the *Epigrammata* has a separate title page and a separate running head, suggesting a firm generic intention. Further, the editors of the Yale edition of More's *Works* state categorically that "the correspondence between More and Erasmus leaves no doubt that More had authorized the publication of his epigrams" (p. 5). Indeed, More was concerned that he himself had not corrected the manuscript copy sent to the printer. In the 1520 edition a number of careless printing errors were corrected, but, except for the addition of eleven new epigrams, More in no way altered the order of the poems.[57]

The *Epigrammata* begins with one long and four shorter epigrams on Henry VIII's coronation. The whole volume is prefaced by the letter to Henry that originally accompanied the five coronation poems when More presented them to the king. In his letter, More apologizes for the tardiness of his tribute (owing, he says, to an attack of gout by the artist who was to illuminate the manuscript) and adds, "I may have robbed them of that characteristic by which they could have given you the greatest pleasure—I mean timeliness" (p. 97).

More's long coronation epigram (no. 19) is a masterpiece of tactful honesty, circumspect advice, and measured praise.[58] Its extraordinary length of almost two hundred lines is evidence of the flexibility of the epigram form. More begins:

> Si qua dies unquam, si quod fuit Anglia tempus,
>   Gratia quo superis esset agenda tibi,

> Haec est illa dies niueo signanda lapillo,
>   Laeta dies fastis annumeranda tuis.
> Meta haec seruitij est, haec libertatis origo,
>   Tristitiae finis, laetitiaeque caput.
> Nam iuuenem secli decus O memorabile nostri
>   Vngit, et in regem praeficit ista tuum.
>
> (ll. 8–15)

[If ever there was a day, England, if ever there was a time for you to give thanks to those above, this is that happy day, one to be marked with a pure white stone and put in your calendar. This day is the limit of our slavery, the beginning of our freedom, the end of sadness, the source of joy, for this day consecrates a young man who is the everlasting glory of our time and makes him your king.]

More goes on to criticize Henry's father explicitly and to praise Henry VIII because

> Sic patriam, ut decuit, praetulit ille patri.
> Nec miror: quid enim non principe fiat ab illo,
>   Cui cultum ingenuis artibus ingenium est,
> Castalio quem fonte nouem lauere sorores,
>   Imbuit et monitis Philosophia suis?
> . . . .
> Ergo alios populi reges timuere, sed istum,
>   Per quem nunc nihil est quod timeatur, amant.
>
> (ll. 115–27)

[He placed, as he should, his country before his father. This preference does not surprise me; what could lie beyond the powers of a prince whose natural gifts have been enhanced by a liberal education, a prince bathed by the nine sisters in the Castalian fount and steeped in philosophy's own precepts? . . . Hence it is that, while other kings have been feared by their subjects, this king is loved, since now through his action they have no cause for fear.]

More simultaneously compliments Henry on what might seem an unfilial act, criticizes his father, and indicates the direction Henry's reign should take—he should be loved rather than feared. More goes on to emphasize Henry's respect for English law, his reduction of the crippling taxes current under Henry VII, and his order to end government reliance on informers. But every compliment that More pays is freighted with implicit warning as well. He tells Henry, for example:

Eneruare bonas immensa licentia mentes
Idque etiam in magnis assolet ingenijs.
At quamuis erat ante pius, mores tamen illi
Imperium dignos attulit imperio.
Nam bona quae pauci sera fecere senecta,
Protinus in primo praestitit ille die.

(ll. 90–95)

[Unlimited power has a tendency to weaken good minds, and that even in the case of very gifted men. But howsoever dutiful he was before, his crown has brought our prince a character which deserves to rule, for he has provided promptly on his first day such advantages as few rulers have granted in extreme old age.]

The opening epigram concludes with praise of Queen Catherine and with hopes for her male offspring.

In this coronation epigram, More initiates a function of the English epigrammatist as educator of princes that will remain central: he is the first of three important sixteenth-century epigrammatists both to hold privileged positions at court and to enclose politic advice and criticism in epigram form. In the seventeenth century, Jonson and Herrick would make that function even more intrinsic to the character of the epigrammatist.

In prefacing his *Epigrammata* with poems of royal praise, More imitates Martial, although More is infinitely more daring than Martial in his use of praise as education. Almost all the rest of the poems on kings and kingship in More's *Epigrammata* are epigrams original to More in conception and purpose, borrowed neither from the Greek Anthology nor from Martial.[59] Among More's 269 epigrams, at least 26 are on kingship, making this the dominant theme among his varied poems.[60] And More's message is stern, for he places little value on the glories and honors of kingship but emphasizes the king's duties and the dangerous corruption to which a monarch is liable to fall prey.

"Death Unassisted Kills Tyrants" (no. 80), for example, takes triumphant pleasure in the destruction of "unjust men" who have oppressed their people:

Duriter es quicunque uiris oppressus iniquis,
Spem cape, spes luctus leniat alma tuos.
Versilis in melius uel te Fortuna reponet,
Vt solet excussa nube nitere dies.
Aut libertatis uindex frendente tyranno,

Eruet iniecta mors miserata manu.
Auferet haec (quo plus tibi gratificetur) et illum,
  Afferet atque tuos protinus ante pedes.
Ille opibus tantis, fastuque elatus inani,
  Ille ferox crebris ante satellitibus,
His neque toruus erit, uultu nec ut ante superbo,
  Sed miser abiectus, solus, inermis, inops.
O quid uita tibi dedit unquam tale? uicissim
  Iam ridendus erit, qui metuendus erat.

[You who have been cruelly persecuted at the hands of unjust men, no matter who you are, take hope. Let kindly hope alleviate your sufferings. A turn of fortune will improve your state—like the sun shining through scattered clouds—or the defender of liberty. Death, touched by pity, will put forth her hand, while the tyrant rages, and rescue you. Death will snatch him away too (the more to please you) and will lay him right before your feet. He who was so carried away by his great wealth and his empty pride, he who once upon a time amid his thronging courtiers was so bold, O, he will not be fierce, will not wear an expression of pride. He will be an object of pity, cast down from his high place, abandoned, helpless, penniless. What gift has life ever given you to compare with this gift? The tables are turned: the man once so fearsome deserves only a laugh.]

More relies here only on death's leveling to overthrow a tyrant. No matter how wicked a ruler may be, there is no suggestion in this epigram that the people should take their revenge themselves. In the coronation epigram, More had stated explicitly that "the anger of the people . . . , common source of civil disturbance," is "a wicked thing" (ll. 142–43). By the end of the *Epigrammata*, however, the sacredness of the king's life will be less certain.

More's epigrams on kingship are remarkably outspoken. "The Difference between a Tyrant and a King" (no. 109), for example, bluntly recalls the more circumspect point made in the coronation epigram:

Legitimus immanissimis
Rex hoc tyrannis interest.
Seruos tyrannus quos regit,
Rex liberos putat suos.

[A king who respects the law differs from cruel tyrants thus: a tyrant rules his subjects as slaves; a king thinks of his as his own children.]

Epigram III posits "That the Good King is a Father not a Master," epigram 112 that he is the head, the people the body of the state. But two epigrams later More lashes out with bitter imprecations against a king who abuses his fatherly role; indeed, More hints at the fragility of the king's power:

> Erigit ergo tuas insane superbia cristas,
>   Quod flexo curuat se tibi turba genu,
> Quod populus nudo surgat tibi uertice, quod sit
>   Multorum in manibus uitaque, morsque tuis.
> At somnus quoties artus adstringit inertes,
>   Haec tua iam toties gloria dic ubi sit?
> Tunc ignaue iaces trunco non impar inani,
>   Aut paulo functis ante cadaueribus.
> Quod nisi conclusus timide intra tecta lateres,
>   In cuiusque foret iam tua uita manu.

[Well then, you madman, it is pride which makes you carry your head so high—because the throng bows to you on bended knee, because the people rise and uncover for you, because you have in your power the life and death of many. But whenever sleep secures your body in inactivity, then, tell me, where is this glory of yours? Then you lie, useless creature, like a lifeless log or like a recent corpse. But if you were not lying protected, like a coward, unseen indoors, your own life would be at the disposal of any man.]

The king's life is ultimately a nightmare of fear, a life to be despised rather than envied, for danger lies everywhere and belies the supposed sovereign power. "On the Anxious Life of Rulers" (no. 238) paints a graphic picture of a haunted life:

> Semper habet miseras immensa potentia curas,
>   Anxia perpetuis sollicitudinibus.
> Non prodit, multis nisi circumseptus ad armis,
>   Non nisi gustato uescitur ante cibo.
> Tutamenta quidem sunt haec, tamen haec male tutum
>   Illum, aliter tutus qui nequit esse, docent.
> Nempe satellitium, metuendos admonet enses,
>   Toxica praegustans esse timenda docet.
> Ergo timore locus quisnam uacat hic? ubi gignunt
>   Haec eadem, pellunt quae metuenda, metum.

[Immense power always brings miserable worries, tormented as it is by ever-present fears. Such a person does not venture out unless surrounded by a large armed guard, does not eat food which has not been tasted in advance. Certainly these precautions are aids to safety; yet they show that a man is not safe if he cannot be safe without them. Thus a bodyguard reveals fear of an assassin's sword. A food-taster manifests fear of poison. And so what place is without fear in such a life?—where even the very means of repelling what is to be feared themselves engender fear.]

"On an Iron Statue" (no. 142), one of the three epigrams on rule that More chose to translate from the Greek Anthology, is atypical of the lyricism we associate with that model:

> Effigiem statuere tibi rex perditor orbis
> Ex ferro, ut longe uilius aere foret.
> Hoc fecere fames, caedes, furor, acris egestas,
> Haec tua quis omnes perdit auaritia.

[To you, the king who ravaged the world, they set up a statue of iron—as far cheaper than bronze. This economy was the result of starvation, slaughter, wrath, and cruel poverty. These are the instruments by which your greed has ravaged all.]

More's choice of this poem from the Anthology is consonant with the stern tone of almost all his political epigrams.

Perhaps the most remarkable aspect of More's epigrams is their occasional flippant disrespect toward kings. In "On Kings, Good and Bad" (no. 115), for example, as Charles Clay Doyle has pointed out, More alters the traditional metaphor of the king as shepherd and his people the flock:

> Quid bonus est princeps? Canis est custos gregis inde
> Qui fugat ore lupos. Quid malus? ipse lupus.

[What is a good king? He is a watchdog, guardian of the flock, who by barking keeps the wolves from the sheep. What is the bad king? He is the wolf.]

Instead of the shepherd, More's king is the dog. Whereas the shepherd expects to profit from the sheep, the dog should only serve and protect them from harm; the dog who "profits" from his sheep is a wolf.

The ultimate implication of More's attitude toward kings is, astonishingly, made explicit in the *Epigrammata*. "The Consent of the People Both Bestows and Withdraws Sovereignty" (no. 121) complicates the apparently passive role of the subjects in "Death Unassisted":

Quicunque multis uir uiris unus praeest,
  Hoc debet his quibus praeest.
Praeesse debet neutiquam diutius
  Hi quam uolent quibus praeest.
Quid impotentes principes superbiunt?
  Quod imperant precario?

[Any one man who has command of many men owes his authority to those whom he commands; he ought to have command not one instant longer than his subjects wish. Why are impotent kings so proud? Because they rule merely on sufferance?]

And epigram 198 answers the ancient question "What is the Best Form of Government" with remarkable frankness:

Quaeris uter melius, Rex ne imperet an ne Senatus.
  Neuter (quod saepe est) si sit uterque malus.
Sin sit uterque bonus, numero praestare Senatum,
  Inque bonis multis plus reor esse boni.
Difficile est numerum forsan reperire bonorum,
  Sic facile est unum saepius esse malum.
(ll. 1-7)

[You ask which governs better, a king or a senate. Neither, if (as is frequently the case) both are bad. But if both are good, then I think that the senate, because of its numbers, is the better and that the greater good lies in numerous good men. Perhaps it is difficult to find a group of good men; even more frequently it is easy for a monarch to be bad.]

More uses as part of his argument for senatorial rule and against a monarchy the very basis of divine right monarchy, except that he sees the king's position as the gift of chance rather than divine intervention:

Alter ut eligitur populo, sic nascitur alter.
  Sors hic caeca regit, certum ibi consilium.
Illeque se factum populo, populum sibi factum
  Scilicet hic ut sint quos regat ipse putat.
(ll. 12-15)

[A senator is elected by the people to rule; a king attains this end by being born. In the one case blind chance is supreme; in the other, a reasonable agreement. The one feels that he was made senator by the people; the other feels that the people were created for him so that, of course, he may have subjects to rule.]

71

More's *Epigrammata* opens with More's praise of the wise and temperate decisions of the new king in his first year. The entire *Epigrammata* was not, however, published until 1518, nine years after Henry's ascension. In this same year, More was first appointed one of the royal counselors and began the career as adviser to Henry that ended with his death seventeen years later. It seems strange, even dangerous, for More to have published his Latin epigrams just at the point when he was beginning to achieve the influence and place at court to which he had long aspired. Certainly the animosity More's epigrams express against kings and their potential for tyranny springs in large measure from More's hatred of Henry VII, and many of the epigrams may have been written before Henry VIII's accession and directed at his father. But that the *Epigrammata* could be read as subversive of the current reign is witnessed by the French poet Germanus Brixius's virulent poem *Antimorus,* published in 1519. Brixius charged that More's coronation poem slandered Henry VII and was therefore an insulting choice of "praise" for his son; and Brixius suggested that Henry VIII, if he cared for the good name of the Tudors, should send More into exile. Richard Marius has argued that More would have had some cause for unease at being publically accused of being disrespectful to Henry: "To send epigrams in manuscript to a new king, joyful at his release from paternal captivity and at his accession to power and resentful of a shrewish father, was one thing; to publish these same epigrams when a king was now accustomed to power, without a son, and threatened by ominous murmurings about the insufficiency of his lineage, was quite another."[61] More lashed out at Brixius with almost rabid anger in his "Letter to Brixius" and in four epigrams attacking Brixius, which he added to the 1520 edition of the *Epigrammata.*

Indeed, in the context of the epigrams' publication at the threshold of More's career, More's argument against monarchical government is audacious in the extreme:

> Rex est in primo semper blandissimus anno,
>   Omni anno consul rex erit ergo nouus.
> Rex cupidus longo populum corroserit aeuo.
> . . . .
> Fallitur, expleri regem qui credit auarum,
>   Nunquam haec non uacuam mittet hirudo cutem.
>   (no. 198, ll. 16–18; 22–23)

[A king in his first year is always very mild indeed, and so every year the consul will be like a new king. Over a long time a greedy king will gnaw away at his people. . . . It is a mistake to believe that a greedy king can be satisfied; such a leech never leaves flesh until it is drained.]

At the end of the epigram on the best form of government, More pauses and addresses himself. He mocks his own powerlessness and remembers the imperfectibility of any human institution. It is a passage that presages a self-mockery and a sense of distance that will characterize all of the important English epigrammatists who will follow More:

> Quaestio sed tamen haec nascitur unde tibi?
> Est ne usquam populus, cui regem siue Senatum
> Praeficere arbitrio tu potes ipse tuo?
> Si potes hoc, regnas: nec iam cui, consule, tradas
> Imperium: prior est quaestio, an expediat.
>
> (ll. 27–31)

[But say, what started you on this inquiry anyway? Is there anywhere a people upon whom you yourself, by your own decision, can impose either a king or a senate? If this does lie within your power, you are a king. Stop considering to whom you may give power. The more basic question is whether it would do any good if you could.]

In the center of the *Epigrammata* is an epigram in which More repeats and makes explicit Martial's metaphor of the emperor-lion and his pet-poet (no. 162). The epigram is framed as a warning to a courtier, but, in the midst of More's daring political poems, it seems ironically applicable to himself:

> Saepe mihi iactas faciles te ad principis aures
> Libere et arbitrio ludere saepe tuo.
> Sic inter domitos sine noxa saepe leones
> Luditur, ac noxae non sine saepe metu.
> Infremit incerta crebra indignatio caussa
> Et subito mors est, qui modo ludus erat.
> Tuta tibi non est, ut sit secura uoluptas.
> Magna tibi est, mihi sit dummodo certa minor.

[You often boast to me that you have the king's ear and often have fun with him, freely and according to your own whims. This is like having fun with tamed lions—often it is harmless, but just as often there is the fear of harm. Often he roars in rage for no known reason, and suddenly the fun becomes

73

fatal. The pleasure you get is not safe enough to relieve you of anxiety. For you it is a great pleasure. As for me, let my pleasure be less great—and safe.]

In 1568, John Fowler printed, as the epigraph to a volume of More's letters, an epigram written by More three years before he was beheaded as a direct consequence of his own insistence on taking the role of adviser to Henry with absolute seriousness.[62] The epigram puns on several levels on More's own name which, in Latin, resembles "morus," the fool, "moror," to linger, and "mors," death itself.[63] It may certainly be read on one level as a mocking commentary on More's role as court jester, the "fool" who tells the king the truth:

> Moraris, si sit spes hic tibi longa morandi:
> Hoc te vel morus, More, monere potest.
> Desine morari, et caelo meditare morari:
> Hoc te vel morus, More, monere potest.
>
> (no. 278)

[You are playing the fool if you expect to stay long here below. Even a fool, More, can tell you that much. Stop playing the fool and contemplate staying in heaven. Even a fool, More, can tell you that much.]

In retrospect, More's execution casts over all his epigrams the shadow of danger.

Sir John Harington, in *The Metamorphosis of Ajax*, tells the story of his two predecessors in the Tudor court, John Heywood and Sir Thomas More. Misacmos, Harington's spokesman, first uses More's broader epigrams to prove that even a poet whose epigrams "flie over all Europe for their wit and conceit" is not above scatological subjects. Yet at first Misacmos will only go as far as quoting one of More's more irreverent epigrams in Latin:

> Te Crepitus perdit nimium si ventre retentes,
> Te propere emissus servat item crepitus:
> Si crepitus servare potest, et perdere numquid,
> Terrificis crepitus, regibus aequa potest.

. . . for I will tell you true, my Muse was afraid to translate this Epigram: and she brought me out three or foure sayings against it, both in Latine and English: and two or three shrewd examples, both of this last poet [More], who died not of the collicke, and of one Collingbourne, that was hanged for a distichon of a Cat, a rat, and a dogge.

Eventually he summons the nerve to translate More's epigram, which, it turns out, is not only scatological but prophetic of More's tragic confrontation—his refusal to make even a verbal concession to save his life.

> To breake a litle wind, sometime ones life doth save,
> For want of vent behind, some folke their ruine have:
> A powre it hath therefore, of life, and death expresse:
> A king can cause no more, a cracke doth do no lesse.

And Harington follows his translation by repeating his Muse's warning "that no man should follow Sir Th. Mores humour, to write such Epigrams as he wrate, except he had the spirit, to speake two such apothegmes as he spake" before his execution.[64] To quote More's epigrams, even to assume his presence, is a reminder of More's wit, daring, and ultimate fate; it is also an indication of the power and the danger of epigram writing.

Thomas More is of peculiar interest to a study of Robert Herrick. Among More's various epigrammatic topics, "the most original for an epigrammatist was kingship. In fact, we know of no other sixteenth-century poet who uses this theme for short poems."[65] In general, More's epigrams were widely imitated by Neo-Latin and English poets and widely anthologized in collections of poetry. His epigrams on kingship, however, remained virtually untouched, perhaps out of caution, perhaps from a lack of sympathy with their radical viewpoint. According to Charles Clay Doyle's list of reprints, translations, and adaptations of More's epigrams in the Renaissance, only Timothe Kendall reprinted any of these epigrams in the sixteenth century. Kendall's *Flowers of epigrammes, out of sundrie the moste singular authours* (London, 1577) offered translations of a number of Greek and Latin epigrams and a smaller number of recent writers, including twenty-eight of More's epigrams, five of them political.[66] Not until the very end of the Protectorate does Doyle note another appearance of the political epigrams, in Pecke's *Parnassi Puerperium* (1659), which translates four.[67] Thomas More was widely recognized in the Renaissance as the first and one of the greatest English epigrammatists. That his original contribution to the genre—starkly critical political epigrams—should have been so carefully avoided is evidence both of the political potential of the epigram and of its danger.

But More's influence on Robert Herrick is crucially important. He provided a precedent for a volume of epigrams with political aphorisms mixed throughout. He provided, too, a strategy of praise which then allowed the possibility of correction, since the structure of More's *Epigrammata* provided a paradigm for royal praise followed by increasingly stringent political aphorisms. Herrick held back both from More's absolute frankness and from his extreme position on kingship. But he followed More's example of using the epigram book as a vehicle for political advice and warning. Whereas More first counsels passive reliance on natural death to end a tyrant's life, he later hints strongly that the people may take the solution to tyranny into their own hands. Herrick, although he acknowledges the possibility that rebellion may end a tyrant's regime, never endorses force. Near the beginning of *Hesperides,* Herrick places an epigram, "Duty to Tyrants" (H-97), that takes a position similar to More's in his early epigram "Death Unassisted Kills Tyrants":

> Good Princes must be pray'd for: for the bad
> They must be borne with, and in ·rev'rence had.
> Doe they first pill thee, next, pluck off thy skin?
> *Good children kisse the Rods, that punish sin.*
> Touch not the Tyrant; Let the Gods alone
> To strike him dead, that but usurps a Throne.

Near the end of *Hesperides,* however, Herrick places an epigram, "Bad Princes pill their People" (H-826), that echoes "Duty to Tyrants" but, tellingly, omits its counsel of submission:

> Like those infernall Deities which eate
> The best of all the sacrificed meate;
> And leave their servants, but the smoak and sweat:
> So many *Kings,* and *Primates* too there are,
> Who claim the Fat, and Fleshie for their share,
> And leave their Subjects but the starved ware.

It is Herrick's sententious political epigrams that have received the least attention from his critics. Perhaps this neglect is due in part to the strategy of reading *Hesperides* in pieces. The complexity of Herrick's epigrams, like More's, is best seen only in context. In part, the neglect is surely due also to the apparent strangeness of Herrick's political epigrams. Seen in the light of More's precedent, however, they seem no longer strange but audacious. Herrick adapted More's example to the circumstances of his own allegiance to the Caroline culture in the civil war. But because of the unique character of More as a mediator of the classical tradition to

England and as victim of his own principles, his reappearance as a ghostly presence in Herrick's volume can tell us a great deal about the intentions of *Hesperides* as an epigram book for another era, where the theory of monarchical authority had become, inevitably, far more complicated.

CHAPTER FOUR

The English Models

&∂૯ઝ. Harington's second example of the relationship between epi-grammatist and king is More's kinsman John Heywood. Heywood married More's niece Joan Rastell, daughter of More's sister Elizabeth and John Rastell. He became an intimate member of More's family circle and was strongly influenced by More. Indeed, according to Gabriel Harvey, "some of Heywood's epigrams are supposed to be conceits and devices of pleasant Sir Thomas More."[1]

Heywood, called by Camden "the great Epigrammatist," was listed by Francis Meres in *Palladis Tamia* as the first of the notable English epi-grammatists.[2] Sir John Davies measured his own accomplishments against Heywood, "which did in Epigrams excell" ("In Haywoodum," no. 29), and Bastard believed he could measure himself against Heywood and Davies both "were I happy, did not fortune frowne" (2.15).[3] Harington decreed, however, in *The Metamorphosis of Ajax* that "This Haywood for his Proverbs & Epigrams, is not yet put downe by any of our countrey, though one [M. Davies] doth in deede come neare him, that graces him more in saying he puts him down."[4]

Heywood's epigrams began appearing in 1556, issued, like Martial's, in batches of one hundred. By 1562, when his *Workes* appeared, there were six hundred epigrams. Also in the *Workes* were Heywood's *Proverbs*, which had already been reprinted three times after their first appearance in 1546. Heywood's poetry remained popular throughout the rest of the sixteenth century; his *Workes* were reprinted four more times.[5] Each of the important English epigrammatists used Heywood as a measure of his accomplishments and as a source; Herrick, for example, directly imitated at least one of Heywood's epigrams in *Hesperides*.[6]

John Heywood was England's last court jester, serving in the reigns of

Henry VIII, Edward VI, and Mary. Sometime after 1558, he fled England because his loyalty to the Catholic religion made Elizabeth's England at best uncomfortable and at worst dangerous.[7] The purpose of Heywood's epigrams was to entertain, and to this end he was willing to make the epigrammatic persona a figure of mockery.[8] Nevertheless, under the rough humor of his epigrams, Heywood insisted upon the old loyalties to the Catholic church, to Mary Tudor, and to old-fashioned morals. In 1534, for example, Heywood wrote a long and passionate poem in praise of Mary Tudor, although Mary was at that time in disgrace with her father. Later, his epigram "Of Rebellion" was the leading poem in his *Sixt Hundred of Epigrams:*

> Against god I dayly offend by frailte:
> But against my prince, or natiue countre,
> With as much as bodkin, when I rebell,
> The next daie after hang me vp faire and well.
>
> . . . .
>
> But beyng true to god, queene, countre, and crowne,
> We shall at all feastes, not hang vp, but syt downe.

The epigram is typical of Heywood's easy narrative style and his pleasure in simple punning. It is typical also in its firm nationalism and its generalized political criticism. By 1561, when the *Sixt Hundred* was published with "Of Rebellion" as its first poem, Heywood was about to flee England as a self-exiled recusant. His epigrams affirm his own devotion, demand an equal loyalty from others, and, at the same time, offer criticism under the thin veil of old saws; for although Heywood borrowed the one hundred poem structure from Martial, the most fruitful source of his epigrams themselves is the proverb.[9] Ironically, while Heywood brought to the epigram a conservative moral standard, a loyalty to the way things used to be, when his epigrams applied the old proverbs against the present times his very conservatism was subversive.

Heywood also wrote longer epigrams that expand into narrative and often take the form of animal fables, concluding with epigrammatic morals.[10] It was this tendency toward expansiveness and explicitness that Ben Jonson would later criticize in English epigram writers who followed Heywood's example. But Jonson was espousing what he believed to be the "old way," the classical rules of epigram writing. The straightforward, proverb-laden English tradition, however, had the value of simplicity and

power. John Heath, an epigrammatist and contemporary of Jonson's, saw
the same awkwardness that Jonson criticized in Heywood but praised as
well Heywood's strength:

> Heywood, th'old English Epigrammatist,
> Had wit at will, and art was all he mist:
> But now a daies we of the moderne frie
> Haue art, and labour with wits penurie.
> Wit is the substance, art the polishment:
> Art does adorne, and wit it does inuent.
> Since then they are so ioyntly link't that neither
> Can well subsist without the helpe of either:
> I gladly could haue wisht with all my hart,
> That we had had his wit, or he our art.
>
> ("Ad modernos Epigrammatistas," 42)[11]

A large part of Heywood's wit lies in the persona of the epigrams, who
presents himself as a buffoon, a court jester whose purpose it is to entertain. The epigram that concludes his *Fifth Book* presents a dialogue sketch
"Of Heywood":

> Art thou Heywood with the mad mery wit?
> Ye forsooth master, that same is euen hit.
> Art thou Heywood that applieth mirth more than thrift?
> Ye sir, I take mery mirth a golden gift.
> Art thou Heywood that hath made many mad plaies?
> Ye many plaies; fewe good woorkes in all my daies.
> Art thou Heywood that hath made men mery long?
> Ye: and will, if I be mad mery among.
> Art thou Heywood that woulde be made mery now?
> Ye sir: helpe me to it now I beseche you.
>
> (5.100)

Such a "merry" man is protected by his own good spirits and ingenuous-
ness from giving offense, no matter what "hit" he may score. In Heywood's circumstances that was wit indeed.

Which brings us back to Harington's story of kings and epigrammatists
in *The Metamorphosis of Ajax.* In 1543 Heywood was indicted for treason
for "attempting . . . to deprive [the king] of . . . his dignity, title and name
of 'Supreme Head of the English and Irish Church,' . . . falsely and traitorously by words, writings and deeds, which are notorious and public.

... and also, falsely and traitorously, with all [his] force and power, to subvert, frustrate, and annihilate the good and praiseworthy statutes and ordinances of . . . the King."[12] Heywood had been part of a group, headed by the pro-Catholic Germain Gardiner, which had accused Archbishop Cranmer of heresy. Gardiner was executed, but, after a public expression of repentance, Heywood was granted a general pardon several months later.

After telling of More's jests on his execution, Harington's Misacmos asks, "what thinke you by Haywood, that scaped hanging with his mirth, the King being graciously and (as I thinke) truely perswaded, that a man that wrate so pleasant and harmlesse verses, could not have any harmfull conceit against his procedings" (p. 102). At least in Harington's review of the episode, Heywood successfully pulled off Martial's feat of presenting himself as amusing enough to be disregarded as a threat.

More and Heywood represent the two extremes at the beginning of the English epigram tradition available to Herrick or any later poet: one classical in inspiration and an accomplished Neo-Latin poet, the other finding his sources in proverbs and expressing them in rough-hewn English; one conscious of the dignity of the poet and his role in the education of princes, the other willing to make the poet a fool in order to inoculate the poems against punishment. Their examples were to be acutely before Harington, Jonson, Bastard, and Herrick.

In the late 1590s the epigram began two decades of popularity that is perhaps related more closely to the upsurge of formal verse satire than to the mainstream of the English epigram's development.[13] Since Davies, Bastard, and Jonson reacted specifically against it, the popular epigram at the turn of the century may be taken as a negative influence on the development of the epigram, but an influence nonetheless.

Joseph Hall, later, as bishop of Exeter, Herrick's ecclesiastical superior, initiated the rage with his *Virgidemiarum, Six Books* (1598), which was quickly followed by Marston's *Certaine Satyres* (1598) and *The Scourge of Villainy* (1598) and by Everard Guilpin's *Skialetheia, Or, A Shadowe of Truth, in certaine Epigrams and Satyres* (1598). In initiating the vogue, Hall prefaced his first book with a manifesto, "his rejection of all poetry except satire," which is notable for professing a poetic stance completely opposed to Herrick's:

> Nor vnder euery banke, and euery tree,
> Speake rymes vnto my oten Minstralsie

Nor caroll out so pleasing liuely laies,
As mought the *Graces* moue my mirth to praise.
Trumpet, and reeds, and socks, and buskins fine
I them bequeath: whose statues wandring twine
Of Yuy, mixt with Bayes, circlen around
Their liuing Temples likewise *Laurell-bound.*
Rather had I albee in carelesse rymes,
Check the mis-ordred world, and lawlesse times.
Nor need I craue the muses mid-wifry,
To bring to light so worth-less Poetry.

(1. Sat. 1, ll. 11.15–26)[14]

In Hall's poetics, indeed in his society, the epigram was aligned with satire in the ranks of "worth-less Poetry" that meant to "check the mis-ordred world, and lawlesse times" rather than with pastoral's "oten Minstralsie." The ecclesiastical authorities, for example, made no distinction between epigram and satire when they issued a decree on June 1, 1599, "that no satires or epigrams be printed hereafter," and that a long list of books be burned by the public hangman, including the works of Hall, Marston, Guilpin, and Davies.[15] Hall (whose *Virgidemiae* was spared conflagration at the last minute) honored the ban and went on to become an Anglican divine who redirected his gift for satire into religious controversy, most notably against John Milton.

But the bishops' ban on epigrams was not honored by others, and in the first decade of the seventeenth century the popularity of epigram collections continued unabated. John Weever's *Epigrams in the Oldest Cut and Newest Fashion* (1599) was in print the year that the ban was issued. *The Letting of Humour's Blood* (1600) was the first of several volumes by Samuel Rowland; Henry Parrot was even more prolific with titles like *The Mous-trap* (1606) and *The Mastive-or Young-Whelpe of the Olde-Dogge* (1615). Many of these collections were exercises in venting spleen and were meant solely to entertain with their topicality and nastiness. Perhaps because they abandoned any attempt to correct the "lawlesse times," they were allowed to pour forth from the press unchecked.

In the *Arte of English Poesie* (1589), George Puttenham explains the psychology of this kind of epigram:

But all the world could not keepe, nor any ciuill ordinance to the contrary so preuaile, but that men would and must needs vtter their splenes in all ordinarie matters also: or else it seemed their bowels would burst, therefore the poet deuised a prety fashioned poeme short and sweete (as we are wont to say) and called it *Epigramma* in which euery mery conceited man might without any long studie or tedious ambage, make his frend sport, and anger his foe, and giue a prettie nip, or shew a sharpe conceit in few verses.[16]

Puttenham recognized that the epigram was, however, potentially dangerous in another way. Puttenham's definition of the epigram, in fact, goes on to explain in more detail the social status of the epigram as an expression of otherwise censured opinion:

this *Epigramme* is but an inscription or writting made as it were vpon a table, or in a windowe, or vpon the wall or mantell of a chimney in some place of common resort, where it was allowed euery man might come, or be sitting to chat and prate, as now in our tauernes and common tabling houses, where many merry heades meete, and scrible with ynke with chalke, or with a cole such matters as they would euery man should know, & descant vpon. (Ibid.)

In other words, epigrams are, in origin and in essence, graffiti.[17] They are displayed in public places to generate discussion, but they are, by their very nature, essentially anonymous because their messages in some way subvert authority, law, and order.

Although Puttenham of course recognizes the textual stage of the epigram's transmission when, thanks to Martial, the genre "came to be put in paper and in bookes, and vsed as ordinarie missiues, some of friendship, some of defiaunce, or as other messages of mirth," he also significantly recorded the practice of the Roman satirists Pasquill and Morphirir "which in time of *Sede vacante*, when merry conceited men listed to gibe & iest at the dead Pope, or any of his Cardinales, they fastened them vpon those Images which now lie in the open streets, and were tollerated, but after that terme expired they were inhibited againe" (pp. 43–44).[18] Historically, the epigram is clearly capable of welling up in satire, lewdness, and contempt whenever the clamp of authority is released.

By the 1590s the influence of Martial was pervasive, in large part because of the use of his poems as models for writing exercises at schools like Winchester (where John Owen, Sir John Davies, Thomas Bastard, and John Heath all studied).[19] In fact, the popular epigrammatists at the turn of the century fell upon Martial's example with a schoolboy's glee, delighting in crude jokes and personal attack. But while they missed any sense of Martial's genius, they did preserve the rough outline of the Martialian epigram book. Most of these volumes, for example, are divided into centuries, and all of them are rooted in the events and personalities of their time. John Weever, in the epistle "To the Generous Reader" at the beginning of his *Epigrams* (1599), makes explicit their ephemeral nature: "Epigramms are much like unto Almanacks, seruing especially for the yeare for the which they are made, then these, (right iudging Readers) being for one yeare pend, and in another printed; are past due before they come from the Presse" (p. 13).[20] In most cases, however, these lesser epigram writers filled their centuries with bad poetry randomly thrown together, and their poems could not survive the year for which they were written.[21]

One of the most popular poets in the Renaissance, whose fame eclipsed even Shakespeare's on the Continent, was an epigrammatist who has today been largely forgotten.[22] John Owen wrote his ten books of epigrams exclusively in Latin, all of them carefully modeled on Martial. Ben Jonson dismissed Owen as "a pure Pedantique Schoolmaster sweeping his living from the Posteriors of litle children, and hath no thinge good in him," and Jonson's judgment is only a little exaggerated.[23] But the Renaissance taste for Owen seemed insatiable. Owen published four centuries of epigrams in 1607, six more in 1612. Before 1622, when all ten books were published together, there were five editions of the first three books. During the seventeenth and eighteenth centuries there were editions of Owen's epigrams published in every country in Europe, including many translations. There were five English translations in the seventeenth century. His astonishing popularity reveals the Renaissance's strong interest in the epigram, and especially in Martial's witty and satirical model.

The first successful imitator of Martial to be published in English was Sir John Davies, whose *Epigrams* appeared together with Marlowe's *Elegies* sometime in the 1590s, probably in 1595 or 1596.[24] The classical epigram belonged so firmly to Martial and his strong literary personality that it made the convention of classical borrowing trickier than it usually was. Sir John Harington addressed—in a Martialian voice but with the rollicking rhyme of Heywood—a poem to Davies about the problem:

> My deer friend *Davys*, some against vs partiall
> Have found we steall some good conceits from Martiall;
> So though they graunt our verse hath some Acumen,
> Yet make they fooles suspect we skant ar trew men
> But *Surrey* did the same, and worthy *Wyatt*,
> And they had praise and reputation by it.
> And *Heywood*, whome your putting down hath raised,

Did vse the same and with the same is praised.
Wherfore yf they had witt that soe did trace vs,
They must again for their own creddits grace vs;
  Or else to our more honour and their greevs
  Match vs at least with honorable theevs.

(McClure 388)[25]

From Martial, Davies borrowed not only conceits but, more importantly, the concept of an epigrammatic persona. Instead of the eager jester of Heywood, who was perfectly willing to make himself the butt of a joke if that was what it would take to make his audience laugh, Davies was a cool, detached observer of the urban scene. Robert Krueger, Davies' modern editor, has described this persona as "the pattern of perfection, . . . a man whose reason so thoroughly controls his will, his affections, his body, and the world around him that he presents to the world an unflawed surface, invulnerable and impassable."[26] The object of Davies' scorn is the "gull," a fop, a coward, and a conceited fool whom Davies draws in authentic detail over and over again in the epigrams. Most particularly, a gull is anyone "so gross and dull" as to think the epigram aimed at him personally. He "knows not what an epigram doth mean":

Which Taxeth under a particular name,
A generall vice that merits publique blame.
                      (I, "Ad Musam")

It is characteristic of Davies to scorn anyone insecure enough to see himself as the scorned and not the scorner.

To some extent, then, Davies achieved the idea of Martial's epigrams but not the spirit, for Davies' persona does not achieve the complexity of Martial's sardonic voice.[27] Martial's observations of Rome are brilliant precisely because he is also randy, greedy, and punctilious about social position (and he knows his readers are too), whereas Davies is detached, cynical, and superior.

Davies imitates the structure of Martial's epigram books as well, but with a dramatic change. Davies' *Epigrams* begins with an introductory poem, "Ad Musam," modeled closely on Martial's opening address to his book (1.3). But halfway through Martial's prototype of one hundred poems, Davies stops and addresses another poem "Ad Musam." In epigram 48 the voice of the persona cracks for the first time. "Ponticus" has envied Davies' fame and attributed it only to high-level patronage; Davies'

85

brand of poetry has gone quickly out of fashion; and worse, all of the epigrams of the 1590s and beyond that "doth but savour of a libel vaine" will
be attributed to his influence. He bids his Muse, as will Jonson and Herrick at midvolume, "peace . . . have done." Unlike Jonson and Herrick,
however, he does not continue after all.

Indeed, like Joseph Hall, Davies did give up epigram writing entirely
after the Bishops' Order of 1599, when both Hall's and Davies' poems were
condemned and Davies' were burned. Both men became distinguished
members of their country's ecclesiastical and judicial authority, respectively, and found other ways of impressing upon their countrymen a need
for correction.

Thomas Bastard, too, gave up the writing of epigrams, but he did not
receive any reward or influence as a result. He died insane and in debt in
1613, apparently abandoned by his patron, Thomas, earl of Suffolk, and
disappointed in his efforts to obtain preferment from James I.

Formally, Bastard's *Chrestoleros* (1598) is relatively sophisticated compared to the epigram collections appearing contemporaneously. Besides
"de subiecto operis sui," its opening catalogue sonnet, there are several
framing poems modeled on Martial's at the beginning of the first book,
and then at the beginning and end of each book thereafter. Rather than
dividing his epigrams into groups of one hundred, Bastard chose to dis-
tribute them evenly over seven books.[28] In a rather labored way, Bastard
imitates Martial's tongue-in-cheek counting of his poems. Midway through
his fourth book, for example, Bastard reminds us of the shape of his
epigram book:

> Reader but halfe my labour is expirde,
> And Poet, matter, witt and all are tyrde.
> Thrise fiftie labours have worne out my veyne,
> An hundred meanings and an halfe remayne,
> Heere would I rest were my first worke to doe.
> Were the last at an end, heere would I to.
>
> (4.29)

In *Chrestoleros* the midpoint is a mechanical marker and a display of classical learning. In the epigram books of Jonson and Herrick, it will become a critical fulcrum that will mark a dramatic change and will color
all that went before it.

To Herrick especially, Bastard would have appeared as the sad example
of a clergyman who committed the double folly of marriage and of epi-

gram writing with no secure social position to support either one. For both of these follies he was well known in the early seventeenth century. At the least, his name together with his marriage made Bastard an irresistible target for epigrammatic wit.[29] Harington's quatorzain on Bastard is by far the wittiest with its pun on Bastard's name and its cutting satire on married clergymen:[30]

Had yow been known to me ear yow wear maryd,
I should have wisht that single yow had taryd.
Yet of your spryte my sperit ys so awfull,
I dare not say soch marriage ys vnlawfull.
Nor dare I say men of soch holy function
Should castrat quite themselvs from such coniunction.
Nor dare I much owr saviour's speeches skann,
To whome twas spoken, "Take it they that cann."
Nor dare I say the word would work more good
Yf preachers wallowd less in flesh and bloud.
Nor dare I say such livyngs wear provided
With crosier staves, not distaves, to be guided.
   Yet least I might be deemd among the dastards,
   I dare say this: "Thy children shall be bastards."
                                        (McClure 358)[31]

Perhaps because Harington admired Bastard's epigrams and his attempt "To work in mens ill manners, good amendment" with verses that "kept within the lists of good sobrietie," Harington had a particular animus against Bastard's failings (2.64; McClure 160). To Harington, Bastard represented, on the one hand, the epigram's potential for the correction of corruption, particularly the corruption of "magistrates." Unfortunately, as we have seen, to Harington Bastard's epigrams also represented compromise and base flattery. Harington, of course, was wealthy and his position relatively secure in comparison with Bastard's "extreme poverty and toiling wretchedness, in the Lord's vineyard," and, significantly, Harington never saw his epigrams published in his lifetime.[32] Bastard may perhaps be forgiven his retreat from political criticism. Jonson would shape the epigram into a tool of subtle irony, but in Bastard's hands it was still a vehicle for bald statement and therefore was crude and dangerous as a device for political advice and correction. Bastard could mount a broad attack on clerical and social abuses, but his indignation was punctured by his qualified flattery of those in high positions.

It is important to remember, however, that in spite of Harington's criticisms of Bastard, he praised him as well for his "prophetic" voice. Late in the last book of *Chrestoleros*, for example, is a powerful and foreboding epigram that explicitly questions both his society and his own poems on that society:

> *Ovr vice is runne beyond all olde mens sawes,*
> And farre authenticall aboue our lawes,
> And scorning virtues safe and goolden meane,
> Sits vncontrolde vpon the high extreame.
> Circes thynne monsters painted out the hue,
> Of fayned filthinesse, but ours is true.
> *Our vice puts downe all prouerbes and all theames,*
> *Our vice excels all fables and all dreames.*
>
> (7.42; italics added)

The epigram starkly denies the careful circumspection of some of his earlier epigrams. Indeed, it denies even the corrective epigrams. No proverbs, no fables, no dreams can imagine the vice the poet sees. Placed at the end of *Chrestoleros*, questioning and, in retrospect, changing all the poems that came before, this epigram reveals the potential of the epigram book to speak in a complex voice.

The epigrams of Sir John Harington are a charming mix of poems to his redoubtable mother-in-law, Lady Rogers; to his wife; and to several principal characters such as "Leda," a wonderful ongoing portrait of a Puritan hypocrite. The character most often and most vividly sketched is "Paulus," who is clearly identifiable as Sir Walter Ralegh. Although there are epigrams in which Harington and Ralegh converse as friends, Harington also recreates Ralegh's vanity, his social climbing, and his homosexuality and condemns Ralegh's servile flattery of the queen and his atheism. "Paulus" appears to be the mirror image of Harington himself; while Ralegh forges his way in the world by shameless flattery and bold physical adventures, Harington remains at home playing the wise fool.[33]

There is a large measure of manifest autobiography in Harington's epigrams. He has poems, for example, about his other literary projects and about intimate details of his domestic wrangles. In this way his poems are similar to Martial's acheivement of psychological truth—an authentic recording of a person's changes of mind and of mood that because they are contradictory are the more realistic.

Harington wrote most of his 430 epigrams in the 1590s, and they circulated freely in manuscript during Elizabeth's reign. A number of Harington's poems are modeled explicitly on Martial's epigrams. But he was equally conscious of the English epigrammatists. He borrowed proverbs and stories from John Heywood, for example, and wrote six epigrams about Heywood himself.[34] Sir Thomas More provided Harington with a model for integrating political commentary into his epigram book and served as a reminder to Harington of the dangers of his position as privileged jester.[35]

Indeed, Harington wrote under circumstances notably similar to those of both More and Heywood. As Elizabeth's godson, Harington was allowed by her a remarkable freedom to chide her in his epigrams and even to criticize her openly. He was, for example, an outspoken proponent of James VI as Elizabeth's successor.[36] But, like Heywood, he protected himself from his sovereign's wrath by playing the harmless joker. Harington incurred Elizabeth's most extreme anger when he was knighted by Essex in Ireland during Essex's treasonous campaign of 1599. Yet even this dangerous association earned him no more than temporary banishment from the court; Elizabeth told Lord Buckhurst, "Go tell that witty fellow, my godson, to get home: it is no season now to foole it here."[37]

It is probable too that Harington was allowed greater license in his epigrams because he kept them out of print. His Muse, Harington says, "never sought to set to sale her wryting"; she therefore "cannot beg applause of vulgar sort, / Free born and bred, more free for noble sport" (McClure 424). Indeed, a reading of Harington's epigrams today is complicated by their double life, first in manuscript and then in print.[38]

The most elegant and authoritative example of Harington's epigrams in manuscript is a holograph presentation copy, probably prepared for Prince Henry's twelfth birthday in 1605.[39] The manuscript is especially interesting because it is carefully arranged to give a distinct sense of chronological progression through historical events and the author's life. It functions on several levels—as an introduction to the poet, as a celebration of the Stuart ascension, and as a lesson in governing. The manuscript is infused with a sense of optimism about the future of England under the Stuarts. Next to the epigrams written under Elizabeth and slyly critical of her reign are juxtaposed epigrams offering an enthusiastic reception to James, the "Bright Northern Starre."

The kind of cumulative message Harington could convey by the arrangement of his epigrams is evidenced in a sequence of three epigrams in the presentation manuscript.[40] In the middle of the sequence Harington placed the epigram "Of Treason" (4.5; McClure 259; 335 in manuscript), an epigram that has since been frequently anthologized:

> Treason doth neuer prosper, what's the reason?
> For if it prosper, none dare call it Treason.

This cynical poem is followed by "The Tragicall Epigram," which is a boldly forthright condemnation of the execution of Mary Stuart, a further interpretation of "treason"'s flexible definition, and a warning to Elizabeth:

> When doome of Peeres & Iudges fore-appointed,
> By racking lawes beyond all reach of reason,
> Had vnto death condemn'd a Queene anointed,
> And found, (oh strange!) without allegeance, treason
> The Axe that should haue done that execution,
> Shunn'd to cut off a head that had been crowned,
> Our hangman lost his wonted resolution,
> To quell a Queene of nobles so renowned.
> Ah, is remorse in hangmen and in steele,
> When Peeres and Iudges no remorse can feele?
> Grant Lord, that in this noble Ile, a Queene
> Without a head, may neuer more be seene.
> (4.82; McClure 336; 336 in manuscript)

In the case of Mary Stuart, Harington argues, the law of treason was twisted beyond recognition. But his most telling and most dangerous gibe is the first poem in the sequence, an epigram "Of Monsters," addressed to Harington's widowed mother-in-law. The epigram lists a series of monsters but concludes, "A headless woman is a greater Monster" (2.93; McClure 189; 334 in manuscript). Since a "headless woman" in Renaissance iconography is an unmarried woman, the cut against Elizabeth is obvious. But coupled with the "Tragicall Epigram" and its wish (or threat) "that in this noble Ile, a Queene / Without a head, may neuer more be seene," Harington's daring is astonishing. Yet each of these epigrams circulated widely in Elizabeth's court and appears in many of the extant Elizabethan and seventeenth-century commonplace books.[41] Grouped together in Harington's epigram book for Prince Henry, they dare even further.

Even in the dedicatory epigram-sonnet that prefaces the Prince Henry manuscript, Harington uses the sestet to make clear that no one will stop his epigrams from recognizing wrongs:

> Yf I whear sin ys wrought, pay shame for wages,
> Let your ritch grace hold my poor zeall excused;
> Enormous acts move modest mindes to rages,
> Which strayght a tart reproofe well gev'n asswages,
> And dewly gev'n yt cannot be refused.
> We do but poynt out vices and detect them;
> Tis you, great prince, that one day must correct them.
> (McClure 347)

Harington's epigrams, then, are meant to be advice to the king. Like Heywood, Harington is willing to amuse, to play the jester, but, again like Heywood, he reserves the jester's right to tell the truth and offer counsel.

Harington indicates his hope that under James his task will be less dangerous and therefore will need to be less cryptic. He goes so far as to offer Prince Henry the "key" to his epigrams when he asks in the dedication of his manuscript that the prince

> Accept a present heer of skribled pages,
> *A work whose method ys to be confused,*
> A work in which my pen yt self engages
> To vse them right that have the world abused.
> (McClure 347; italics added)

Harington's "method" in the epigrams has been to be just "confused" enough so that he can plead innocence and coincidence for any criticism implied by an analogy, a key word, or an amusing thrust with serious intent.

But now under the Stuarts Harington tells Henry that the poet hopes to be able to speak more freely:

> Now to more serious thoughts my soule aspyers,
> This age, this minde, a Muse awsteare requires.
> Now for those fayned joyes true joyes do spring,
> When I salute my sovraigne lord and king.
> *Now we may tell playn truth to all that ask,*
> *Our love may walke bare-faste without a mask.*
> (McClure 427, ll. 9–14; italics added)

It is notable that when Harington's epigrams were finally published after his death, neither this poem nor the dedicatory poem was included.

🙰 Herrick's debt to the sixteenth-century English epigram tradition is significant. Herrick relies heavily throughout *Hesperides* on Heywoodian proverbs, for example, in a way completely unlike Ben Jonson, who scorned such explicitness. An early georgic poem like "A Country Life," for example, is studded with italicized proverbs such as "*A wise man ev'ry way lies square*" or "*Wealth cannot make a life, but Love*" (H-106, ll. 98, 128). A random cluster of late epigrams yields "*The more we get, / The more on ycie pavements we are set*" (H-1032), "*Like will to like, each Creature loves his kinde*" (H-1043), and "*No man dies ill, that liveth well*" (H-1059). Herrick uses this adages to reaffirm traditional loyalties and values in a way very similar to Heywood's avowedly moral purpose.

Furthermore, like Heywood, More, and Harington, Herrick devises a harmless persona who can express potentially dangerous opinions with impunity. Jonson specifically rejected the convention of the epigrammatic jester and chose a voice of serious moral weight. Herrick may have learned a bitter lesson from the example of his poetic father: to take a public moral stance is potentially to expose the self to public shame earned by degrading compromises necessitated by political allegiance or the marketplace. Herrick's persona, in contrast, is not so much the fool or jester but an innocuous penner of elegant conceits and a court poet of skillful panegyrics, a guise that safely envelops his stringent epigrams in apparent innocence. Herrick thus solves the problem that Thomas Bastard, his fellow West Country pastor and epigrammatist, could only deal with awkwardly—the yoking of flattery with political and social criticism. Bastard is manifestly one of Herrick's epigrammatic models for the opening of *Hesperides*. But Bastard's pause at midvolume and bitter denunciation of his society and his own poetry about that society at the end of *Chrestoleros* also serve as a model for Herrick's formal development of his book.

Herrick is specifically indebted to the *Meditations* of Joseph Hall as a source for a surprisingly large number of epigrams in *Hesperides*. Herrick may be indirectly indebted to Hall as well. In *Virgidemiarum*, Hall had articulated the other side of poetry, rejecting the Muse and lashing out in decidedly unpretty attacks. Herrick would integrate both the poetic sweetness and the angry gall into one volume.

Sir John Harington was the most innovative of Herrick's English predecessors before Jonson. He further developed the epigram book's "confused method," which enabled him to offer advice to a sovereign while claiming innocence and coincidence if he were called to task for any apparent criticisms. Harington's epigrammatic strategy underlies the "method" of *Hesperides* as well, for Herrick's "delight in disorder" is a protective barrier against too close a reading of single poems.

Harington arranged his epigrams in a way that suggests both an autobiographical narrative and a history of his times. This underlying narrative thread throughout Harington's four books is a precedent for the complex development of political commentary, persona, verse form, and mood in *Hesperides*.

Finally, *Hesperides* may be indebted, too, to the epigram's twin form, the sonnet, and in particular to the example of Michael Drayton. Joan Ozark Holmer has documented the collaboration among a coterie of fairy court poets in the 1620s: Michael Drayton, Sir Simeon Steward, William Browne, and Robert Herrick. Their influences and shared images are so intimately intertwined that scholars have debated the exact authorship of several of the fairy poems.[42]

The work upon which Drayton lavished the most intense care is his sequence of sonnets which began as *Ideas Mirrour: Amours in Quatorzains* when it was first published in 1594, but that metamorphosed into *Idea,* an entirely different work. In 1599, 1600, 1602, 1605, and 1619, Drayton published continually revised and rearranged versions of *Idea* until by 1619 the sonnet sequence had altered radically from the highly conventional poems of 1594. A major impetus for change at the beginning of this process was the criticism of the original *Ideas Mirrour,* criticism voiced in epigrams by Sir John Davies, by Guilpin in *Skialetheia (Or, A Shadowe of Truth, in certaine Epigrams and Satyres),* and the more general criticism of the sonnet mode of Hall and of Marston's epigram book, *Scourge of Villainy.*[43] The evolution of Drayton's sonnet sequence is thus a dramatic enactment of the conflicting poles of the two related forms, sonnet and epigram, toward lyricism, on the one hand, and mockery, on the other. Finally, *Idea* rests someplace in the middle.

The sonnet that first introduced Drayton's 1599 edition of *Idea* and remained in all subsequent editions as his "Argument" warns his readers what not to expect and tells them how to read the ensuing sequence:[44]

> Into these Loves, who but for Passion lookes,
> At this first sight, here let him lay them by,

And seeke else-where, in turning other Bookes,
Which better may his labour satisfie.
No farre-fetch'd Sigh shall ever wound my Brest,
Love from mine Eye a Teare shall never wring,
Nor in AH-MEES my whyning Sonnets drest,
(A Libertine) fantastickly I sing:
My Verse is the true image of my Mind,
Ever in motion, still desiring change;
And as thus to Varietie inclin'd,
So in all Humours sportively I range:
  My Muse is rightly of the ENGLISH straine,
  That cannot long one fashion intertaine.[45]

(italics added)

Drayton's proposal is extraordinary: he will sing "fantastickly"; *Idea* will reflect his moods, his changing opinions, so that the variety that the volume contains will not be dictated merely by rhetorical principle but will be "the true image of [his] mind."[46] Indeed, *Idea* itself changed constantly over the years as Drayton grew increasingly skillful as a poet and skeptical about the very genre within which he worked. What Drayton proposes in his liminal poem may be read as a radical theory for the kind of poetic sequence that Herrick will develop in the interplay of lyric and epigram that is *Hesperides.*[47]

CHAPTER FIVE

"Father Ben": Jonson's *Epigrammes*, *The Forrest*, and *Under-wood*

As one of the self-professed "Sons of Ben," Herrick openly admitted the special relationship that his own poetry had with Jonson's:

> When I a Verse shall make,
> Know I have praid thee,
> For old *Religions* sake,
> Saint *Ben* to aide me.
>
> (H-604)

We cannot understand Herrick's procedures as an epigrammatist without a preceding grasp of Jonson's, not only in his own *Epigrammes*, the first of his collections of verse to be published, but also in *The Forrest* and *Under-wood*. And in order to understand Jonson, we need to gain some critical perspective on what exactly it meant for him, especially at the beginning of his career, to commit himself to the "classical" tradition in poetry and thereby to deny himself (and his readers) much of what they had come to expect in the mixed genes of the genre that had emerged in the early seventeenth century.

Ben Jonson told Drummond of Hawthornden "that when Sir John Harrington desyrd him to tell the Truth of his Epigrames, he answered him that he loved not the Truth, for they were Narrations and not Epigrames." With that equivocation Jonson consigned Harington to the ranks of the "new" way, the English perversion of the classical epigram tradition that Jonson attacked in "To my Meere English Censurer" (18) and intended to outshine.[1] Jonson's remark becomes more complicated, however, if we place it in the context of the actual publication history of his epigrams and of Harington's. Jonson's *Epigrammes. I. Booke* appeared as the first of his collected poems in the 1616 *Works*. It is possible that they had already been published in 1612. Although there is no extant copy of such an edition, it was entered in the Stationers' Register for that year, and William Drummond included among "bookes red be me anno 1612 . . . Ben Jhonsons epigrams."[2]

While Harington had written most of his epigrams two decades earlier, they were not published until 1615, either closely following or anticipating Jonson's *Epigrammes. I. Booke,* and three years before Jonson's conversation with Drummond. In 1618, a second, expanded edition of Harington's epigrams appeared (which was reprinted in 1625 and 1634). Harington is, in one sense, then, a contemporary and a rival of Jonson, and Jonson's remarks can be read in that context.[3] One must wonder, too, what Jonson did think of the "truth" of Harington's epigrams. He deflected the question with a semantic play to the question of form. But the question remains, and it is an important one. In the dedication of his *Epigrammes,* for example, Jonson asks Pembroke for his protection for the *Epigrammes* because "truth, and libertie" need a high-ranking patron. "Truth" is the key word in the dedication. Jonson therefore squirms uneasily at the thought that he may have praised where praise was not deserved, offending against "truth" by flattery.

Harington also prided himself on the "truth" of his epigrams and resented Jonson's flippant answer. In his epigram "That his Poetrie shall be no fictions, but meere truths," Harington creates a "narration" whose plot is a confrontation between Jonson, as "Momus," the carping critic, and himself. The epigram begins as "Harington" has begun to compose a reply to Jonson. In typically self-mocking fashion, Harington says that his reply is already sixteen lines long, a narration within a narration, when he hears that "Momus" has found fault with "Harington"'s use of yet another literary term:

> Scant wrate I sixteene lines, but I had newes,
> *Momus* had found one fault, past all excuse,
> That of *Epistle* I the name abuse.
> No, gentle *Momus,* that is none abuse,
> Without I call that *Gospel* that ensues,
> But read to carpe, as still hath been thine vse:
>> Fret out thine heart to search, seeke, sift and pry,
>> Thy heart shall hardly giue my pen the ly.
>>> (1.1; McClure 2)

Harington is, after all, disarmingly frank about why and for whom he writes. In "Of his Muse" (McClure 424) he elaborates on the point of his quarrel with Jonson about the truth of epigrams:

> I near desearvd that gloriows name of Poet;
> No Maker I, nor do I care who know it.
> *Occasion oft my penn doth entertayn*
> *With trew discourse; let others Muses fayn;*
> *Myne never sought to set to sale her wryting;*
> In part her frends, in all her selfe delighting
> She cannot beg applause of vulgar sort,
> Free born and bred, more free for noble sport.
> My Muse hath one still bids her in her eare;
> Yf well disposd, to write; yf not, forbear.
>
> (italics added)

Harington here articulates the limits of the epigram as art. Occasional, terse, undecorated, it is a form that pushes poetry as close as possible to plain statement and thus highlights the tension in poetry between "fayn-ing" and "trew discourse."[4] Harington chooses unvarnished truth as appropriate for the epigram and so, like Hall, rejects the artifice of poetry.

Ben Jonson, on the other hand, did aspire to "that gloriows name of Poet." He aspired, too, to elevate the epigram, certainly above the level to which it had been dragged by the popular epigrammatists of the turn of the century, but also to a higher plane than that of the epigrams of Davies and Harington.[5] In epigram 18, for example, Jonson implies that his "Meere English Censurer" will scorn him, both for joining the scurrilous company of the English epigrammatist of the 1590s *and* for writing an epigram book so different from theirs. He laughs at the Censurer's ignorance and parochialism:

> To thee, my way in *Epigrammes* seemes new,
> When both it is the old way, and the true.
> Thou saist, that cannot be: for thou hast seene
> *Davis,* and *Weever,* and the best have beene,
> And mine come nothing like. I hope so. Yet,
> As theirs did with thee, mine might credit get:
> If thou'ldst but use thy faith, as thou didst then,
> When thou wert wont t'admire, not censure men.
> Pr'y thee beleeve still, and not judge so fast,
> Thy faith is all the knowledge that thou hast.[6]

Jonson publicly abjured the English way of epigrams and turned to Martial as his primary model, aiming for complex, tightly constructed poems spoken by an urbane voice.

Since Jonson was committed to modeling the English epigram on the classical example, it would seem that he had in some way to integrate the praise of rulers into *Epigrammes*. But it was against Jonson's nature to adopt the groveling stance of Martial's epigrammatic persona. In the epigram "To the Ghost of Martial" (36), he acknowledged the problem and tried to explain it away:

> *Martial,* thou gav'st farre nobler *Epigrammes*
> To thy *Domitian,* than I can my *James:*
> But in my royall subject I passe thee,
> Thou flattered'st thine, mine cannot flatter'd bee.

Whether the poems sustain this premise is open to question. Those to James in *Epigrammes* are restrained and reasonable (4, 5, 35, 36, 51). But when Jonson praises James indirectly by way of men highly placed in his government who therefore act as an extension of Jacobean policy, his strategy seems often designed to maintain his own dignity.[7] Thomas Howard, earl of Suffolk, for example, is identified, first of all, as the people's favorite: "Which, by no lesse confirm'd, then thy kings choice, / Proves, that is gods, which was the peoples voice" (67). More problematic is the epigram in praise of Robert, earl of Salisbury (63). Jonson asks:

> Who can consider thy right courses run,
> With what thy vertue on the times hath won,
> And not thy fortune; *who can cleerely see*
> *The judgement of the king so shine in thee*
> . . . .
> And can to these be silent, Salisburie?
>
> (ll. 1–10; italics added)

Since Jonson suspends the syntax almost to the poem's conclusion and retains its statement in the form of a question, this praise, although apparently wholehearted, can also be read as ironic. Nor does the couplet that ends the poem resolve the ambiguity:

> Curst be his *Muse,* that could lye dumbe, or hid
> To so true worth, though thou thy selfe forbid.

Since Salisbury was infamous for his system of spies and his rigid control of possible libels, Jonson's implication that Salisbury would "forbid" the recognition of "so truth worth" is potentially sarcastic.

This epigram is paired with another to Salisbury upon his accession to Lord Treasurer in 1608, a poem that also mentions the king's wisdom in choosing his advisers. It is one of Jonson's most tortuous poems, virtually impossible to read through without stopping, doubling back, and puzzling out meanings. Midway through, the gnarled compression eases, and Jonson finally delivers the expected compliment:

> But I am glad to see that time survive,
> > Where merit is not sepulcher'd alive.
> Where good mens vertues them to honors bring,
> > And not to dangers. *When so wise a king*
> *Contends t'have worth enjoy, from his regard,*
> *As her owne conscience, still, the same reward.*
> These (noblest Cecil) labour'd in my thought,
> > Wherein what wonder see thy name hath wrought?
> *That whil'st I meant but thine to gratulate,*
> *I'have sung the greater fortunes of our state.*
>
> (64, italics added)

But Jonson's "owne conscience" remained decidedly uneasy with what Salisbury's "name hath wrought." Earlier in *Epigrammes*, there is yet another poem to Salisbury, written in the same elliptical style:

> What need hast thou of me? or of my *Muse?*
> > Whose actions so themselves doe celebrate;
> Which should thy countries love to speake refuse,
> > Her foes enough would fame thee in their hate.
> 'Tofore, great men were glad of *Poets:* Now,
> > I, not the worst, am covetous of thee.
> Yet dare not, to my thought, lest hope allow
> > Of adding to thy fame; thine may to me,
> When in my booke, men reade but *Cecill's* name,
> > And what I write thereof finde farre, and free
> From servile flatterie (common *Poets* shame)
> > As thou stand'st cleere of the necessitie.
>
> (43)

The equation Jonson sets up at the end of the poem may be read either as clever praise or as an indictment, not only of Cecil, but of himself, purveyor of "servile flatterie (common *Poets* shame)."

Directly following the two poems on Salisbury's accession to Lord Treasurer is the crucial poem "To my Muse" (65), placed at the formal center of *Epigrammes*. There Jonson recoils with revulsion at the thought that greed or desire for place should have induced him to flatter:

> Away, and leave me, thou thing most abhord
>   That hast betray'd me to a worthlesse lord;
> Made me commit most fierce idolatrie
>   To a great image through thy luxurie.

In rejecting the epigrammatic Muse, "thou thing most abhord," Jonson lashes out not only at his own book of epigrams but at the whole classical tradition he is imitating. The "abhord" epigram can be a whore, can be Martial's fawning expediency, the prostitute dancing at the Saturnalian feast. In the middle of *Epigrammes*, Jonson questions not only his book itself but the dialogue he is carrying on back through a form.[8] He sends the Muse to her next "unluckie" master:

> Get him the times long grudge, the courts ill will;
>   And, reconcil'd, keepe him suspected still.
> Make him loose all his friends; and, which is worse,
>   Almost all wayes, to any better course.

But Jonson now wants to be left with the happier Muse of poverty, who "shall instruct my after-thoughts to write / Things manly, and not smelling parasite." After this noble and passionate declaration, however, the poet's stance suddenly and disconcertingly changes, and the poem comes to an abrupt stop:

> But I repent me: Stay. Who e're is rais'd,
>   For worth he has not, He is tax'd, not prais'd.

Perhaps the Muse of poverty looked a bit thin for the poet's taste. Perhaps, after all, an epigrammatic twist at the end of this agonized outcry can set the whole moral position of the book straight. Perhaps. Certainly, at the end, the poet allows the epigrammatic Muse to stay and by so doing he allows into the margin of his book all of the "masters" she has served before. Jonson faces here the inherent ambivalence of the genre, accepts it, and enunciates a strategy to make it work for him.

In the volume as a whole he recreates, it seems fair to say, the opposing purposes—correction and flattery—that Harington and Bastard had played out a generation earlier. Herford and Simpson call "literary foppery" Jonson's imitation of Martial's role of poet to Caesar, but in his book devoted to "truth," Jonson holds himself aloof from the excesses of praise which Martial wallows in to the point of parody.[9]

Because Jonson's epigrams have an avowedly moral purpose, they are easily read as an indirect criticism of society. However, by committing himself in *Epigrammes. I. Booke* to the classical model and rejecting the English way, Jonson forfeited the opportunity to use the epigram as a vehicle for direct political criticism or counsel. His anxiety about this self-imposed restriction may be revealed in his jealous criticism of Harington's epigrams, and it may also be revealed by the fact that there never was an *Epigrammes. II. Booke*. Certainly, in the dedication of *Epigrammes* to Pembroke, Jonson creates an elaborately ambivalent frame for the poems, alternately avowing their innocence of any subversive meaning and hinting broadly that they may be read as dangerous after all. "Though they carry danger in the sound," Jonson says, "when I made them, I had nothing in my conscience, to expressing of which I did need a cypher." This already tentative statement is then heavily qualified by the words that follow:

But, if I be falne into those times, wherein, for the likenesse of vice, and facts, every one thinks anothers ill deeds objected to him; and that in their ignorant and guiltie mouthes, the common voyce is (for their securitie) BEWARE THE POET, confessing, therein, so much love to their diseases, as they would rather make a partie for them, then be either rid, or told of them: I must expect, at your Lo: hand, the protection of truth, and libertie, while you are constant to your owne goodnesse.[10]

Finally, even the constancy of Pembroke's goodness is shadowed by a proviso. And Pembroke, the most generous patron of his age, was son of the countess of Pembroke, nephew of Sir Philip Sidney, and one of "the incomparable pair of brethren" to whom Shakespeare's first folio is dedicated. *Epigrammes* remains as a standard of morality which few can attain, critical both in its praise and in its blame.

On one point only does Jonson disassociate himself from Martial entirely. Jonson's epigrams abjure the "lewd, prophane, and beastly phrase, / To catch the worlds loose laughter, or vaine gaze" (2, "To my Booke"). Whereas Martial had advised, "Let Cato not enter my Theater," in Jonson's "Theater" it is those men immersed in "riot," "pride," and "self-love" who should stay away, but there "CATO, if he liv'd, might enter without scandall."

But Jonson does not banish the "lewd, prophane, and beastly phrase" entirely; instead, in a gesture that curiously resembles the bowdlerization of epigram books by nineteenth-century scholars, he gathers a large mass of scatology and raw satire and places it at the end of his volume. Jonson's final epigram, 133, "On the Famous Voyage," is an extraordinarily long epigram that can be read as yet another gibe at Harington, since it is certainly a "narration" and is also, in part, an imitation and a satire of *The Metamorphosis of Ajax*.[11] The mock-heroic "Voyage" begins "I sing" and invokes Hercules as its Muse and guide through an ordurous hell. All the careful circumspection of *Epigrammes. I. Booke* is stripped away in this poem, ending the volume on a note of rude laughter, confirmation perhaps of Puttenham's psychological insight into the nature of the epigram and evidence that coarseness is an irrepressible part of the genre. Placed strategically as the last poem in the volume, "On the Famous Voyage" serves also to demonstrate the epigram book's tendency as a genre to deconstruct itself, to mock itself and its own pretensions. The moment of self-doubt about his own rectitude which Jonson placed at midvolume in "To my Muse" is reasserted in the primitive, Rabelaisian humor of the end.

In the body of *Epigrammes*, however, Jonson's purposes are expressly moral—to satirize corruption and folly and to praise excellence. In this Jonson is not, in fact, returning the epigram to the old way but conforming to the English model of satiric correction. And the epigram of praise, conventional since Martial, Jonson uses in a new way as moral exemplar counterbalancing the satiric epigrams.[12] In epigram 102, for example, Jonson again addresses William, earl of Pembroke, and goes so far as to call Pembroke's name alone "an *Epigramme*, on all man-kind; / Against the bad, but of, and to the good."

Epigrammes is carefully arranged to convey a dramatic sense of good and evil; Pembroke is an actor

> . . . in this strife
> Of vice, and vertue; wherein all great life
> Almost, is exercis'd: and scarse one knowes,
> To which, yet, of the sides himselfe he owes.
>
> (102)

The first half, as Edward Partridge has observed, is dominated by satiric epigrams directed against pseudonymous fools like Don Surly and Sir Voluptuous Beast.[13] The second half, however, is dominated by specifically named men and women held up as models of goodness: "so many good, and great names (as my verses mention on the better part) to their remembrance with posteritie" ("To the Great Example of Honor and Vertue . . . William, Earle of Pembroke," p. 3). The poem on flattery, "To my Muse," is the pivot upon which the drama of the volume turns, since it is the moment of the poet's self-revelation. Although the second half of *Epigrammes* is, on balance, an affirmation of human goodness, Jonson is careful never to lose sight of the essential qualification that he imposes at midvolume on all his poems of praise: "Who e're is rais'd, / For worth he has not, He is tax'd, not prais'd." Just as guilty readers find themselves in the anonymous epigrams, so the named reader will find his own guilt in any undeserved praise. The epigram is, thus, a touchstone for truth, a philosopher's stone that can turn gold to lead. Only a few readers will be "good" enough to read Jonson's epigrams without finding their own guilt written between the lines. Lucy, countess of Bedford, for example, the woman who appears in *Epigrammes* more frequently than any other, is one of the privileged few:[14]

> . . . *Satyres,* since the most of mankind bee
>   Their un-avoided subject, fewest see:
> For none ere tooke that pleasure in sinnes sense,
>   But, when they heard it tax'd, tooke more offence.
> They, then, that living where the matter is bred,
>   Dare for these poemes, yet, both aske, and read,
> And like them too; must needfully, though few,
>   Be of the best: and 'mongst those, best are you.
>
> (94)

The epigrams of praise are more than occasional pieces; they are intended to serve as emblems of virtue, regardless of their literal truth. In his dedication, Jonson told Pembroke, "if I have praysed, unfortunately, any one, that doth not deserve; or, if all answere not, in all numbers, the pictures I have made of them: I hope it will be forgiven me, that they are no ill pieces, though they be not like the persons" (p. 3).

In *Epigrammes,* then, Jonson set out to reform the English epigram and bring it closer to the Roman model, although he was sensitive to the problematic nature of that model. He therefore retained, in a muted form, the convention of praise for Caesar transformed to celebration of an exemplary ruling class, while relinquishing the English epigram's tradition of direct political comment. He used Martial's century structure to dramatize a world of folly and greed. The most dramatic point in the book is its center, where the persona confronts his own folly and therefore rejects his Muse. "To my Muse," however, alters the entire conception of the book, for once he confronts his own weakness, the persona can see the ambiguous nature of his flattery. He can bid his Muse "Stay" after all and write on. The final note of *Epigrammes. I. Booke* is self-mockery: the carefully compacted epigrams explode into a rambling mock epic that celebrates the "lewd and beastly" that the rest of the volume had abjured and instead "praises" two "horride knaves."

Herrick is conventionally honored as Jonson's most worthy son. Yet the extent and depth of Herrick's debt to Jonson have not been measured, except in isolated poems. I believe a detailed discussion of the structure and persona of *Hesperides* must come back to Jonson's epigrams over and over again, both as a model and as an influence against which Herrick reacted.[15] The personal crisis at the midpoint of *Epigrammes* that alters the poet's stance in the rest of the book, for example, is reflected in *Hesperides,* although the outcome is different, since the "Herrick" persona is incapacitated rather than freed by disillusionment. Certainly *Hesperides* combines poems of praise and coarse poems of "satire" in a mix that resembles *Epigrammes,* although Herrick does not intend Jonson's moral purpose or sense of dramatic conflict between good and evil.

Hesperides, of course, contains a much wider variety of poems than *Epigrammes*—the epigrams surround epistles, songs, love lyrics, epithalamia, for example—but for this medley Herrick could find precedents in Jonson's other poetry. In the preface to *Under-wood,* Jonson had said that its title grew "out of the Analogie" to the title of *The Forrest* because both were derived from the classical term "sylva," a collection "in which there were workes of divers nature, and matter congested" (p. 117). The title of Herrick's poems can be read as growing by another analogic step from *The Forrest* and *Under-wood* to *Hesperides.* Both *The Forrest* and *Under-wood* contain epigrams that are markedly different in conception and presentation from *Epigrammes* and that exert a significant influence on Herrick.

Many of the poems in *The Forrest,* for example, may be seen as epigrams that Jonson pushed to the limit of the form. They are long, discursive, experimental in meter. "To Sir Robert Wroth," for example, a poem that influenced Herrick specifically in several poems, is modeled in part on an epigram of Martial, but edges over generically into verse epistle. Alastair Fowler has pointed out the deliberate shape of *The Forrest,* which he argues is Jonson's generic innovation, in contrast to the randomness traditionally associated with "sylva": "*The Forrest* has come a very considerable distance from the rough spontaneous gathering pretended by Statius and disliked by Quintilian. It is highly polished and, at least in part, articulated into a structured sequence whose arrangement or 'disposure' must have been planned from a fairly early stage."[16] Fowler argues that the pattern of *The Forrest* is one of gradual retirement from the world and increasing aspiration toward heaven. Certainly the first poem in this serious volume, "Why I Write Not of Love," is an introduction and explanation of what is to come: Cupid has fled the constraint of his rhymes and so "wonder not, / That since, my numbers are so cold, / When *Love* is fled, and I grow old." Herrick would develop the same conflict between Cupid and poet into a recurrent motif of loss, age, and a changing poetic voice. *The Forrest* also contains groups of obviously articulated poems, perhaps the most significant being a sequence of three poems at the center of the book. The "Song. To Celia" (9), for example, is followed by an untitled poem beginning "And must I sing?" The heavy rhyme and satirical argument of this poem mock facile, conventional, and commissioned poetry. Jonson rejects Cupid, Hercules, Bacchus, Venus:

> Nor all the ladies of the *Thespian lake,*
> (Though they were crusht into one forme) could make
> A beautie of that merit, that should take
>
> My *Muse* up by *commission:* No, I bring
> My owne true fire. Now my thought takes wing,
> And now an *Epode* to deepe eares I sing.

Indeed, the following poem is an epode, on true virtue and true love. *Hesperides* too is studded with such small sequences, and Herrick certainly intends the entire volume to be read as a structured sequence.

But *Under-wood* is Herrick's closest model for *Hesperides.* The mix of poetic forms in *Under-wood* is, for one thing, more marked, although the poems are, in general, grouped together by genre.[17] Of the ninety-one poems in *Under-wood,* twenty-six are specifically labeled as epigrams or epitaphs, and at least another dozen are uncontestable epigrams. Conservatively, therefore, one-third of *Under-wood* is epigrammatic. Moreover, Jonson opens the book with an epigraph from Martial (1.25), "Cineri, gloria sera venit" [Glory comes too late to the ashes of the dead]. And either Jonson or his editor concludes *Under-wood* with a translation from Martial (8.77):

> *Liber,* of all thy friends, thou sweetest care,
>   Thou worthy in eternall Flower to fare,
> If thou be'st wise, with 'Syrian Oyle let shine
>   Thy locks, and rosie garlands crowne thy head;
> Darke thy cleare glasse with old *Falernian* Wine;
>   And heat, with softest love, thy softer bed.
> Hee, that but living halfe his dayes, dies such,
>   Makes his life longer then 't was given him, much.
>
> (91)

It is, therefore, this book of Jonson's that *Hesperides* most closely resembles, although Herrick takes the idea of epigrams included in a "sylva" several steps further, using variety to achieve a play of form against form.

In *Censorship and Interpretation,* Annabel Patterson has described *Under-wood* as a "retrospective of Jonson's career."[18] Although the volume was published posthumously as part of the folio *Works* of 1640–41, Jonson had prepared it for publication before his death, and his controlling hand is clearly visible throughout most of the volume. The occasional poems arranged in roughly chronological order "interrogate each other" in light of the perspective of time and experience (p. 132). *Under-wood* can therefore, Patterson argues, be read as an explanation of the poet's relationship with society and an assertion of his "personal identity in defiance of societal pressures" (p. 126).

Jonson is able to achieve this complex purpose in part because of the mix of form, epigrammatic and lyric, which *Under-wood* contains. It is a stunningly sophisticated variation on the irony and self-realization of "To my Muse" in the center of *Epigrammes. Under-wood* is, in a way, an epigram book freed from the constraint of a single form but realizing more fully the epigram book's function: a commentary on contemporary society that records the voice of the poet in a series of seemingly disconnected yet actually interdependent statements.

Throughout *Under-wood,* for example, Jonson is concerned with two major themes—true friendship and flattery—which often intertwine. In the "Epistle to a Friend, to Perswade Him to the Warres" (17), probably written about 1620 when English volunteers were rallying to the support of the Elector Palatine, Jonson argues that to stay in England and "flatter my good Lord" is "To lose the formes, and dignities of men" (ll. 146–47). Instead, Jonson urges:

> Friend flie from hence; and let these kindled rimes
> Light thee from hell on earth: where flatterers, spies
> Informers, Masters both of Arts and lies;
> Lewd slanderers, soft whisperers that let blood
> The life . . .
> .   .   .   .   .   .
> . . . lowd
> Boasters, and perjur'd, with the infinite more
> Praevaricators swarme.

Above all else, Jonson tells his friend, value "honesty" and "truth" (ll. 177, 179); to live otherwise is a "hell on earth." Jonson is stating at length here, and in other poems such as "An Epistle Answering to One That Asked to Be Sealed of the Tribe of Ben" (49), the same moral revulsion from abject flattery that he had dramatized at the midpoint of *Epigrammes*.[19]

In its latter half, *Under-wood* becomes pronouncedly epigrammatic. There Jonson places a series of occasional epigrams, dated and arranged chronologically from 1629 to 1635, that documents his years as a Caroline poet (nos. 64-84). As Patterson has observed, these epigrams of praise are preceded by a poem simply (and safely) entitled "An Epigram" (63), but which is almost certainly addressed to Bishop Williams and which, she argues, "alter[s] the character of Jonson's Caroline lyrics."[20] Jonson congratulates his unnamed subject that "you [who] have seene the pride, beheld the sport, / And all the games of Fortune, plaid at Court" "are got off thence, with cleare mind, and hands / To lift to heaven" (63, ll. 1-2, 7-8). With wrenching and self-destructive irony, Jonson follows "An Epigram" with another, "To K. Charles for a 100. Pounds He Sent Me in My Sicknesse," which initiates a sequence of conventional court epigrams praising or consoling Charles and Henrietta Maria on the events of court life—births, deaths, anniversaries. Underlying the epigrams is a note of desperation as Jonson begs the king for the patronage Charles's father had granted the poet (78), attempts to bully the king's household into sending Jonson his promised gift of sack (70), or pleads with Lord Treasurer Weston in an "Epistle Mendicant" (73). At the end of "An Epigram on the

Princes Birth 1630" (67), which calls Prince Charles the "Prince of flowers" growing in the garden of the "Lilly, and the Rose," Jonson appends an epigraph from Martial that seems extraneous to the poem:

> ———Non displicuisse meretur
> Festinat Caesar qui placuisse tibi.

[He deserves not to displease you, Caesar, who hastes to please you.]

This explicit bid for favor at the end of a poem whose dainty, conventional conceits are uncharacteristic of Jonson's intellectually rigorous style sounds a pathetic and obsequious note.

And where the poems to the Stuarts may be understandable as the duty of a court poet, the poems to Lord Treasurer Weston and his family are painful in their abasement. Indeed, these poems can be painfully bad as poetry. The epigram celebrating Weston's investiture as earl of Portland (75) begins, for example:

> Looke up thou seed of envie, and still bring
>   Thy faint, and narrow eyes, to reade the *King*
> In his great Actions: view whom his large hand,
>   Hath rais'd to be the *Port* unto his *Land!*

With the succession of Charles I in 1625, Jonson lost the privileged position, and much of the patronage, he had enjoyed under James. And after his stroke in 1628 and the failure of his late plays, Jonson became a marginal figure in Caroline culture. As his Caroline epigrams reflect his attempt to regain favor, they play out before us a humiliation that must have been profound—especially since to flatter, for Jonson, is "To lose the formes and dignities" of man.

It can be argued that *Under-wood* provided Herrick with a model for a complex and unified volume, a way of gathering together the work of a lifetime. This is not to say, however, that *Hesperides* makes the same statement about poet and society that Jonson does. Although both poets write about themselves and about Caroline England, the relationship between poet and society in Jonson and Herrick is, as we shall see, radically different. Jonson has been a public poet, implicated in the world he writes of by his praise, self-condemned by his own failures of judgment, and finally forced to make his voice serve necessity. Herrick, even in his occasional poems, inhabits a private world. In the end he will not be the poet standing apart, but the artist imprisoned in his own dying world. "Herrick" is his own artistic creation, and when the frame of "Hesperides" begins to disappear, when the fantastical garden is shattered by reality, the poet is violated within it and dies. It is because of this emphatically *literary* persona, this fictive autobiography, that *Hesperides* conveys its extraordinary sense of a sustained narrative.

I have argued that Herrick cannot be understood without a grasp of what his predecessors in the genre of epigram, and epigram book, contributed. The figures examined hitherto were all strong individuals, with strong literary personae, whose contributions permanently affected the expectations that a reader would bring to a book of epigrams. But there were also other developments and expectations, not associated with particular persons or models, of which Herrick would have been aware, and which probably affected his practice. One development, for instance, was a blurring of the boundaries between epigram and song. At the turn of the century, Thomas Campion marked the beginning of a revolution in English music in his *Booke of Ayres* (1601). The preface of Campion's volume articulated the principles of the new "cult of the ayre or solo song," that is, performance by a single voice accompanied by a single instrument, as opposed to the older polyphonic madrigal.[21] The result of this musical simplicity was a greater range for poetic complication, since the words became significantly more important, often dramatic, when sung by a single voice. Campion, who was himself a poet as well as a musician, stressed the relationship between music and poetry, choosing to describe this new musical form by analogy to poetic form:

What Epigrams are in Poetrie, the same are Ayres in musicke, then in their chiefe perfection when they are short and well seasoned. . . . A naked Ayre without guide, or prop, or colour but his owne, is easily censured of everie eare, and requires so much the more invention to make it please. And as *Martiall* speakes in defence of his short Epigrams, so may I say in th' apologie of Ayres, that where there is a full volume, there can be no imputation of shortnes. (p. 15)[22]

Campion's analogy initiated an association between the epigram and the song that, later in the century, became so close that the two forms were virtually indistinguishable.

Both Jonson and Herrick composed songs to be sung by a single voice. When Jonson included his songs in *The Forrest* and *Under-wood* he carefully labeled them as songs and even, in *Under-wood,* his "workes of divers nature, and matter congested," grouped most of them together near the beginning of the book. "Epigram" and "Song" therefore stand clearly separate in Jonson's poetry. By the eighteenth century, however, the distinction between epigram and song was so effaced that one epigrammatist remarks that although he has "heard much good discourse spent in shewing the difference between a Song and an Epigram; I protest that between an English Song and an English Epigram, I know of none but the length."[23]

Hesperides stands somewhere between this later confusion and Jonsonian clarity. Swinburne called Herrick England's "greatest song-writer," but it is frequently difficult to decide where his songs end and his epigrams begin. Some poems are entitled "songs," many are entitled "epigrams," but many more have no generic title. Most songs are in tetrameter; most coarse and sententious epigrams are in pentameter couplets; but many poems in *Hesperides* shift easily between these two categories. Lyric and epigram are, for Herrick, two tones of one voice—its modulation complex and full of implication, its meaning often contradictory—but the voice is the same. Louise Schleiner has proposed that the writing of simple song-texts had an overall effect on Herrick's poetry; she argues that the brevity of Herrick's poems, "their relative density or bareness of imagery, their smoothly flowing rhythms, and their more or less fully developed argumentation—were influenced by the demands of the song-text as genre."[24] Any one of these attributes, however, could be ascribed to the influence of the epigram as well. To say that Herrick is primarily a song writer or primarily an epigrammatist is to miss the close relationship between the two forms, a relationship that Herrick's poetry brought to its highest pitch of complexity and tension.

ॐ Richard Flecknoe, a respectable poet in spite of the infamy he has gained as Dryden's byword for bad poetry, opens his 1673 collection of *Epigrams made at several Times upon several Occasions* with a "Proemium of Epigrams," which repeats Campion's connection between song and epigram but goes on to shed an interesting light on another function of the epigram in the seventeenth century:

> What Airs in point of Musick are the same,
> In point of Writing is your Epigram,
> For short and sprightly, and both these and those
> When th'ear expects it always comes to th' close.

'Tis but a few lines, but those like Gold well try'd
Out of the dross of many lines beside,
And says not much, but i' th' Laconick way,
Comprises much, i' th' little it does say.
In euery Kind, be th' writing what it will,
'Tis that most takes and most delights you still,
And adds to all the rest, no less a Grace,
Then Wit to Sence, or Beauty to the Face.
Poets can't write, nor Orators declame,
But all their Wit, is chiefly Epigram;
And both in Verse, and Prose, and everything,
Your Epigram is writing for a King.

                          (A₂v; italics added)

Flecknoe accepts the identification of epigram and song because of their shared compression and strong sense of closure. He echoes Thomas Pecke's notion that epigrams are the essence of poetry, the soul of wit. But while Flecknoe's poem articulates the virtual identity between epigram and song, it also makes explicit what was implicit in the tradition derived from Martial—that one of the genre's essential functions was "writing for a King." In the seventeenth century, especially after the publication of Jonson's 1616 Folio, the minor contributors to Jacobean and Caroline culture took this for granted.[25] Even volumes of satirical epigrams included apparently anomalous poems of lavish praise. John Davies of Hereford, for example, one of the most popular writers of the early seventeenth century, calls his volume of epigrams *The Scourge of Folly,* but includes a very long section of epigrams "On Worthy Persons," James being preeminent.[26] Thomas Freeman's excellent book of epigrams, *Rubbe, and a great cast* (1614), begins with a series of epigrams to the royal family carefully arranged in order of rank from James to the Elector Palatine and then on to the nobility of England. On a more humble scale, Thomas Bancroft dedicated his *Two Bookes of Epigrammes* (1639) to "two top-branches of Gentry," Sir Charles Shirley and William Davenport.

Or epigram volumes could be devoted entirely to praising the king. Perhaps the best demonstration of the epigram's use as royal panegyric is a sumptuous volume published in 1626 in honor of Charles's ascension and marriage, *Anagrammata Regia.* This is a collection of poems in English and Latin, each of which seizes upon a piece of royal symbolism and draws it out to the limits of ingenuity. A great deal is made, for example, of Henrietta Maria as the Lily of France, Charles as the Red and White Rose; Henrietta Maria as myrrh and frankincense, Charles as a type of Christ. Another favorite metaphor presents Charles as Solomon and Henrietta Maria as his bride in the Song of Songs.

Royal propaganda by way of epigram, especially propaganda couched in such nearly blasphemous terms, was liable to criticism within the genre itself. *The Mirror of New Reformation* (1634), for example, is a book of epigrams by a Catholic intended to convert "the Impartial Protestant Reader."[27] The author includes the conventional epigrams of praise for the king, but the king in the *Mirror* is God, a neat criticism, by implication, of the lengths that epigrammatists had gone to in praise of earthly kings.

Epigrams could also be "writing for a King" in another sense as well. The aphoristic wisdom of the epigram can be read both as advice *to* the king and as a general statement of the stable values of good citizenship that a king wishes to see in his subjects. The wisdom of Solomon in Proverbs is the ultimate source of this sententiousness. James I, of course, carefully associated himself with Solomon and his wisdom, and Charles I attempted to transfer that association to himself.[28] A "Justice Epigram" in Robert Hayman's *Quodlibets* (1628) makes explicit the parallel between king and epigram as social regulators:

> Kings doe correct those that Rebellious are,
> And their good subjects worthily preferre;
> Just Epigrams reprove those that offend,
> And those that vertuous are, she doth commend.
>
> (39)

George Herbert offered James I another explanation for the appropriateness of "royal" epigrams. He began his *Musae Responsoriae* (written in the 1620s; published in 1662), a defense in forty epigrams of Anglican ritual against the attack of the Scottish reformer Andrew Melville, with an epigram "To the King: The reason for a project of epigrams":

> Cum millena tuam pulsare negotia mentem
>   Constet, & ex illâ pendeat orbis ope;
> Ne te productis videar lassare Camoenis,
>   Pro solido, CAESAR, carmine frusta dabo.
> Cùm tu contundis *Catharos*, vultúque librísque,
>   Grata mihi mensae sunt analecta tuae.

[Since a host of things
Dilates your mind, and the world
Hinges on its influence,
And lest I seem to tax you
With tiring verses,
I shall give to you, Caesar,
Not one but several songs.
When you beat down the Puritans
With your books and learning,
The crumbs of your table
Are precious to me.][29]

But the functions of flattering kings, advising them, and imitating their regulatory functions do not often sit well together, especially in light of the epigram's other role as a vehicle of all-out satire.

In the English Renaissance, the epigram could serve as a vehicle for praise, for counsel, for sharp criticism, or for any combination of these. It thus filled an important official place in cultural propaganda and yet was also allowed to question authority and play even more subversive roles. Although Bastard and Jonson had attempted to reform the genre, scurrility was an irrepressible part of its nature. It could be brought to serve a moral purpose, but its tendency was to serve only wit. Within this smallest of poetic forms were yoked explosive contrarieties.

Brought together in a "book," the epigram could expand exponentially. The structural possibilities of one hundred brief poems were fertile, especially since a persona could emerge who was conscious of the irreconcilable double purpose of his poetry, to praise and to subvert, to correct and to blaspheme. Jonson, in his three collections of poetry, *Epigrammes. I. Booke, The Forrest,* and *Under-wood,* first brought the classical epigram book to its highest point in English literature but then experimented with a volume of mixed forms that used the epigrams embedded in it as cryptic commentary on the lyric poems.

All of these rich possibilities were available to Robert Herrick in collating the poems he had written over four decades. To read *Hesperides* in the light of the epigram book prevents us from making the typical modernist gestures—repressing the scurrilous epigrams and isolating lyrics and epigrams and reading them alone without their contextual ironies and qualifications. It enables us to read *Hesperides* as an integrated volume, whose poems are not only tied to each other but have complex filiations also with other "books" of epigrams in the classical and more recent past.

Part Three

HESPERIDES

Nicholas Poussin, "Et in Arcadia ego"
(courtesy of the Louvre)

CHAPTER SIX

Hesperides and the Classical Epigram: Martial or Anacreon?

.𝒱𝒮𝒞𝒱. Critics have come to no conclusive position on the structure or lack of structure in *Hesperides*. Alexander Grosart, at one extreme, was so offended by the coarse epigrams that he believed that Herrick could have had nothing to do with the arrangement or even with the choice of poems printed in *Hesperides*.[1] He and other early editors either eliminated the coarse epigrams or printed them separately in an appendix.

Floris Delattre, the author of the first scholarly work on Herrick, and L. C. Martin, Herrick's first modern editor, have suggested that *Hesperides* is somehow structured chronologically—that is, in the order in which the poems were composed.[2] There are so many exceptions to a theory of arrangement by date of composition, however, that it becomes an untenable and, indeed, a deceptive oversimplification. Most subsequent critics have followed Delattre's lead in regarding any deviation from chronology as an example of the rhetorical principle of variety and contrast, but this again is an oversimplification, since it fails to recognize the curious dialogues and relationships that take place between the "contrasting" poems or the long sequences of "like" poems that Herrick places throughout *Hesperides*.[3]

Certainly the greatest source of confusion about the order of the poems in *Hesperides* has been the place of the epigrams. Only in the twentieth century have the epigrams been given any sort of critical appraisal; before that, the coarse epigrams were dismissed out of hand as loathsome and obscene, and the rest of the epigrams were simply ignored. Modern criticism is more appreciative of the cynicism, wit, and plain style of the epigrams, but the main critical thrust has been simply to group them into manageable categories—coarse epigrams, epigrams of praise, sententious epigrams—and to discuss them separately from one another and from the body of *Hesperides*.[4]

Such critical sorting out and rearranging is understandable in light of the sheer number of epigrams; they make up at least half of the poems in *Hesperides*. Indeed, given a broader definition of the epigram which would include the brief lyrics, the epigrams make up almost the entire volume. Reading Herrick's poems out of their formal context, however, means losing the resonance, wit, and ambiguity that they gain within their own sequences. Rather than being an anomaly in *Hesperides* and therefore a structural problem, the epigrams are the key to the structure of the volume.

The 1,130 poems of *Hesperides* obviously cannot be read in one sitting, yet Herrick intended that his book be read "unto the end" (H-6) and in sequence. Since Herrick did not number his poems or divide them into centuries, there is no clear formal indication of natural divisions among the poems. Yet unless we select out kinds of poems or subjects, it is extremely difficult to discuss *Hesperides*. Granting the arbitrary nature of this division, I shall discuss *Hesperides* in terms of eleven centuries, since, generically, *Hesperides* most closely resembles an epigram book. When *Hesperides* is divided into clearly marked parts, even if the division is temporary and artificial, it is possible to make specific observations about the change and development of themes and genres in Herrick's poems. Such groupings must be done with extreme caution and with the constant proviso that Herrick himself does not give explicit indication of any divisions between the poems. An interesting case may be made for division by centuries, however, if the royal poems are seen as markers for nine "books" in *Hesperides*, with Martial's poems to Domitian at the beginning of his epigram books as a classical precedent.[5] The possibility of "books" dedicated to the Stuarts is suggestive and, to an extent, can contribute to a coherent reading of *Hesperides* as a formal structure. I wish, however, to avoid positing any rigid demarcation. A discussion of *Hesperides* in terms of centuries seems to me both to be sanctioned by the formal make-up of the book and to be loose enough not to impose any unwarranted constraints. It is useful as a way of grouping poems for discussion without always having to separate them into kinds. It is useful as well as a marker indicating the development of themes or changes in the generic make-up of the volume.

It seems appropriate at this point to address Herrick's harshest twentieth-century critic. In *The Classics and English Renaissance Poetry: Three Case Studies* (1978), Gordon Braden assessed Herrick's debt to Martial, Anacreon, and Horace. Braden applied considerable learning and wit to his analyses, but his basic premise is peculiar: since Herrick is influenced by Martial, therefore he should duplicate Martial's achievement exactly. Any deviation from the classical example can only be a mistake, proof of shallow reading or lack of poetic stature. (Confusingly, Braden's objection to Herrick's use of Anacreon is the opposite. He felt that Herrick resembles Anacreon *too* closely and shows poor taste in his choice of models.) Because Herrick echoes lines, but directly translates few complete poems, Braden argued that his "response is primarily to moments of verbal grace rather than to structures of meaning"; Herrick is "almost premental"; and he concluded that Herrick "decontextualizes" the classics, that he learned "the heft or timbre of his authors' voices but none of their specific intentions." Braden thus dismissed "the prejudice" that "deeper congruences somehow obtain" (pp. 176, 174, 177).

Braden admitted that Herrick's imitation of Martial "is the most persistent and overt" ("whatever deeper affinities may be lacking"); "of all the classical oeuvres, the *Epigrammata* is the one that Herrick's book most resembles as a book" (p. 180). Yet, according to Braden, Herrick has a "problem" in that he does not follow Martial's layout closely enough (p. 182). He does not divide his poems into books, nor does he number his poems.[6] Braden concluded, therefore, that Herrick has "fudged," that he has "missed or ignored the joke" of Martial's arbitrary structure, that Herrick's "imitation" of Martial is "soft" (pp. 182, 184).

Braden chose to disregard the fact that Herrick is writing within a rich tradition that continued to develop after Martial.[7] He did not consider the possibility that the disparities between Herrick and Martial might be conventions of the Renaissance epigram or innovations on Herrick's part rather than unimaginative mistakes. All in all, Braden's brand of intertextual criticism, however brilliant when applied to Horace and Herrick, is at its most vulnerable here. His dismissal of Herrick's epigrams comes down finally to the level of personal innuendo—compared to Martial, Herrick is not a man's man.

Nevertheless, the specific question of structure which Braden raises needs to be answered. Why did Herrick leave his poems unnumbered and scattered in profusion across a large volume of poetry? What is the structural principle underlying *Hesperides?* Can and should *Hesperides* be read as a book of epigrams? The best place to begin to look for answers is again in the formal opening that Herrick provides for *Hesperides.*

✦✦✦ Eight poems make up the introduction to *Hesperides,* nine including the dedicatory epigram to Prince Charles. Besides "The Argument of his Book" there are a "lyric" poem to Herrick's Muse, four epigrams to his book, one to "the soure Reader," and finally an epigram with directions on "When he would have his verses read." The eight poems form a web of allusion to earlier epigram writers; along with the imitation of Bastard there are variations on poems by Heywood, Harington, and Jonson.[8] The second poem, "To his Muse," is particularly significant for a reading of *Hesperides,* since it dramatizes the Hesperidean persona. It is also a variation, as we shall shortly see, on the third poem of Martial's first book of epigrams.[9]

The poet-persona who had been foregrounded insistently in the "Argument" was speaking to the reader. In the second poem in *Hesperides,* he speaks in a way to himself or to the force that motivates his writing. "To his Muse" is, quite simply, funny, as are so many of Herrick's poems. The poet is exasperated, pleading, and stymied by his willful alter ego; he opens the poem with a question:

> Whither *Mad maiden* wilt thou roame?
> Farre safer 'twere to stay at home:
> Where thou mayst sit, and piping please
> The poore and private *Cottages.*
> Since *Coats,* and *Hamlets,* best agree
> With this thy meaner Minstralsie.
> There with the Reed, thou mayst expresse
> The Shepherds Fleecie happinesse:
> And with thy *Eclogues* intermixe
> Some smooth, and harmlesse *Beucolicks.*
> There on a Hillock thou mayst sing
> Unto a handsome Shephardling;
> Or to a Girle (that keeps the Neat)
> With breath more sweet then Violet.
> There, there, (perhaps) such Lines as These
> May take the simple *Villages.*
> But for the Court, the Country wit
> Is despicable unto it.
> Stay then at home, and doe not goe
> Or flie abroad to seeke for woe.

Contempts in Courts and Cities dwell;
No *Critick* haunts the Poore mans Cell:
Where thou mayst hear thine own Lines read
By no one tongue, there, censured.
That man's unwise will search for Ill,
And may prevent it, sitting still.

The persona plumps to a conservative conclusion with a tidy adage, but
whether the Muse will follow his advice is not at all clear. Even the
strained, almost ridiculous rhyme of "intermixe" and "Beucolicks" forces
us to look askance at the poet's plea. And, in fact, the question that opens
the poem implies that the "Mad maiden" *will* roam, regardless of the
poet's reluctance to leave safety and humble pleasures. Herrick's sense of
humor is the quality of his poetry that has been most neglected by critics
who have isolated his poems from each other and have failed to credit his
poetic voice with subtlety. In fact, the conflict that "To his Muse" implies
between poet and Muse signals the beginning of the self-mocking contra-
dictions that bedevil the poet throughout *Hesperides* and that have led a
critic like DeNeef, for instance, to argue that there are a number of different personae operating in *Hesperides*.

"To his Muse" has been read by critics as a key poem in establishing the
pastoral nature of *Hesperides,* or at least in defining the "pastoral persona"
as opposed to, for example, the epigrammatic or courtly personae.[10] On
the literal level of the conflict between poet and Muse which the dramatic
monologue creates, however, an exclusively "pastoral" reading of the
poem is incomplete and skews our response to the rest of *Hesperides*. "To
his Muse" is further complicated by its source in the opening of Martial's
first book. Martial's epigram is also a dramatic monologue, where the
poet warns his book:

Argiletanas mavis habitare tabernas,
    cum tibi, parve liber, scrinia nostra vacent?
nescis, heu, nescis dominae fastidia Romae:
    crede mihi, nimium Martia turba sapit.
maiores nusquam rhonchi: iuvenesque senesque
    et pueri nasum rhinocerotis habent.
audieris cum grande sophos, dum basia iactas,
    ibis ab excusso missus in astra sago.
sed tu ne totiens domini patiare lituras
    neve notet lusus tristis harundo tuos,

aetherias, lascive, cupis volitare per auras.
i, fuge! sed poteras tutior esse domi.

[You prefer to inhabit the shops of the Argiletum, although, little book, my cylinders have plenty of space for you. You don't know—alas!—you don't know the scorn of mistress Rome: believe me, the crowd of Mars' descendants is only too clever. Nowhere will you hear louder snorts: both young and old, and even boys, have rhinoceros-noses. Just when you've heard a tremendous "Bravo!", just while you're throwing kisses to the audience, you will shoot up to the stars, flung up from a shaken-out blanket. But, so as not so often to suffer the erasures of your master, and so that his stern pen may not keep on marking your playful lines, you are keen, you mischievous creature, to fly through the airy breezes: go on then, be off with you; but you could have been safer at home.][11]

The similarities between Martial's introductory epigram and Herrick's serve, first of all, to contradict Braden's contention that Herrick could not hear the "specific intentions" of classical poems. It serves as well to mark *Hesperides* very clearly as a book of epigrams, or rather as an innovation in the epigrammatic tradition—epigram and pastoral combined in a volatile partnership. Like the "Argument," "To his Muse" alters the *content* of a well-known model in the genre, as a signal pointing to Herrick's own innovation, but an innovation that could not exist, could not even be recognized, without a prior recall of the tradition.

Herrick's borrowing of Martial's poem had been anticipated by other Renaissance epigrammatists. Sir John Davies, for example, begins his *Epigrams* with a poem, "Ad Musam. I," that is clearly meant to capture Martial's spirit:

> Flie merry Muse unto that merry towne,
> Where thou mayst playes, revels, and triumphes see,
> The house of fame, and Theatre of renowne,
> Where all good wits and spirits love to be.
>
> Fall in betwene their hands, that praise and love thee,
> And be to them a laughter and a jest;
> But as for them which scorning shall reproove thee,
> Disdayne their wits, and thinke thyne owne the best.
>
> But if thou finds any so grose and dull,
> That thinke I do to privat Taxing leane:
> Bid him go hang, for he is but a gull,

And knowes not what an Epigramme doth mean;
Which Taxeth under a particular name,
A generall vice that merits publique blame.

Davies' bravado, however, misses the point of Martial's reluctance to let his poems go out into a fickle urban world. Simply "disdayne" the man who reproves you, Davies directs, "Bid him go hang." Davies comes closer to the point of Martial's amused cynicism in his last epigram, "Ad Musam. 48," where he rejects epigram writing in dismay at the transience of his popularity. Since Davies had not initially been prepared for rejection by a world of "gulls," he must ask in the end, "What fame is this that scarse lasts out a fashion?" Without an awareness of the possibility of failure, Davies' persona is unequipped to face criticism and simply stops writing altogether at midvolume.

Ben Jonson had also played upon the theme of Martial's poem in his second epigram but had changed it to suit his own conception of his epigram book. Unlike Martial and his epigrams, Jonson and his book are at first in perfect harmony. Jonson sends his book forth to "let men know / Thou art not covetous of least selfe fame, / Made from the hazard of anothers shame." Jonson's conflict with his Muse comes instead at midvolume and is of a more private nature.

In light of Martial's epigram and the earlier Renaissance variations on it, then, Herrick's opening poem, "To his Muse," is more than simply a pastoral signal. It is instead both a tongue-in-cheek mockery of the poet's preference for a pastoral stance and an indication that these "poems of the West Country" will have both a wider audience and greater ambitions, that *Hesperides* is to be a book of epigrams set in a pastoral world and that that incongruity can be both amusing and satiric.

Perhaps the best representation of the yoked opposites of *Hesperides* is its frontispiece.[12] There the bust of a living Herrick is mounted on a monument, suggesting a tombstone, a strange combination of life and death, of nature and art. Behind the monument is a landscape filled with the clichés of poetic pastoralism: Pegasus, the fount of Helicon, wreaths of flowers borne by Cupids. Upon the monument itself is carved an epigram (or epitaph) on Herrick, written by a minor contemporary poet.[13] The frontispiece serves as an emblem of the volume of poems to follow. On a carved monument stands a living bust—a bizarre visual summary of Herrick's fascination with his own death and burial and his concomitant belief that his poetry will survive his age. In the foreground of a decorative pastoral world, emblematic of lyric poetry, stands an epigram starkly outlined in black, a visual and theoretical summary—both pretty Cupids dancing to music and epigrams carved in stone—of the poems to follow.

The "Argument" and "To his Muse" are the only two of the eight opening poems which are not obviously epigrams, yet both, after all, are drawn directly from the epigrammatic tradition. Since the entire opening is shot through with allusions to the epigram books that preceded Herrick, both the pretty subjects listed in the epigrammatic catalogue poem and the poet's plea for a pastoral career in "the simple Villages" sit even more pointedly in a mocking, epigrammatic context. It is notable, for example, that the "cleanly-Wantonnesse" of the "Argument" is balanced, or qualified, by the use of Martial's "epigrammaton linguam" in the extreme anality of the fifth poem:

> Who with thy leaves shall wipe (at need)
> The place, where swelling *Piles* do breed:
> May every Ill, that bites, or smarts,
> Perplexe him in his hinder-parts.

Herrick also borrows Martial's insight into the nature of coarse poetry and women:[14]

> To read my Booke the Virgin shie
> May blush, (while *Brutus* standeth by:)
> But when He's gone, read through what's writ,
> And never staine a cheeke for it.
>
> (H-4)

The one thing that each of Herrick's opening epigrams points to is "his Book," an entity unto itself that the poet addresses repeatedly. He directs the reader's attention to his book as a whole, not only in the "Argument," but in the epigram "To the soure Reader," who is asked only to "read'st my Booke unto the end."

Finally, in the eighth of these preliminaries, the poet tells us "When he would have his verses read," an allusion to Martial's prefatory epistle to his first book of epigrams: as Martial had insisted that his epigrams were intended for a holiday audience during the Saturnalia, and that "Cato [should] not enter my theatre," so Herrick directs:

> In sober mornings, doe not thou reherse
> The holy incantation of a verse;

But when that men have both well drunke, and fed,
Let my Enchantments then be sung, or read.
When Laurell spirts 'ith fire, and when the Hearth
Smiles to it selfe, and guilds the roofe with mirth;
When up the *Thyrse* is rais'd, and when the sound
Of sacred *Orgies* flyes, A round, A round.
When the *Rose* raignes, and locks with ointments shine,
Let rigid *Cato* read these Lines of mine.

In Jonson's *Epigrammes*, the governing metaphor is a variation on the "Theater" of Martial's first book, but in Jonson's "Theater" even Cato "might enter without scandall." Herrick, however, here invites Cato and the reader into an entirely new metaphoric frame, a party of friends supplied with plenty of wine in a warm room after dinner. Although "rigid Cato" might normally be scandalized, in such a convivial context even he may read these poems with pleasure. Here in this poem, borrowed in part so clearly from the introductions to the epigrams of both Martial and Jonson, Herrick seems to be alluding, however, not to his epigrams but to his lyric poems. As in the "Argument" and "To his Muse," Herrick artfully combines lyric and epigrammatic form and content.

Herrick's epigrams themselves are generally sarcastic about those who drink too much and counsel, especially at the end of *Hesperides*, that

Excesse is sluttish: keepe the meane; for why?
Vertue's clean Conclave is sobriety.

(H-1109)

And in the final renunciation of the poetic life that makes up the very end of *Hesperides* is a two-line epigram on "Abstinence" (H-1117). But the lyric poems use drunkenness as the primary metaphor for both poetic inspiration and the good life.

"When he would have his verses read" is, in fact, a revealing test case for a reading of *Hesperides* as a volume defined by the epigram, alone and in tension with lyric poetry. Placed at the threshold of *Hesperides*, it is closely related in language, imagery, and theme to several of Herrick's most important lyric poems and to Herrick's Anacreontic epigrams. Does it therefore weaken a reading of Herrick's volume as an epigram book in conception?

"To live merrily, and to trust to Good Verses" (H-201), for example, enacts the "time" for poetry which "When he would have his verses read" describes:

> Now raignes the Rose, and now
>   Th'*Arabian* Dew besmears
> My uncontrolled brow,
>   And my retorted haires.

Herrick drinks a toast to a series of classical poets, Homer, Vergil, Ovid, Catullus, until:

> Wild I am now with heat;
>   O *Bacchus!* coole thy Raies!
> Or frantick I shall eate
>   Thy *Thyrse,* and bite the *Bayes.*

> Round, round, the roof do's run.

He drinks to Propertius, and then to Tibullus. But the death of Tibullus reminds him of a "Text," Ovid's lament for Tibullus (*Amores* 3.ix). Indeed, this text forms an insistent undercurrent throughout Herrick's poems. Ovid's agonized cry of loss at the urn of Tibullus is filled not only with grief but with triumph at the power of song to survive death. The epitaph Herrick placed on his title page, for example, is from this same "Text": "Effugient avidos Carmina nostra Rogos" [Song alone escapes our funeral pyre].[15] In the spinning drunkenness of "Trust to Good Verses," the memory of Tibullus's urn, the physical emblem of death, is a sobering vision:

> Now, to *Tibullus,* next,
>   This flood I drink to thee:
> But stay; I see a Text,
>   That this presents to me.

> Behold, *Tibullus* lies
>   Here burnt, whose smal return
> Of ashes, scarce suffice
>   To fill a little Urne.

It is literally a vision. The poet stops in mid-verse, with a glass raised half-way to his lips, "But stay; I see a Text." The graven epitaph, the physical monument of death, sobers the drunken celebration. After all, the sweet madness of drink provides a false euphoria. It is only good verses that will survive.

Perhaps Herrick's most successful lyric, certainly his most successful on the power of wine, is "His age, dedicated to his peculiar friend, Master John Wickes" (H-336).[16] "His age" begins with a translation from Horace's second ode on the inexorable passing of time and goes on to argue for the power of friendship to make what there is of life a private pleasure. Up to this point the poem is relatively conventional in its classical themes and its Cavalier emphasis on friendship, but midway through Herrick makes the poem very much his own.[17] He imagines his old age:

> When with the reume,
> The cough, the ptisick, I consume
> Unto an almost nothing,

a time when he and Weeks will meet again. Herrick is obsessed throughout *Hesperides* with his own aging, frequently enacting little dialogues with different mistresses about his advanced years, his gray hairs, his blindness, lameness, impotence. "His age" is the most delicate and fully realized of these imaginings, in part because it is not presented as unconscious fantasy but dramatically as the projected fantasy of a middle-aged poet. When he is old, he will have his imagined son sing his lyric poems to the two old friends, and the poems he will wish to have conjured up will be lyrics—"The Lilly in a Christal," "The Primrose," the "Julia" poems, a piece "of a higher text," perhaps religious. And hearing these lyrics of his youth, "Herrick" will "reare / Mine aged limbs above my chaire," "Flutter and crow, as in a fit / Of fresh concupiscence, and cry / *No lust theres like to Poetry*." A "frantick crazie man," he shall "Repeat the Times that I have seen!" weeping and doting, and ask his son to spice their ale. He and Weeks shall drink to all those friends, "High sons of Pith," who have celebrated his poems with him in the past. The pair shall drink "Untill our tongues shall tell our ears, / W'are younger by a score of years," until the fire dies; "We'l then to bed, / Farre more then night bewearied."

Lyric poetry, then, here and elsewhere in *Hesperides*, is associated with a happy madness, with friendship and with drunkenness. But the whole scene imagined in "His age" is tinged just slightly with the ludicrous and pathetic. The old man Herrick drunk on memory and wine, flapping about the table with tears in his eyes, drinking until he falls into bed or into the longer sleep of the grave—this is an ambiguous fantasy for a man to have about himself. Robert Halli, Jr. has read "His age" as an enactment and celebration of poetic immortality, but it can equally be read as a fantasy of obscurity and failure. The self-portrait of the old debauchee, rheumy, consumptive, coughing himself away, is a picture with which the coarse epigrams are also obsessed. The old man, the old wife, drinking in the kitchen are images freighted with mockery and distaste in *Hesperides*.

In *Hesperides*, "the Mystick *Thyrse*" (l. 135) of lyric poetry is also the thyrse of drunken celebration. Herrick draws on several classical sources for his poems of drinking and inspiration, but chief among them are the Anacreontic epigrams from the Greek Anthology, which he credits explicitly several times. Herrick's adaptation of the Anacreontic pose of the drunken old man has been particularly excoriated by Braden; it is a pose he called "a repertoire of bits, like that of a clown" (p. 207). "Taken as a whole," Braden argued, "the Anacreontea propose a lyric oeuvre as a closed system of motifs, as though the writing of poetry were merely the display, over and over again, of the intrinsically poetic. . . . The Anacreontea . . . allow their poeticisms to remain in a deliquescent repose, never really challenging their own validity" (p. 208). This may be a fair assessment of the Anacreontea; but Braden again goes too far, positing a simplistic equation between Renaissance poet and classical source: "Certainly the routines of that stock character are used widely throughout *Hesperides*, and are in fact the terms in which Herrick's literary personality is generally recalled" (p. 214).

Herrick's literary personality is far more complex than the Anacreontic poems, which make up a small number of the sum of *Hesperides* and are certainly "challenged" by the epigrams of praise, satire, and advice that surround them, as well as by the lyrics to friends and the lyrics on the realities of country life. Especially pertinent here are Herrick's companion poems, "The fare-well" and "The Welcome to Sack" (H-128 and -197). The "Welcome" is the second poem of the pair, placed at the end of the second century, just three poems before "To live merrily." It is the poet's erotic wooing of his "Spouse" back again after their separation. Who but she "can bring / More love unto my life, or can present / My *Genius* with a fuller blandishment?" (ll. 54–56). He vows that if he ever leaves her vitalizing blood again, his numbers may "all / Run to a sudden Death, and Funerall" (ll. 89–90). The connection between drink and inspiration is explicit in this long metaphor where the Canary Isles and the Isles of Hesperides seem one and the same.

But prefacing this reconciliation is, of course, the divorcement between poet and sack. Herrick's "fare-well," although couched in amusingly literary terms, is an entirely realistic swearing off of the bottle because

> . . . Nature bids thee goe, not I.
> 'Tis her erroneous self has made a braine
> Uncapable of such a Soveraigne,
> As is thy powerfull selfe. . . .
> . . . .
> . . . what's done by me
> Hereafter, shall smell of the Lamp, not thee.

It is important to remember that this conflict between wine and sobriety, between a fantastic vision and reality, indeed, between inspiration and death, is not resolved here in the second century but defines the persona's personality throughout *Hesperides*.

In a small lyric at midvolume, for example, the poet himself articulates the impotence of the drink-inspired lover:

> Whither dost thou whorry me,
> *Bacchus*, being full of thee?
> This way, that way, that way, this,
> Here, and there a fresh Love is.
> That doth like me, this doth please;
> Thus a thousand Mistresses,
> I have now; yet I alone,
> Having All, injoy not *One*.
>
> (H-415)

Drink makes the difference between a life lived in imagination and one lived in reality.

Braden put heavy emphasis on Herrick's conscious identification with "Anacreon," a poet constructed by early Renaissance scholars from a number of poets in the Greek Anthology. Braden devoted eighteen pages to arguing that Anacreon is not a strong persona and one page concluding that, therefore, Herrick must not be either (pp. 196–214). Herrick's fictive relationship with Anacreon is indeed clear, especially in "The Apparition of his Mistresse calling him to Elizium," the long and important poem placed at the formal center of *Hesperides* (H-575). Herrick's "Mistresse" promises to

> . . . bring thee *Herrick* to *Anacreon*,
> Quaffing his full-crown'd bowles of burning Wine,
> And in his Raptures speaking Lines of Thine,
> Like to His subject; and as his Frantick-

> Looks, shew him truly *Bacchanalian* like,
> Besmear'd with Grapes; welcome he shall thee thither,
> Where both may rage, both drink and dance together.

But this promised introduction is part of an extended fantasy, a dream that ends abruptly at daybreak. It can be paired with another dream at the very end of *Hesperides* where Herrick has a vision of Anacreon flushed, his hair oiled:

> And as he spake, his mouth ranne ore with wine.
> Tipled he was; and tipling lispt withall;
> And lisping reeld, and reeling like to fall.
>
> (H-1017)

Anacreon fondles a "young *Enchantresse*" but, because he is so drunk, he can do no more. She, in anger, gives his wreath to Herrick, "Since when (me thinks) my braines about doe swim, / And I am wilde and wanton like to him." This combination of poetic wantonness and physical impotence seems rather a mixed blessing. Braden's guess is that Herrick used it as a "cover" for his choice of chastity. Perhaps.

It is well to remember that there are other models in *Hesperides*. The apparition who guides the poet to the dream-Elizium takes him as well to the new "chiefe" of poets, "Thy Father Johnson." Jonson, too, is associated by Herrick with drink, but he transcends its power. As "nobly wild" as "those *Lyrick* Feasts" with Jonson were at "The *Sun*, / The *Dog*, the triple *Tunne*," "yet each Verse of thine / Out-did the meate, out-did the frolick wine" (H-911). Herrick, in "A Bacchanalian Verse" (H-653), drinks to Jonson's memory over and over but can "thrive / In frenzie ne'r like thee." Jonson himself specifically refused entrance to the "Tribe of Ben" to "those that meerely talke, and never thinke, / That live in the wild Anarchie of Drinke" (*Under-wood*, 49, ll. 9–10). The Anacreontic pose is, after all, a pose only, a temporary state, certainly not the defining limits of Herrick's literary persona. "The bad season," for example, combines in one poem the conflict of reality and the lure of "sacred Orgies." The beginning of the poem is grounded very firmly in the realities of the 1640s—the Stuart dream seems finished. But *if* the dream were restored, if Charles and Henrietta Maria were back on the throne, then:

> I sho'd delight to have my Curles halfe drown'd
> In *Tyrian Dewes*, and Head with Roses crown'd.

And one more yet (ere I am laid out dead)
Knock at a Starre with my exalted Head.

(H-612)

His wish here at midvolume is couched in the terms of "When he would have his verses read": the anointed curls, purple dew, crown of roses. It is a desperate wish for escape, a wish that the Anacreontic poem "On him-selfe" (H-170) makes explicit:

I Feare no Earthly Powers;
But care for crowns of flowers:
And love to have my Beard
With Wine and Oile besmear'd.
This day Ile drowne all sorrow;
Who knowes to live to morrow?

or "A New-yeares gift sent to Sir Simeon Steward" (H-319), which invites Steward to drown out the news of Parliament and king in wine and to "Sit crown'd with Rose-buds, and carouse, / Till *Liber Pater* twirles the house / About your eares" (ll. 41–43).

But these are only escapes and are portrayed as such. There is always the "sober morning" when reality has to be faced again, and, increasingly toward the end of the volume, the persona does face reality in spare epigrams. In place of the poet knocking his head against the stars, there is Tom Blinks:

. . . his Nose is full of wheales, and these
Tom calls not pimples, but *Pimpleides:*
Sometimes (in mirth) he sayes each whelk's a sparke
(When drunke with Beere) to light him home, i'th'dark.

(H-834)

Balanced against the "Helicon" of the Stuarts, their Hesperides of Plea-sure, are epigrams like "Pleasures Pernicious" (H-1087):

Where Pleasures rule a Kingdome, never there
Is sober virtue, seen to move her sphere.

Most chilling of all, placed at the end of this volume devoted in such large measure to good fellowship and good friends, is the final epigram before the formal closing poems, "Distrust" (H-1121):

> What ever men for Loyalty pretend,
> *'Tis Wisdomes part to doubt a faithfull friend.*

What, then, is the import of "When he would have his verses read"? Does it mean that *Hesperides* is primarily a volume of lyric poetry that Herrick intends us to read in the same drunken frenzy in which it was written?

Herrick's conception of poetry extends far beyond Anacreon's Greek Anthology epigrams and the drunken daze of "sacred Orgies." In the ongoing narrative structure of *Hesperides,* a structure made possible by the model of Martial's epigram book and enriched by the examples of Harington and Jonson, the "Raigne of the Rose" falters and ends. In constant tension with the languorous Anacreontic epigrams are the mocking epigrams that savage such a pose, the poems of realistic advice to kings, and Herrick's very personal poems to friends and family. It is much more appropriate to take as a model of *Hesperides* the sly and sardonic books of Martial, where drunken poets and their poses are to be mocked as surely as any other fool. Indeed, in *Hesperides* Herrick finally questions the idea of poetry itself as pleasurable and decorative. The Anacreontic poems are one part of an ongoing dialectic between the ideal and the real, between imagination and experience. "When he would have his verses read" is an invitation to a book that must face, at last, the "sober morning."

CHAPTER SEVEN

The *Hesperides* of Herrick's "Saints" and "Heroes"

✥✥✥. Curiously, one of Herrick's most beautiful and moving poems, the epigram to his father's memory, has rarely been addressed by his critics.[1] It is one of a group of poems, the epigrams of praise, that have been almost completely neglected since *Hesperides* was published. The neglect of the epigrams of praise, poems that were important to Herrick personally and are essential to the structure and import of *Hesperides*, may perhaps be attributed to the critical myth of Herrick as a craftsman of pure art and fantasy. The reality of flesh-and-blood people in *Hesperides*, however, must alter our perception of the whole volume.

Herrick's father had died, an apparent suicide, when Herrick was fourteen months old. In the first century of *Hesperides*, Herrick addresses "the reverend shade of his religious Father" (H-82) and begs forgiveness:

> That for seven *Lusters* I did never come
> To doe the *Rites* to thy Religious Tombe:
> That neither haire was cut, or true teares shed
> By me, o'r thee, (*as justments to the dead*)
> Forgive, forgive me; since I did not know
> Whether thy bones had here their Rest, or no.

The poem opens in a rush of enjambment atypical of Herrick's more characteristic end-stopped lines. The anxiety and guilt of these opening lines inform the rest of the brief poem, which is essentially an offering, a placation of the ghost of his father. The poet brings the offerings traditional for a Graeco-Roman, not a Christian, burial and performs the ceremonial rites. But this is not enough to placate the spirit of the father nor the deep need of the son:

> I come to pay a Debt of Birth I owe.
> Thou gav'st me life, (but Mortall;) For that one

133

> Favour, Ile make full satisfaction;
> For my life mortall, Rise from out thy Herse,
> And take a life immortall from my Verse.

That the father shall live forever through his son's genius seems a fitting conclusion to the poem and a resolution of Herrick's guilt and remorse. But the poem does not rest so easily on its closing lines. They answer and echo too closely the note of insistency that the title of the poem introduced. The title informs the reader that this is to be a poem "To the *reverend* shade of his *religious* Father" (italics added). Yet his father's imputed suicide would mean expulsion from all Christian grace and from eternal salvation. Since the closing couplet seems to be offering another kind of eternity as a substitute for the one his father cannot have, the end of the poem, in effect, undercuts the exculpation that the title promises it will be. The words that remain most insistent after a reading of the poem to Herrick's father are "Forgive, forgive me."

Herrick's poem to Nicholas Herrick alerts us to several aspects of the epigrams of praise. First is Herrick's hope, expressed in almost all of these poems, that his epigrams will create a realm of immortality, an Hesperides where his chosen people can live forever. But "To the reverend shade of his religious Father" also indicates the levels of psychological complexity that these poems can plumb. In the deeply felt poems to his immediate family, to John Weeks, his closest friend, and to Ben Jonson, his poetic father, for example, Herrick reveals doubts and anxieties that are hidden beneath the polished surface of most of his poems. In the epigrams of praise for patrons and public figures, Herrick reveals his ambivalence about putting his poetry in the service of money and influence.

Because Herrick is a poet of magic phrases (even a single word like "liquefaction" is memorable), critics have often borrowed his phrases as the symbolic foundation for their argument. For Roger Rollin, for example, *Hesperides* is "This Sacred Grove"; for A. Leigh DeNeef, Herrick's art is "This Poetick Liturgie." Yet the poems from which these potent phrases have been drawn are precisely those poems that have rarely been factored into an overall reading of *Hesperides*.[2] It is particularly important to include Herrick's epigrams of praise in any holistic reading because they are concerned as much with his "Book" and his art as they are with the people he praises. In the only critical work devoted to the epigrams of praise, Helen Marlborough has faulted Herrick for this egocentricity; but to do so is to read Herrick on terms other than his own.[3] Herrick is intensely concerned with the power of art to grant immortality. His epigrams are simply the "Hesperides" of his heroes who will live forever in his book—"the pure Starres the praising Poetrie" (H-444).[4]

To John Selden (H-365), for example, Herrick declares:

> A City here of *Heroes* I have made,
> Upon the rock, whose firm foundation laid,
> Shall never shrink, where making thine abode,
> Live thou a *Selden*, that's a Demi-god.

The sacrilegious undertone here in the echo of Christ's words to Peter on the founding of the Christian church, "Upon this Rock I will build my church, and the powers of death shall not prevail against it," is characteristic of the volume as a whole. Indeed, Herrick's amalgam of secular with Christian symbols and vocabulary has been the primary critical problem for readers of Herrick in the twentieth century. The emphasis on ceremony which has prevailed in Herrick criticism for the last decade, for example, is one way of explaining and justifying Herrick's heretical equation of art with religion and pagan deities with Christ.[5]

Another way to read Herrick's "religion" of art is to look closely at the epigrams that articulate it. Reading the lyrics on love's religion is complicated by the Renaissance convention of speaking of love in religious terms.[6] Since, however, the use of religious terminology in epigrams is unique to Herrick, it is easier to isolate his intentions here. In the critical sixth century, for example, Herrick addresses an epigram to himself where he articulates the purpose of the epigrams of praise, at least as he sees that purpose at midvolume:

> Th'art hence removing, (like a Shepherds Tent)
> And walk thou must the way that others went:
> Fall thou must first, then rise to life with These,
> Markt in thy Book for faithfull Witnesses.
>
> (H-507)

The small poem is heavily freighted with biblical references. The "Shepherds Tent" is from Isaiah 38:12, "Mine age is departed, and is removed from me as a shepherd's tent." The biblical gloss connects the epigram with the other poems at midvolume that lament the changing times and, because of them, chart a new course for Herrick's poetry. The final line is borrowed from the prophecy of Daniel 12:1, "Thy people shall be delivered, every one that shall be found written in the book." Herrick says elsewhere that his book of poetry is a "Testament" (H-977); that the immortality which his poetry offers shades into "Life eternall" (H-392). When he says that Penelope Wheeler shall be a "Saint" in "this Poetick Liturgie" (H-510), when he includes Stephen Soame as

> . . . one of my righteous Tribe:
> A Tribe of one Lip, Leven, and of One
> Civil Behaviour, and Religion.
> A stock of Saints; where ev'ry one doth weare
> A stole of white, (and Canonized here)
>
> (H-545)

there is an element of literal truth to Herrick's promise. He declares to Sir Thomas Heale (H-869) that "the *Magick* of my powerfull Rhymes" will stand "'Gainst all the indignation of the Times." Leah Marcus has argued in convincing detail the anti-Puritan strategies of *Hesperides'* pastoral poems and of *Noble Numbers's* childlike epigrams.[7] Similarly, in the epigrams of praise, Herrick's "Saints" are an antidote to the Puritan saints, such as "Zelot" (H-666) and "Peason" (H-843), two probable references to William Prynne, whose ears were lopped in 1633 as punishment for a supposed insult to the queen in *Histriomastix.*[8] About Zelot, for example, Herrick asks with scathing contempt,

> Is *Zelot* pure? he is: ye see he weares
> The signe of *Circumcision* in his eares

and about Peason he constructs an ugly pun:

> Long Locks of late our Zelot *Peason* weares,
> Not for to hide his high and mighty eares;
> No, but because he wo'd not have it seen,
> That Stubble stands, where once large eares have been.

Herrick's "Saints," in marked, deliberate contrast, are "the Generation of [his] Just" ("To his worthy friend, Master Arthur Bartly," H-664). Later Herrick promises "his Friend, Master J. Jincks" (H-859) that he will place him

> . . . here among my righteous race:
> The bastard Slips may droop and die
> Wanting both Root, and Earth; but thy
> Immortall selfe, shall boldly trust
> To live for ever, with my Just.

Herrick borrows this epigram from the Wisdom of Solomon 4:3, "the multiplying brood of the ungodly shall not thrive, nor take deep rooting from bastard slips, nor lay any fast foundation." The seasons of *Hesperides* are filled with Herrick's secular "calendar" of saints (H-444) as an antidote to a new order.

The preeminent "Saint" in Herrick's calendar is Ben Jonson. There are five poems to Jonson, placed early, middle, and late in *Hesperides*. Each one of them appears to have been written after Jonson's death in 1637. The first of the early pair of epigrams to Jonson (H-382 and H-383) details the degeneration of the stage "After the rare Arch-Poet JOHNSON dy'd":

> For men did strut, and stride, and stare, not act.
> Then temper flew from words; and men did squeake,
> Looke red, and blow, and bluster, but not speake:
> . . . .
> *Artlesse the Sceane was;* and that monstrous sin
> Of deep and *arrant ignorance* came in.

Herrick predicts that only Jonson can revive the stage, but leaves hope that Jonson may somehow return:

> . . . all witt
> In utter darkenes did, and still will sit
> Sleeping the lucklesse Age out, till that she
> Her Resurrection ha's again with Thee.

At midvolume (H-604) Herrick dedicates a lyric "Prayer" to Jonson:

> When I a Verse shall make,
> Know I have praid thee,
> For old *Religions* sake,
> Saint *Ben* to aide me.
>
> Make the way smooth for me,
> When I, thy *Herrick*,
> Honouring thee, on my knee
> Offer my *Lyrick*.
>
> Candles Ile give to thee,
> And a new Altar;
> And thou Saint *Ben*, shalt be
> Writ in my *Psalter*.

And it is preceded by an epigram that is an unmistakable echo of Jonson's epigram "To the Reader," which opens *Epigrammes:*

> Pray thee, take care, that tak'st my booke in hand,
> To reade it well: that is, to understand.

Herrick's parallel epigram is addressed "To his Booke":

> Be bold my Booke, nor be abasht, or feare
> The cutting Thumb-naile, or the Brow severe.
> But by the *Muses* sweare, all here is good,
> If but well read; or ill read, understood.

The relationship between these poems shows how close are lyric and epigram in *Hesperides*. Herrick can rhyme his own name with "Lyrick" but in the contiguous poem construct a pointed imitation of a Jonson epigram. Jonson had carefully marked "song" and "epigram" and had placed them together. In a complex imitation of Jonson, when Herrick writes lyrics he will still pay tribute to Jonson, but the tribute he pays is to enroll Jonson in his world of epigrams, his "Psalter" of saints.

The final pair of poems to Jonson, one epigram and one lyric, sounds a different note, one of finality. The first poem (H-910) is an epitaph ("Here lyes *Johnson* with the rest / Of the Poets; but the Best"). The next is an ode to Jonson and the "*Lyrick* Feasts / . . . at the *Sun*, / The *Dog*, the triple *Tunne*." The final stanza is an acknowledgment of Herrick's debt to Jonson and a warning that this inspiration is finite:

> My *Ben*
> Or come agen:
> Or send to us,
> Thy wits great over-plus;
> But teach us yet
> Wisely to husband it;
> Lest we that Tallent spend:
> And having once brought to an end
> That precious stock; the store
> Of such a wit the world sho'd have no more.

The specific debt Herrick owes Jonson in his lyric poems has been commented on extensively. "Delight in Disorder" is a variation on Jonson's song "Still to be neat" from *Epicoene,* for example; "The Country

Life" borrows from "To Robert Wroth." Herrick's debt to Jonson's epigrams is pervasive but more diffuse, because Herrick conceives of his book in terms very different from Jonson's. The governing metaphors of *Epigrammes* are the commonwealth and the theater. Jonson's book is essentially dramatic and corrective, since the epigrams of praise and the satiric epigrams act out a conflict of good and evil. Because Jonson carefully delineates those qualities that have earned each person a place in his book, his epigrams of praise are moral exemplars.

The governing metaphors of *Hesperides'* praise epigrams are, by contrast, static; the poems and the people they enshrine may be, for example, stars or statues. The most important metaphor is the Book itself—Psalter, Testament, Calendar, Poetick Liturgie. Herrick's praising epigrams may therefore suffer in comparison with Jonson's moral weight and purpose. But Herrick's epigrams of praise are concerned more with their own power of preservation than with the qualities of the people they enshrine. They reveal more about the poet than the praised. And the epigrams of praise allow us to test the hypothesis that *Hesperides* is best understood as a coherent, well-planned epigram book.

There are more than one hundred of these praising epigrams, and it is very clear that Herrick has arranged them in a deliberate order with clearly marked signposts. Indeed, in 1876 Alexander Grosart suggested that Herrick had collected his epigrams of praise in a separate manuscript and had intended to publish them as a separate book.[9] Grosart believed too that Herrick never intended to publish the rest of the epigrams, but that they had been extracted from him by an ill-advised publisher and jumbled together with the epigrams of praise and the "true" *Hesperides* poems; and Grosart concluded that "the Poet himself had nothing to do with the arrangement or disarrangement" of the resulting volume. Grosart's argument here is on the same plane as that of those critics who have argued that the portrait on the frontispiece could not possibly be of Herrick because he could not have been so ugly nor had such a big nose. Grosart can claim "disarrangement" only because he first excises the epigrams of praise from the volume. The careful placement and marked progression of these epigrams through the "Book" absolutely contradict Grosart and other critics, Delattre and Martin among them, who have found complete confusion, intentional or not, in *Hesperides*.[10]

In his use of the praise epigrams to provide us with explicit markers of our place within the book, Herrick imitates the way Martial mocks and objectifies his "book" by counting poems and announcing where we are and how far we have to go. In the middle of *Hesperides* (H-510), for example, Herrick tells his cousin, Penelope Wheeler,

> Next is your lot (Faire) to be number'd one,
> Here, in my Book's Canonization:
> Late you come in; but you a Saint shall be,
> In Chiefe, in this Poetick Liturgie.

Herrick devises for Doctor Alabaster (H-763) a particularly witty compliment based on his location in the latter half of *Hesperides:*

> Nor art thou lesse esteem'd, that I have plac'd
> (Amongst mine honour'd) Thee (almost) the last:
> In great Processions many lead the way
> To him, who is the triumph of the day,
> As these have done to Thee, who art the one,
> One onely glory of a million,
> In whom the spirit of the Gods do's dwell,
> Firing thy soule, by which thou dost foretell
> When this or that vast *Dinastie* must fall
> Downe to a *Fillit* more *Imperiall.*

To his sister-in-law, Susanna Herrick, very late in the book (H-977) he explains:

> The Person crowns the Place; your lot doth fall
> Last, yet to be with These a Principall.
> How ere it fortuned; know for Truth, I meant
> You a fore-leader in this Testament.

And that is the extent of the poem. Simply to be named seems to be enough for Herrick, especially in these many little epigrams to his cousins, nephews and nieces, and in-laws. Another late epigram makes this clear. Its title, "To his kinsman Master Thomas Herrick, who desired to be in his Book" (H-983), is perhaps an allusion to Jonson's "Epistle Answering to One That Asked to Be Sealed of the Tribe of Ben":

> Welcome to this my Colledge, and though late
> Tha'st got a place here (standing candidate)
> It matters not, since thou art chosen one
> Here of my great and good foundation.

Whereas Jonson had imposed a long list of restrictions for membership in his circle, Herrick's desideratum is simple and clear. Just to ask is enough to enroll his nephew in the "great and good foundation." A late epigram simply entitled "To a Friend" (H-906) reveals the powerful magic that Herrick ascribes to his book and the words within it. Herrick directs:

> Looke in my Book, and herein see,
> Life endlesse sign'd to thee and me.
> We o're the tombes, and Fates shall flye;
> While other generations dye.

The physical presence of their names "sign'd" in the book guarantees them "Life endlesse."

At the beginning of *Hesperides'* final century, Herrick places an epigram "On his Booke" (H-1019) that signals its conclusion and makes clear what Herrick believes his book will grant himself and "his":

> The bound (almost) now of my book I see,
> But yet no end of those therein or me:
> Here we begin new life; while thousands quite
> Are lost, and theirs, in everlasting night.

This epigram pushes to the extreme Herrick's often-used metaphor of his "Saints," his "Elect." To be excluded is to live in the darkness of silence which lies outside Hesperides, the garden of immortality. The epigram anticipates the fulfillment of the promise Herrick had made his father at the beginning of "his Book," the promise of "a life immortall" in his son's verse that all of *Hesperides* is constructed to fulfill.

The most explicit and complicated allusion to the physical "Book" of *Hesperides* is an epigram to Michael Oldisworth, the member of Parliament from Plymouth, Devon and from Salisbury (H-1092):

> Nor thinke that Thou in this my Booke art worst,
> Because not plac't here with the midst, or first.
> Since Fame that sides with these, or goes before
> Those, that must live with Thee for evermore.
> That Fame, and Fames rear'd Pillar, thou shalt see
> In the next sheet *Brave Man* to follow Thee.
> Fix on That Columne then, and never fall;
> Held up by Fames *eternall Pedestall.*

"Fames *eternall Pedestall*" is clearly a reference to the penultimate poem in *Hesperides*, "The pillar of Fame" (H-1129). We do not see it on the next page, however, as the poem might lead us to expect. The allusion is both more complicated and more disjunctive. "The pillar of Fame" does indeed follow "To the most accomplisht Gentleman Master Michael Oulsworth" on the next sheet of the gathering as it would have appeared before being folded, bound, and cut. It is therefore a reference to the actual printing process, and this epigram is presumably one of the very last poems Herrick wrote for publication.

It therefore bears further scrutiny. Michael Oldisworth had been secretary to William Herbert, third earl of Pembroke, Lord Chamberlain, and dedicatee of Jonson's *Epigrammes*. In 1637 Oldisworth became secretary to Pembroke's brother, Philip Herbert, earl of Pembroke and Montgomery, who had succeeded his brother in the office of Lord Chamberlain. Oldisworth had strong parliamentarian sympathies, and he was widely credited by royalists for Pembroke's allegiance to the parliamentary cause. In 1640, Oldisworth was elected from both Plymouth, Devon and Salisbury and sat on both the Short and the Long Parliament. Oldisworth testified at Laud's trial, alleging Laud's efforts to deprive Pembroke of his right as Lord Chamberlain to appoint the royal chaplains. Pembroke himself was elected to the House of Commons and was made one of the two masters of the prerogative office. His defection from the king's cause was particularly conspicuous because of his prominence, and particularly painful to loyal royalists.

Since Oldisworth was believed to be the mastermind behind Pembroke's rise in the parliamentary order, he was excoriated ruthlessly by royalist pamphleteers. From 1648 to 1650, a number of satiric tracts appeared, allegedly signed by "Oldisworth," giving crude and illiterate accounts of the earl's parliamentary career, such as "Newes from Pembroke and Montgomery, or Oxford Manchestered by Michael Oldsworth and his Lord" (1648), which satirically describes the earl's presence in Oxford to supervise the parliamentary visitation at the last royalist stronghold. Another Oldisworth tract "describes" Pembroke's final farewell to the king. In another, Pembroke is made to say, "I love my man, Michael Oldsworth, because he is my mouth, and prays for me."[11]

Herrick may have included Oldisworth in *Hesperides* because of his connection with Devonshire, although he probably knew Oldisworth already in his capacity as secretary to the earl, since Herrick also seems to have received patronage from Pembroke.[12] But Michael Oldisworth represents everything Robert Herrick might be assumed to loathe, everything the supposedly royalist *Hesperides* should attack. How, then, should we read Herrick's epigram to Oldisworth, strong in its praise as it stands but made stronger still in its association of Oldisworth with the "pillar of Fame," Herrick's monument against time and the Times at the end of *Hesperides?* An important part of the compliment the epigram pays is its place in the volume. Oldisworth is not to think himself "worst" because he is not among the first of Herrick's subjects. Oldisworth is of the new order, and praise for him therefore ends the volume that has seen the deterioration of the hierarchical values enshrined in its beginning.

There is a special category of praising epigrams in *Hesperides* that deserves examination, as a test of the argument for careful ordering.

The relationship between poet and patron in the Renaissance is acted out in *Hesperides* by epigrams to several wealthy men. The poems to Sir Clipseby Crewe, a friend of Herrick's at Cambridge, are characteristic. The first poem to Crewe, an epithalamion on the occasion of Crewe's wedding in 1625 (H-283), is typical of the kind of poem that court poets produced for patrons. It is a beautiful poem, framed by references to Hesperides, the star traditionally associated with the wedding night.

In the fifth century, on the other hand, is a poem complaining of Crewe's unkindness and the end of their familiarity with each other (H-426). Later in the same century is another expression of hurt (H-489), this time making clear that Crewe's "fault" is a cessation of patronage after Herrick moved to Devonshire:

> Since to th'Country first I came,
> I have lost my former flame:
> And, methinks, I not inherit,
> As I did, my ravisht spirit.
> If I write a Verse, or two,
> 'Tis with very much ado;
> In regard I want that Wine,
> Which sho'd conjure up a line.
> Yet, though now of Muse bereft,
> I have still the manners left
> For to thanke you (Noble Sir)
> For those gifts you do conferre

> Upon him, who only can
> Be in Prose a *gratefull man.*

The complaint is made palatable by its cleverness, this "Prose" in singsong octosyllabic couplets. Herrick clearly implies that the "wine" required for inspiration should be supplied by patronage and that, given enough "wine," this prose could become inspired poetry. Herrick makes the terms of his relationship with Crewe so explicit that all later poems to Crewe must be read in light of this overt deal.

Therefore, when we read several poems later a touching epigram to Lady Crewe, "Upon the death of her Child" (H-514), consoling her with the idea of her child's peaceful sleep after pain, we must be conscious of the relationship of patronage at the same time that we are charmed and moved. The poems to the Crewes are arranged so that we must be conscious of what Herrick is doing on several levels at once.

The small tribute to the dead child seems to have healed the rift that the sequence of poems implies between patron and poet, for it is closely followed by an ode to Crewe (H-544) inviting him to the country to partake of "Lyrick Wine" in Herrick's enchanted cell. The final poem to Crewe (H-620) is an outright request: "Give me wine, and give me meat" and a frank statement of the terms of barter:

> 3. Give me these (my Knight) and try
>   In a Minutes space how I
>   Can runne mad, and Prophesie.

> 4. Then if any Peece proves new,
>   And rare, Ile say (my dearest *Crew*)
>   It was full enspir'd by you.

This is not, however, the end of the story. Late in *Hesperides,* forming a counterpoint to the early epithalamion, is an epitaph on the death of Lady Crewe in 1639:

> This Stone can tell the storie of my life,
> What was my Birth, to whom I was a Wife:
> In teeming years, how soon my Sun was set,
> Where now I rest, these may be known by *Jet.*
> For other things, my many Children be
> The best and truest *Chronicles* of me.
>
> (H-978)

The poems to Lord and Lady Crewe thus form a small story, interwoven throughout *Hesperides*, of a poet's public life and the events in the life of his patron. They reveal as well how unabashed Herrick was in asking for support.

At Cambridge, Herrick also met John Weeks (or Wicks), who appears to have remained Herrick's close friend for the rest of his life.[13] The careers of the two men in the Anglican church are parallel in many ways, but their level of success differed greatly. Weeks was a fellow at St. John's College, Cambridge, when Herrick entered in 1613. In 1617, Weeks went to Oxford to study divinity, while Herrick moved to Trinity Hall, Cambridge, and studied law, graduating M.A. in 1620. The next record we have of Herrick's life is his ordination, with John Weeks, as deacon and then priest by the bishop of Peterborough in 1623. Weeks's career then prospered: he was rector of Shirwell in northern Devonshire in 1627 and was still there in 1634; he was dean of St. Burian, Cornwall; he was chaplain to Archbishop Laud; he was, like Herrick, a friend of Endymion Porter. Marchette Chute suggested that it may have been Weeks who interceded with Porter to have Herrick appointed as one of the chaplains for the Isle of Rhé expedition in 1627. Weeks, too, was a chaplain on that ill-fated expedition. In 1630, the year Herrick assumed his living at Dean Prior, Weeks attempted unsuccessfully to snare the living at Deptford, which was within walking distance of Dean Prior. Weeks was one of the two licensers of the 1640 edition of *Shakespeare's Poems*, in which Herrick's "The Primrose," "The Apparition of his Mistresse," and "To a Gentlewoman, objecting to him his gray haires" appeared. In the context of Herrick's very scanty biography, the relative wealth of information we have about his friend fleshes out at least one aspect of Herrick's life. It reveals, as well, the startling difference in ecclesiastical success between the two men. The poems to Weeks might seem more properly discussed in a context other than Herrick's relationships with patrons, except that Herrick seems, toward the end, painfully aware of his dependence on his friend.

There are three poems to Weeks in *Hesperides*. The first and most successful, "His age" (H-336), is Herrick's fantasy of the two friends as old men remembering their youth together. The second, "A Paranaeticall, or Advisive Verse, to his friend, Master John Wicks" (H-670), urges Weeks to take pleasure out of life rather than to work hard: "let / Thy servant, not thy own self, sweat." It is the final poem to Weeks, an epigram very late in *Hesperides*, that interests me here. It is full of the anguish that rises in Herrick's voice in the last centuries of the volume. It is hard to resist associating this poem, "To his peculiar friend Master John Wicks" (H-1056), with Herrick's expulsion from Dean Prior. The poem opens hopefully and with a touch of humor:

> Since shed or Cottage I have none,
> I sing the more, that thou hast one;
> To whose glad threshold, and free door
> I may a Poet come, though poor;
> And eat with thee a savory bit,
> Paying but common thanks for it.

His mood swings quickly to suspicion, however:

> Yet sho'd I chance, (my *Wicks*) to see
> An over-leven-looke in thee,
> To soure the Bread, and turn the Beer
> To an exalted vineger;
> Or sho'dst thou prize me as a Dish
> Of thrice-boyl'd-worts, or third dayes fish;
> I'de rather hungry go and come,
> Then to thy house be Burdensome;
> Yet, in my depth of grief, I'de be
> One that sho'd drop his *Beads* for thee.

His anger turns to pleading in the final couplet. That his range of emotion, from dignity to anger and then to self-abasement, should be occasioned by asking John Weeks for help reveals the state of mind dramatized at the end of *Hesperides*. In "His age" Herrick had been able to invite Weeks to his house for a drink and a reminiscence under his own roof:

> If we can meet, and so conferre,
> Both by a shining Salt-seller;
>   And have our Roofe,
> Although not archt, yet weather proofe,
>   And seeling fre,
> From that cheape *Candle baudery:*
> We'le eate our Beane with that full mirth,
> As we were Lords of all the earth.

But now he has no "shed or Cottage." The anger and discomfort of this last poem to Weeks is evidence of Herrick's need for a place, a place protected by his own household lars. Dispossessed of this space, his voice becomes bitter.

Endymion Porter was one of the leading patrons of the arts in Stuart England. The five poems addressed to Porter in *Hesperides* are a study in the artistic system of patronage and poetic support and advice to the Stuart hegemony. Porter contributed "Oyl of Maintenance" to Jonson, Davenant, May, and Dekker as well as to Herrick. Herrick's poems are bracketed by an early and a late epigram on Porter's generosity (H-117, H-1071). At midvolume are two poems that seem characteristic of Stuart sentiments in the 1630s. The first is a pastoral dialogue between Endymion Porter and "Lycidas Herrick" (H-492). Endymion asks why Lycidas has laid aside his pipe. The poet replies that it is because of Endymion's absence from the country and his presence "Where Shepheards sho'd not keep. / I meane the Court." Endymion promises to return quickly, and Lycidas agrees to sing again. The dialogue is then followed by a coda with a blunt reminder of what Herrick hoped to get in return for his fancy:

> And my most luckie Swain, when I shall live to see
> *Endimions* Moon to fill up full, remember me:
> Mean time, let *Lycidas* have leave to Pipe to thee.

The second pastoral poem to Porter is one of Herrick's better-known long poems, "The Country life," addressed to Porter under his title, "Groome of the Bed-Chamber to his Majesty" (H-662), and therefore probably written in the 1620s when Porter held this significant office. The poem seems not so much a compliment to Porter as advice to his master. It is both a flattering statement of Charles's policy of urging the English nobility to return to their land and leave the court and a veiled suggestion that the king should engage himself personally in the ruling of his country. It seems much more likely, for example, that it is Charles rather than Porter whom Herrick is addressing when he says,[14]

> . . . thou dost know,
> That the best compost for the Lands
> Is the wise Masters Feet, and Hands.
> There at the Plough thou find'st thy Teame,
> With a Hind whistling there to them:
> And cheer'st them up, by singing how
> The Kingdoms portion *is the Plow.*

> This done, then to th'enameld Meads
> Thou go'st; as thy foot there treads,
> Thou seest a present God-like Power
> Imprinted in each Herbe and Flower.
>
> (ll. 22–32)

The second half of the poem enunciates the country pleasures of hunting and festivals (most of which Herrick memorializes in other poems throughout *Hesperides*). "The Country life" ends neatly with the bitter-sweet reflection borrowed from Vergil's *Georgics* (2.458):

> O happy life! if that their good
> The Husbandmen but understood!
> Who all the day themselves doe please,
> And Younglings, with such sports as these.
> And, lying down, have nought t'affright
> Sweet sleep, that makes more short the night.

"The Country life" appears to be a fully rounded poem, its conclusion logical and complete, if conditional. But Herrick has added at the end of the poem the phrase "*Caetera desunt . . .*" [the rest is lacking . . .] The suggestion of incompletion at the end of this georgic poem on the country life and, by implication, on the Stuart idyll, reinforces the note of regret and nostalgia that the final lines had introduced. The phrase recalls the disclaimer "Desunt nonnulla" at the beginning of his *poetic* idyll, "The Apparition of his Mistresse calling him to Elizium," a century earlier. It is possible that Herrick added the phrase sometime after the composition of the poem. In any case, it further reinforces the sense of faltering ideals at midvolume.

Herrick has an ode to Endymion Porter which introduces us to one of the strangest pairings of lyric and epigram in *Hesperides*. "An Ode to Master Endymion Porter, upon his Brothers death" (H-185) is complicated, first of all, by some uncertainty about its subject. It has been suggested that the ode concerns the death of one of Porter's brothers—either Edmund, who died in 1628, or Gyles, who died about 1645, but both of Herrick's modern editors believe that it almost certainly concerns the death of Herrick's own brother, who is addressed in the following epigram.[15] The poem is further obscured by a confusion about its speaker or speakers. The final and most disturbing question we must ask is why Herrick would address to his court patron a poem on such a personal and tragic subject.

Alexander Grosart suggested that the first stanza of the four-part ode is spoken by Porter himself.[16] The presence of two speakers in the ode is indicated by the address in the first stanza to "Herrick" and in the second to "Porter." Since Herrick used the dialogue form again in his pastoral eclogue between Endymion Porter and Lycidas Herrick, it seems probable that he intends this ode to be read as a dialogue as well. Herrick's usual clarity of reference is missing here, however. The ode's obscurity may be attributed to its genre, but it seems more likely that this poem was, for some reason, difficult for Herrick to write.

"Porter" opens the poem with a stanza of consolation, arguing that out of apparent death, life again revives:

> Not all thy flushing Sunnes are set,
> > *Herrick*, as yet:
> Nor doth this far-drawn Hemisphere
> Frown, and look sullen ev'ry where.
> Daies may conclude in nights; and Suns may rest,
> > As dead, within the West;
> Yet the next Morne, re-guild the fragrant East.

The speaker uses the governing metaphor of *Hesperides* itself to comfort the poet.

The next stanza answers the opening consolation and is clearly spoken by the bereaved Herrick:

> Alas for me! that I have lost
> > E'en all almost:
> Sunk is my sight; set is my Sun;
> And all the loome of life undone:
> The staffe, the Elme, the prop, the shelt'ring wall
> > Whereon my Vine did crawle,
> Now, now, blowne downe; needs must the old stock fall.

But the poet quickly revives and lavishes extravagant praise on his patron:

> Yet, *Porter*, while thou keep'st alive,
> > In death I thrive:
> And like a *Phenix* re-aspire
> From out my *Narde*, and Fun'rall fire:
> And as I prune my feather'd youth, so I
> > Doe mar'l how I co'd die,
> When I had Thee, my chief Preserver, by.

Herrick's rapid recovery seems incongruous following the gravity of his loss and the depth of the grief he first expresses.

The tone of the final stanza is even more disturbing. It begins with Herrick's expression of total recovery:

> I'm up, I'm up, and blesse that hand
> Which makes me stand
> Now as I doe; and but for thee,
> I must confesse, I co'd not be.

Porter has become here "the staffe, the Elme, the prop, the shelt'ring wall" to replace the support that Herrick's brother had lent him previously, a sentiment appropriate enough in the context of the poem. The concluding lines, however, alter the terms of the ode so abruptly that it is difficult to be sure what is being said or even who is speaking:

> The debt is paid: for he who doth resigne
> Thanks to the gen'rous Vine;
> Invites fresh Grapes to fill his Presse with Wine.

Since the conclusion develops the image of the vine from the second stanza, it seems logical that the vine should be the poet here. The debt that is paid must then be Herrick's to Porter for his encouragement after Herrick's depression over his brother's death. Herrick's payment is therefore this poem itself and further tributes to come. It seems a callous and uncomfortable way to end the ode, for it introduces the imagery of poetry as payment and implies that future payment can be forthcoming.

It is possible, too, that the final three lines are spoken, not by Herrick, but by Porter, thus balancing Porter's speech at the beginning of the poem. Spoken by Porter, the lines would mean that the patron regards Herrick's debt to him as discharged by this poem and that he promises to invest the poet with "fresh grapes" to fuel new poetic endeavors. Such a reading would make the vine imagery in the poem inconsistent, but Herrick frequently refers elsewhere to patronage as a gift of wine.

However we read the poem, its placement directly before the epigram "To his dying Brother, Master William Herrick" (H-186) is disturbing. Because Herrick's grief at his brother's death is anticipated and assuaged before it is articulated, the force of the epigram is dramatically lessened. The epigram begs William Herrick to delay his death until the brothers can bid each other farewell. Once his brother dies, Herrick promises that

... I will bequeath my heart
Into thy loving hands: *For Ile keep none*
To warme my Breast, when thou my Pulse art gone.
No, here Ile last, and walk (a harmless shade)
About this Urne, wherein thy Dust is laid,
To guard it so, as nothing here shall be
Heavy, to hurt those sacred seeds of thee.

(italics added)

The poet's promise to his brother must seem hollow coming directly after he describes turning from his brother's grave to a new source of support. The conjunction of the two poems, especially in their reverse order, darkens once again the image of the public poet who trades poetry for patronage. The confused, garbled nature of the "Ode" may testify to the discomfort the poet feels.

There is a final, late epigram to Porter that seems hyperbolic but innocuous enough at first glance (H-1071). The epigram, however, echoes and debases imagery that Herrick had previously reserved for the Stuarts alone. Herrick had built the epigram "To Prince Charles upon his coming to Exeter" (H-756) around the image of Charles's poets as "Prophets" keeping watch and praying for Charles's success in ending the civil war. At the very end of *Hesperides*, Herrick applies that image elsewhere:

When to thy Porch I come, and (ravisht) see
The State of Poets there attending Thee:
Those *Bardes*, and I, all in a *Chorus* sing,
We are Thy *Prophets Porter; Thou our King.*

The echo of Herrick's Stuart poems is particularly audible here because the epigram to Porter is placed next to two of the most outspoken political epigrams in *Hesperides*. Next to this rather cutting advice, for example,

No man so well a Kingdome Rules, as He,
Who hath himselfe obaid the Soveraignty.

(H-1074)

the recycling for a rich patron of Herrick's vocabulary of Stuart praise sounds at least equivocal.

Besides William Herrick, Herrick had two other brothers, both of whom he addresses in *Hesperides*. Herrick's poem to his oldest brother, Thomas, is one of his most famous, "A Country life: To his Brother,

151

Master Thomas Herrick" (H-106). It was written on the occasion of his brother's leaving London about 1610 to become a gentleman farmer and is therefore one of Herrick's earliest poems. It is an accomplished example of the georgic poem counseling Stoic pleasure in the simple life and arguing against the corrupting and unhappy luxury of cities and court.[17] Placed very early in the book, the poem to Thomas Herrick is important to the pastoral mood of *Hesperides'* beginning, while the many epigrammatic *sententiae* embedded within it suggest the shape of the volume as a whole.

The classical poem becomes most particular and immediate when Herrick praises Thomas specifically for leaving his mercantile career in the city. Instead,

> . . . thou at home, blest with securest ease,
>   Sitt'st, and beleev'st that there be seas,
> And watrie dangers; while thy whiter hap,
>   But sees these things within thy Map.
> And viewing them with a more safe survey,
>   Mak'st easie Feare unto thee say,
> *A heart thrise wall'd with Oke, and Brasse, that man*
>   *Had, first, durst plow the Ocean.*
> But thou at home without or tyde or gale,
>   Can'st in thy Map securely saile:
> Seeing those painted Countries; and so guesse
>   By those fine Shades, their Substances:
> And from thy Compasse taking small advice,
>   Buy'st Travell at the lowest price.
>
> (ll. 69–82)

In the country, Thomas can hear with wonder, rather than fear, "of States, of Countries, Courts, and Kings," happier to hear of the world's activities than to witness them (ll. 83–88). That Thomas Herrick's country venture was a failure, and that he was thereafter forced to become dependent on his uncle's grudging generosity does not change the accomplishment of the poem. "A Country life" stands near the entrance of *Hesperides* as a testimony to Stoic virtue and pastoral happiness. Like "The Country life to Endymion Porter," it embodies the cultural program current in the Stuart reign.

But at the far other end of *Hesperides*, Herrick placed, as the final epigram of praise in the volume, a poem to his third brother. "To his Brother

Nicolas Herrick" (H-1100) echoes and seems to correct the early poem to Thomas Herrick. Nicholas Herrick, two years older than Robert Herrick and a year younger than Thomas, chose a life very different from either of his brothers'. He was a merchant who traveled and traded in the Levant. He embodied everything that Thomas Herrick rejected in turning to a country life and everything that Herrick deprecated in praising Thomas's choice to stay at home and see the world through books and maps. What Herrick chooses late in *Hesperides* to praise about Nicholas's life is therefore startling:

> What others have with cheapnesse seene, and ease,
> In Varnisht maps; by'th'helpe of Compasses:
> Or reade in Volumes, and those Bookes (with all
> Their large Narrations, *Incanonicall*)
> Thou hast beheld those seas, and Countries farre;
> And tel'st to us, what once they were, and are.
> So that with bold truth, thou canst now relate
> This Kingdomes fortune, and that Empires fate.

His brother has seen the roses of Sharon, the present Jerusalem, Calvary, and the "Saviours Sepulcher." One has only to listen to him to "see / The truth of Travails lesse in bookes then Thee." The credibility of those "large Narrations, *Incanonicall*" is debunked as exaggeration, if not fiction. At the same time, the pun on "travails" adds a note of amusement and reservation to the compliment.

Nevertheless, that the final person Herrick chose to praise in *Hesperides* is a brother who lived a life actively engaged in the world is further evidence of the disillusionment with a poetic life and with pastoral ideals at the end of *Hesperides*. It distinguishes "truth" from "Bookes . . . Narrations." It coincides with the many epigrams in the latter half of *Hesperides* that urge practical action, especially on the king. It rejects remaining passively at home in "securest ease," feeling morally superior to the turmoil of politics and rulership.

At the beginning of *Hesperides* is a small lyric poem, "Upon Mistresse Elizabeth Wheeler, under the name of Amarillis" (H-130). This slight poem spins the fancy that "Robin-Red-brest" (one of Herrick's names for himself) covers the sleeping Amarillis with leaves, thinking her dead, but then is overjoyed when she awakens. At the other end of *Hes-*

perides is another pastoral poem to Elizabeth Wheeler, "under the name of Amarillis" (H-1068), a dialogue between shepherdess and poet. The poet's argument and his situation are, however, the complete reverse of the usual pastoral posture of the shepherd inviting the woman to come and live an ideal country life with him (of which Herrick has several in *Hesperides*). Here it is Amarillis who will leave for the country and "Herrick" who remains at court. The arguments that "Herrick" offers Amarillis are a series of reversals of the main tenets of the rest of his lyric poems. He asks her:

> What have the Meades to do with thee,
>   Or with thy youthfull houres?
> Live thou at Court, where thou mayst be
>   The *Queen* of men, not flowers.
>
> Let Country wenches make 'em fine
>   With Poesies, since 'tis fitter
> For thee with richest Jemmes to shine,
>   And like the Starres to glitter.

Herrick wrote "A Dialogue betwixt himselfe and Mistresse Elizabeth Wheeler" early in his career, perhaps as early as his years as a goldsmith's apprentice and before he went to Cambridge (1607–1613). Elizabeth Wheeler was his neighbor as a child, daughter of a prominent goldsmith like Herrick's father and uncle.[18] She married in 1613, but before that resided alternately in London and in the county. This poem, then, is one of Herrick's earliest, probably written about the same time as "A Country life." Its placement at the very end of *Hesperides* is evidence of Herrick's careful arrangement of the book, for, no matter when it was composed, it belongs in the urbane London world at the end of *Hesperides*.

The poem bidding farewell to Amarillis, the epigram of praise for Michael Oldisworth, the commendation of his brother Nicholas, conclude Herrick's "Testament" of praise. It is a testimony to Herrick's family loyalty, to his worldly fortunes, and to the times that shaped them. It is, above all else, a testimony to his belief in the power of poetry to endure.

CHAPTER EIGHT

The Mocking Epigrams

꩜ Ben Jonson begins *Epigrammes* with a famous warning about the reader's responsibility:

> Pray thee, take care, that tak'st my booke in hand,
> To reade it well: that is, to understand.

Herrick places an epigram in *Hesperides* that is a close imitation of Jonson's, but Herrick addresses his epigram not to the reader but "To his Booke," and places it not at the beginning of his poems but at midvolume:

> Be bold my Booke, nor be abasht, or feare
> The cutting Thumb-naile, or the Brow severe.
> But by the *Muses* sweare, all here is good,
> If but well read; or ill read, understood.
>
> (H-603)

I believe we may read Herrick's epigram "To his Booke" as explicit directions for two possible readings of *Hesperides*. The epigram suggests, at the very least, that the competent and friendly reader will find everything here "good" and that even a poor or malicious reader will understand the book and that therefore the book will still be "good," if on different terms. But Herrick may be suggesting a much more radical critical strategy: if we read "well," then we will find that all in the book is "good"; but if we read "ill," *then* we will understand. I would like to try to "understand" *Hesperides* by reading it "ill," or, more accurately, by reading carefully, in the context of the whole volume, those epigrams that Herrick's readers have usually taken "ill."

Herrick's "mocking" epigrams have earned him the scorn of his critics, even their impassioned venom.[1] Variously called coarse, vulgar, or sportive by critics, these epigrams number about one hundred fifty, or more, depending on one's margin of vulgarity. On the occasion of the first complete edition of *Hesperides* since 1648 (1823, edited by Thomas Maitland), Robert Southey declared:

We have lately seen the whole of Herrick's poems republished, a coarse-minded and beastly writer, whose dung-hill, when the few flowers that grew therein had been transplanted, ought never to have been disturbed. Those flowers indeed are beautiful and perennial; but they should have been removed from the filth and ordure in which they are embedded.[2]

They were expunged from most nineteenth- and early twentieth-century editions of Herrick's poetry. Even today, they are never anthologized.

In recent years, however, the mocking epigrams have attracted considerable attention from critics who have attempted to explain Herrick's inclusion in *Hesperides* of these profoundly disturbing poems. In his unpublished but influential dissertation of 1958, Richard Ross argued that to Herrick the coarse epigrams represent the "nature" that is opposed to the "art" of his lyric poems.[3] John Kimmey saw Herrick as a "keen satirist" in these poems, one who exposes imperfections both physical and spiritual.[4] A. Leigh DeNeef believed that Herrick's purpose in the "sportive" epigrams is not satirical; rather, he is simply forcing the reader to confront brutal reality.[5] Antoinette Dauber emphasized their anality and argued that Herrick is allowing the reader to release a childish pleasure.[6] Robert Halli, Jr., in his article "Robert Herrick's Epigrams on Commoners," presented them as the antithesis of Herrick's lyric images of beauty, innocence, and wealth.[7]

Beyond his choice of title, Halli does not emphasize the class distinction that the mocking epigrams draw. It is remarkable, however, that Gubbs and Skinns, Doll and Skurffe, and the other targets of Herrick's wit are all poor (or nouveau riche), uneducated members of the lower class. Jonson's satiric epigrams, by comparison, although they cover the spectrum of urban life from "My Lord Ignorant" to "Groome Ideot," concentrate mainly on titled fools and court hangers-on. And while Jonson targets moral flaws, Herrick is fascinated almost exclusively with physical grotesqueries and physical sins. Floris Delattre argued that these epigrams are the product of Herrick's unhappiness in Devonshire and that their subjects are the "rude" and "rocky" Devonshire peasants.[8] Delattre's thesis is intriguing, but oversimplified.

Like Jonson, Herrick aspired to be the poet of the privileged classes. The best-known expression of Herrick's social prejudices is "The Hock-cart, or Harvest home: To the Right Honourable, Mildmay, Earle of Westmorland" (H-250), which begins:

> Come Sons of Summer, by whose toile,
> We are the Lords of Wine and Oile:
> By whose tough labours, and rough hands,
> We rip up first, then reap our lands.

Herrick implies that he is speaking not only for Westmorland and other landowners of his class but for himself as well, the poet and master of ceremonies for the "Lords of Wine and Oile." At the laborers' celebration, the "smirking Wine" (l. 36) of poetry and finer pleasures is not supplied, but Herrick invites the celebrants to partake freely of

> . . . that, which drowns all care, stout Beere;
> Which freely drink to your Lords health,
> Then to the Plough, (the Common-wealth).

Herrick expresses here the same sentiments that he will to Endymion Porter in "The Country life": "The Kingdoms portion [or source of wealth] is the Plow" (H-662, l. 28).[9] In "The Country life," Herrick urges Porter (and, by implication, the king) to remember the importance of English agriculture. In "The Hock-cart," the proposition is explained from the bottom up: the labor of the rustics perpetuates the power and wealth of their lords. At the end of the poem, his attitude toward the laborers is made more brutally clear than in any comparable seventeenth-century poem:

> Feed, and grow fat; and as ye eat,
> Be mindfull, that the lab'ring Neat
> (As you) may have their fill of meat.
> And know, besides, ye must revoke
> The patient Oxe unto the Yoke,
> And all goe back unto the Plough
> And Harrow, (though they'r hang'd up now.)

But, granting his class assumptions, Herrick's final words to Westmorland's farmhands are still surprisingly harsh, almost bitter:

> And, you must know, your Lords word's true,
> Feed him ye must, whose food fils you.
> And that this pleasure is like raine,

> Not sent ye for to drowne your paine,
> But for to make it spring againe.

This savagely frank version of the true purpose of the workers' feast shatters the festival gaiety of the rest of the poem.

Herrick has been so insistently seen as a royalist, and that position is usually seen as so simple, that even when a reader hears the ambivalence at the end of this poem, he or she may recognize it only as an anomaly in *Hesperides*. Peter Stallybrass, for example, uses Herrick as his primary evidence for the use by the Stuart hegemony of rural festivals as "bread and circuses" for the English lower class.[10] But Stallybrass is "surprised" at "the extent to which the 'disinterested, gratuitous relationship' of the lord to his workers is revealed as 'overt domination.' . . . For the last three lines mark a strange *reversal* of that common ideological maneuvre through which (contested) human history is transformed into (uncontested) natural process. . . . The lines are so radically ambivalent that they threaten to subvert the ethic of 'communal reciprocity' which is central to the rural idyll" (p. 247). But Stallybrass chooses finally to ignore the subversion that he hears in order to make Herrick suit his thesis.

On the other hand, it has been argued by Richard Lougy that the attitude Herrick expresses in "The Hock-cart" is ironic and that he is actually in sympathy with the laborers and, indirectly, is criticizing Westmorland's cruelty.[11] Such a reading, appealing but anachronistic, depends not only on inverting all of the poem's explicit statements but also on isolating it from its larger Hesperidean context.

In this chapter, I shall argue that the social content of "The Hock-cart," which is capable of more than one interpretation, is part of a larger structure of social ambivalence, in which Herrick's uneasy sense of his own status frequently expresses itself by debasing those of whose inferiority to himself he can be reasonably certain. His debasing equation of the farm laborers with oxen at the end of "The Hock-cart" operates at the same social and rhetorical level as most of the mocking epigrams. Yet even on the subject of the Dean Prior community Herrick admits his ambivalence. He declares them "A people currish; churlish as the seas; / And rude (almost) as rudest Salvages" ("To Dean-bourn," H-86) and, in "Discontents in Devon" (H-51), moans:

> More discontents I never had
> Since I was born, then here;

Where I have been, and still am sad,
In this dull *Devon-shire.*

But he also admits:

Yet justly too I must confesse;
I ne'r invented such
Ennobled numbers for the Presse,
Then where I loath'd so much.

The ambivalence Herrick names here and enacts throughout *Hesperides* is encapsulated, for example, in a "mistresse" poem like "The Wake" (H-761):

Come *Anthea* let us two
Go to Feast, as others do.
Tarts and Custards, Creams and Cakes,
Are the Junketts still at Wakes:
Unto which the Tribes resort,
Where the businesse is the sport:
Morris-dancers thou shalt see,
Marian too in Pagentrie:
And a Mimick to devise
Many grinning properties.

All this is what Herrick had promised he would sing of in the "Argument," "*May-poles, Hock-carts, Wassails, Wakes,*" cakes and country festivals. But the poet's tone as he describes the event to "Anthea" becomes increasingly sardonic:

Players there will be, and those
Base in action as in clothes:
Yet with strutting they will please
The incurious Villages.
Neer the dying of the day,
There will be a *Cudgell*-Play,
Where a *Coxcomb* will be broke,
Ere a good *word* can be spoke:
But the anger ends all here,
Drencht in Ale, or drown'd in Beere.
Happy Rusticks, best content
With the cheapest Merriment:

> And possesse no other feare,
> Then to want the Wake next Yeare.

The critical argument that Herrick's art is devoted to ceremony as a way of defeating transiency must be qualified to some extent by a poem like "The Wake," where Herrick jeers at the simple happiness and cyclical sense of surety such ceremonies can give. Any sense of envy the poem conveys is tempered by its tone of condescension. Herrick's ceremonialism may serve the social order, but it does so with significant hesitations and undercurrents. His ceremonialism may also celebrate the continuity of life, but it is, like all ceremonies, a highly self-conscious act. DeNeef has pointed out that the irony of "The Wake" lies in the sophisticated persona who cannot share the rustics' pleasures. The price he must pay for his superiority is the taste of pleasure jaded.[12] The poem may be read, then, as ambivalent both about the rustic ceremony and about the sophistication that prevents poet and imaginary mistress from taking part.

Herrick's ambivalence about the "churlish" members of his own parish is, however, only one aspect of a still larger contradiction in *Hesperides,* a conflict between the modes of praise and abuse that extends to every subject and ultimately involves the poet himself and his view of his own work. In mixing praise and satire throughout his epigram book, Herrick had, of course, the precedent of Jonson. But whereas Jonson's satiric epigrams are best considered in conjunction with the epigrams of praise, since together they create the conflict and resolution of *Epigrammes,* Herrick's mocking epigrams work in direct tension with his lyric poems of delicate beauty and finally bring into question the ontological status of beauty itself.

In the center of *Hesperides,* the epigram "Upon Jack and Jill" (H-498) dramatizes the conflict of poetry and "reality" in *Hesperides:*

> When *Jill* complaines to *Jack* for want of meate;
> *Jack* kisses *Jill,* and bids her freely eate:
> *Jill* sayes, of what? says *Jack,* on that sweet kisse,
> Which full of Nectar and Ambrosia is,
> The food of Poets; so I thought sayes *Jill,*
> That makes them looke so lanke, so Ghost-like still.
> Let Poets feed on aire, or what they will;
> Let me feed full, till that I fart, sayes *Jill.*

"Upon Jack and Jill" is one of the many poems in *Hesperides* that makes explicit the generic tension between lyric and epigram. A great deal of the humor of *Hesperides* and also its poignancy derives from Herrick's derision of his own "poetic" character.

In other words, Herrick not only subverts the things he praises but subverts the act of praise. Robert Halli, Jr., for example, has pointed out that "almost every source of delight in Herrick's poems on imaginary mistresses has its antithesis in the coarse epigrams." If sexuality is "innocent, sacred, and mysterious" in the "cleanly-Wanton" poems of *Hesperides*, it is coarse, sinful, and mercantile in the epigrams.[13] If wealth and luxury are signs of exalted place and character in the lyric poems, especially those written for patronage, any grubbing attempt to escape from or to disguise poverty is revealed and despised in *Hesperides'* mocking epigrams. If the lyric poems and the epigrams of praise are fragrant with incense and perfume, the coarse epigrams reek of rotting teeth, sour breath, and excrement. But above all else, throughout *Hesperides* Herrick mocks himself, "Jack" the poet who lives on air and loves his own imaginary version of "Jill."

In the first century of *Hesperides*, for example, an ambiguous interplay between lyric beauty and harsh epigrammatic wit connects two poems on blindness and fidelity. In "Being once blind, his request to Biancha" (H-98), Herrick pleads with one of his idealized mistresses that "When Age or Chance has made [him] blind," Biancha will lead him by her perfumes and her effulgent light. But in the following epigram, lovely Biancha becomes discordant Blanch, a woman who because she still "swears her Husband's lovely; when a scald / Has blear'd his eyes" (H-99) is cruelly mocked by the poet for her fondness. The disquiet these poems produce is characteristic of the disturbing irony that plays beneath the surface of *Hesperides* and sometimes shatters the poet's lyric illusions. At the same time that Herrick values poetry as fictive and celebratory, he also sees it as a veneer and an artifice that he has created to cover a grim reality.

In the second century, Herrick has a conventional pair of love poems addressed to a woman named Dorothy Keneday (H-122 and -123). In the first poem, the epigram on "His parting from" her, the poet mourns that when he left she did not cry, she "Whose heart, whose hand, whose ev'ry part spake love." The lyric "The Teare sent to her from Stanes," the second poem of the pair, picks up the image of crying. His tear is to glide down the Thames to her:

> To that coy Girle;
> Who smiles, yet slayes
> Me with delayes;
> And strings my tears as Pearle.

The poem then elaborates, in six stanzas, a plea for her love, portraying the woman as cruel and the poet as helplessly in thrall.

Following the poems on tears to Dorothy Keneday is an epigram "Upon one Lillie, who married with a maid call'd Rose" (H-124), whose slight conceit seems harmless:

> What times of sweetnesse this faire day fore-shows,
> When as the Lilly marries with the Rose!
> What next is lookt for? but we all sho'd see
> To spring from these a sweet Posterity.

But the epigram on the flowers and their children is followed by "An Epitaph upon a child" (H-125) that reminds us that flowers are associated in *Hesperides* mainly with death:

> Virgins promis'd when I dy'd,
> That they wo'd each Primrose-tide,
> Duely, Morne and Ev'ning, come,
> And with flowers dresse my Tomb.
> Having promis'd, pay your debts,
> Maids, and here strew Violets.

Capping this whole sentimental sequence of tears and wooing and marriage, however, is one of Herrick's rawest and most violent epigrams, "Upon Scobble" (H-126):

> *Scobble* for Whoredome whips his wife; and cryes,
> He'll slit her nose; But blubb'ring, she replyes,
> Good Sir, make no more cuts i'th'outward skin,
> One slit's enough to let Adultry in.

In four lines, Herrick here ravages marriage, sexuality, and tears, deliberately destroying the fragile mood of fanciful melancholy that the preceding poems had so artfully created. These five poems are typical of the way Herrick develops *Hesperides*. At any point in the book, similar sequences play against each other to puncture and destroy lyric elegance. Indeed, late in *Hesperides* is a sardonic epigram, "Upon Faunus" (H-986), that punctures the balloon of pastoralism's innocent mythology:

We read how *Faunus,* he the shepheards *God,*
His wife to death whipt with a *Mirtle Rod.*
The Rod (perhaps) was better'd by the name;
But had it been a Birch, the death's the same.

The epigram makes clear that underneath the poet's fables and euphe-
misms are cruelty and death.

Besides "To the Virgins" and "Corinna's going a Maying,"
Robert Herrick is best known today for his poems on women's clothing,
such as "Delight in Disorder." These lyrics suggest that a woman is made
more alluring by artful suggestion rather than by bold revelation of her
beauty and, furthermore, that the artfulness of a woman's appearance
should be disguised as a careless naturalness. Implicit in all these poems
on woman's beauty is the parallel argument that poetry, like a woman,
should place "art above nature" without appearing to do so.

Herrick makes his aesthetic theory explicit in "The Lilly in a Christal"
(H-193) in a series of images borrowed from two of Martial's epigrams
(4.22; 8.68).[14] Herrick lists a number of examples of the heightened attraction of beauty that is veiled. Put grapes or cherries, for instance, in a glass:

> . . . and they will send
>   More beauty to commend
> Them, from that cleane and subtile skin,
>   Then if they naked stood,
> And had no other pride at all,
>   But their own flesh and blood,
>   And tinctures naturall.

> Thus Lillie, Rose, Grape, Cherry, Creame,
>   And straw-berry do stir
>   More love, when they transfer
> A weak, a soft, a broken beame;
>   Then if they sho'd discover
> At full their proper excellence;
>   Without some Scean cast over,
>   To juggle with the sense.

It becomes apparent only at the end of "The Lilly in a Christal" that it is, as well, advice to women on how to arrange themselves in order to attract men. The "Christal'd Lillie" should be "A Rule, how far to teach, / Your nakednesse must reach." In the last stanza, examples are dispensed with and Herrick becomes direct:

> So though y'are white as Swan, or Snow,
>   And have the power to move
>   A world of men to love:
> Yet, when your Lawns and Silks shal flow;
>   And that white cloud divide
> Into a doubtful Twi-light; then
>   Then will your hidden Pride
>   Raise greater fires in men.

Spoken to a woman on the subtleties of erotic attraction, "The Lilly in a Christal" is, at the same time, the fullest exposition of Herrick's aesthetic theory. It seems to offer clarity and fixity of image and of theory in the contradictory world of Herrick's book of poetry.

But this surety is immediately destroyed. Two poems later, in a stunningly cynical reversal of "The Lilly in a Christal," Herrick gives advice in "Upon some women" (H-195) to "Thou who wilt not love" and rips away the veil he had so artfully drawn over a woman's nakedness:

> Learne of me what Woman is.
> Something made of thred and thrumme;
> A meere Botch of all and some.
> Pieces, patches, ropes of haire;
> In-laid Garbage ev'ry where.
> Out-side silk, and out-side Lawne;
> Sceanes to cheat us neatly drawne.
> False in legs, and false in thighes;
> False in breast, teeth, haire, and eyes:
> False in head, and false enough;
> Onely true in shreds and stuffe.

"Upon some women" expresses the anti-aesthetic of the mocking epigrams that see the "In-laid Garbage" under the silk and lawn; when it exposes and destroys women's "art," it must also call into question Herrick's theory of lyric poetry: "Sceanes to cheat us neatly drawne."

Between "The Lilly in a Christal" and "Upon some women" is an epigram in which Herrick addresses his book of poems as if it were a woman:

> Like to a Bride, come forth my Book, at last,
> With all thy richest jewels over-cast:
> Say, if there be 'mongst many jems here; one
> Deservelesse of the name of *Paragon:*
> Blush not at all for that; since we have set
> Some *Pearls* on *Queens,* that have been counterfet.

The image of his book as a woman artfully enameled with jewelry seems elegantly consonant with "The Lilly in a Christal," the poem that it follows, since it makes explicit the metaphor of poetry as a woman, "over-cast" with flattering decoration. But she is not to be ashamed if some of her jewels are "false," for Herrick has falsely praised false queens before. The epigram is actually poisonous in its cynicism about Herrick's poetry, about the subjects of his poetry, and about the poet himself, especially because it is followed by the devastating exposé of "Upon some women."

We may feel superior to Southey and his squeamishness about the coarse side of *Hesperides,* but there are epigrams among Herrick's poems that must be repulsive, no matter how liberated, or dulled, our sensibilities. Antoinette Dauber has attempted to explain these "foul" epigrams as a conscious strategy by Herrick to "cure" the epigram of its inherent coarseness and at the same time to provide a psychological catharsis for the reader. But her argument distorts the coarse epigrams by putting them in a falsely positive light.

There are dark moments in *Hesperides* that cannot be explained away. The element of disgust, which has made readers who cherish the "lyric" Herrick avoid *Hesperides* as a whole, cannot be denied. For Herrick sees and dwells upon things that readers of lyric poetry would rather not see. The inclusion of these excremental and self-consuming moments challenges at its very root the humanist conception of poetry as somehow a "better" or more precious form of discourse. Even early in *Hesperides* in the predominantly lyric half of the volume, Herrick insists upon the dualism of his vision. In an epigram abrupt with disgust, Herrick contrasts our ideas of cleanliness with the brutal actuality of bodily process:

> *Sudds* Launders Bands in pisse; and starches them
> Both with her Husband's, and her own tough fleame.

And he immediately follows it with one of his loveliest poems, "To the Rose. Song" (H-238), the first lines of which are borrowed directly from Martial's lines "I, felix rosa, mollibusque sertis / nostri cinge comas Apollinaris" (7.89). Herrick's "Song" begins, "Goe happy Rose, and enterwove / With other Flowers, bind my Love." But a stanza later it introduces something that, in the immediate aftermath of the epigram, sounds jarringly familiar:

> Say (if she's fretfull) I have bands
> Of Pearle, and Gold, to bind her hands.

The repetition of "bands," the key word from "Upon Sudds," and the implied colors, yellow and white, make the lyric, for one startling and undermining moment, repulsive.

The use of identical images over and over again in Herrick's poetry has been called by Gordon Braden "a kind of . . . aural decor, a texture of minute fixations" for which Braden slighted Herrick as "a man with nothing really to say or find out or in general to get at, but with a keen disposition, quickly expended and quickly renewed, to write in a certain way."[15] In order to come to this conclusion, however, Braden must ignore the startling nuances and the intense incongruities that those "minute fixations" produce. For instance, Braden could have cited Herrick's fascination with the teeth of his mistresses. But Herrick is equally obsessed by the rotting teeth and empty mouths of "Glasco" (H-129), "Bridget" (H-419), "Ursly" (H-543), "Franck" (H-728), and "Mudge" (H-965), among others.[16] Indeed, in a telling crossover from the coarse epigrams to the beautiful lyrics, Herrick advises women "to hide their teeth, if they be rotten or rusty" (H-738):

> Close keep your lips, if that you meane
> To be accounted inside cleane:
> For if you cleave them, we shall see
> There in your teeth much Leprosie.

This harsh epigram is closely followed by a "mistress" poem to Julia, which by this point the reader has come to expect to be dainty in its poetic fancy.[17] But "The Candor of Julias teeth" (H-741) comes very close to crossing the line between poetic elegance and disgust. The epigram to Julia's teeth reads:

> White as *Zenobias* teeth, the which the Girles
> Of Rome did weare for their most precious Pearles.

Uncharacteristically, Herrick's epigram is an incomplete sentence, left open as if Herrick drew back from making the analogy explicit. Zenobia was the black queen of Syria, kept a prisoner in Rome for many years. The image of her teeth worn as jewelry is, at best, disquieting.

The elements of Freudian anality, cannibalism, and self-consumption in Herrick's poetry, which this poem hints at, constitute the most disturbing aspect of Herrick's poetry.[18] It is only a small step from the analogy of Julia's teeth with Zenobia's to an epigram like that "Upon Madam Ursly" (H-668):

> For ropes of pearle, first Madam *Ursly* showes
> A chaine of Cornes, pickt from her eares and toes:
> Then, next to match *Tradescant's* curious shels,
> Nailes from her fingers mew'd, she shewes: what els?
> Why then (forsooth) a Carcanet is shown
> Of teeth, as deaf as nuts, and all her own.

There is a curious sense that Herrick is mocking his own poetic "fixations," devouring his own images. At midvolume, "Art above Nature, to Julia" (H-560) catalogs the intricacies and beauty of Julia's dress and the arrangement of her hair, concluding that "mine eye and heart / Dotes less on Nature, then on Art." The poem is, however, followed by an epigram "Upon Sibilla" (H-561), which also, shockingly, describes the details of a woman's toilet:

> With paste of Almonds, *Syb* her hands doth scoure;
> Then gives it to the children to devoure.
> In Creame she bathes her thighs (more soft then silk)
> Then to the poore she freely gives the milke.

To complete the process of this mockery of "art," Herrick follows the epigram on "Syb" with an epigram of praise to his niece Bridget Herrick. The aspect of her beauty that Herrick praises makes a connection unavoidable:

> Sweet *Bridget* blusht, and therewithall,
> Fresh blossoms from her cheekes did fall.
> I thought at first 'twas but a dream,
> Till after I had handled them;
> And smelt them, then they smelt to me,
> As Blossomes of the *Almond* Tree.

The epigram seems innocent and charming if it is not read after the preceding poem. But read together, the description of Bridget sounds very different. The blush that falls tangibly from her cheeks like petals and smells like almonds echoes the almond paste Syb feeds her children. Herrick's "handling" and "smelling" of the "Blossomes" is therefore tinged with the fetishistic.[19]

The case for Herrick's epigrams of self-consumption as self-parody is strongest in a series of epigrams directly preceding the final Stuart epigram, "TO THE KING, Upon his welcome to Hampton-Court." First, an epigram of praise to Elizabeth Finch (who has not been identified) recommends to her a strategy of hoarding in the face of adversity (H-958):

> Hansome you are, and Proper you will be
> Despight of all your infortunitie:
> Live long and lovely, but yet grow no lesse
> In that your owne prefixed comelinesse:
> Spend on that stock: and when your life must fall,
> Leave others Beauty, to set up withall.

Then in "Upon Ralph" (H-959), an extremely coarse epigram, Herrick seems to delight in Ralph's neurotic hoarding of his body parts:

> *Ralph* pares his nayles, his warts, his cornes, and *Raph*
> In sev'rall tills, and boxes keepes 'em safe;
> Instead of Harts-horne (if he speakes the troth)
> To make a lustie-gellie for his broth.

Finally, in the next poem Herrick addresses "his Booke":

> If hap it must, that I must see thee lye
> *Absyrtus*-like all torne confusedly:
> With solemne tears, and with much grief of heart,
> Ile recollect thee (weeping) part by part;
> And having washt thee, close thee in a chest
> With spice; that done, Ile leave thee to thy rest.

The poet packing the bits of his dismembered book of poems into a box is so strongly reminiscent of Ralph saving his warts and toenails to make his soup that the parody is unmistakable. Such self-parody absolutely denies Braden's dismissal of *Hesperides* as "a book about dainty things lived with more or less on their own terms" (p. 155). Just as all his dainty mistresses have their doubles in the disgusting women of the coarse epigrams, so too Herrick duplicates himself in the distorted mirror of the mocking epigrams. The drunkards, the poverty-stricken louts, the poet who "writes in Prose, how sweet all Virgins be" but smells bad himself (H-802), each reflects Herrick's fears about himself. "Skurffe" (H-480) swears by his nine fingers because "a Fellon eate the Tenth away," and a century later Herrick writes an epigram "Upon the losse of his [own] Finger" (H-565). The supreme accomplishment of *Hesperides* is its portrayal of the poet's mind; in this complex mix, the coarse epigrams are Herrick's barely suppressed nightmares and self-doubts.

As we have seen, wine is Herrick's symbol both for poetic inspiration and for poetry's release from grim reality. It also symbolizes Herrick's cherished connection with the king and the "Lords of Wine and Oile." At the end of *Hesperides,* however, even the wine of "sacred Orgies" is lost or renounced. There are numerous bacchanalian verses in *Hesperides,* Anacreontic in inspiration and frivolous in their exhortation to drink to happy distraction. Compare, however, this terse poem in the tenth century (H-988):

> Drinke up
> Your Cup,
> But not spill Wine;
> For if you
> Do,
> 'Tis an ill signe;
>
> 2. That we
> Forsee,
> You are cloy'd here,
> If so, no
> Hoe,
> But avoid here.

Once one has become hopelessly drunk, one is no longer welcome here. There must be a degree of control or one passes into another order and must leave the bounds of lyric celebration. Preceding this "Bachanalian Verse" is an epigram on "The Quintell" (H-987), a jousting post set up for sport at weddings and festivals in the seventeenth century. In this epigram, Herrick erases the boundary line he has maintained throughout *Hesperides* between the mocking epigrams and the pretty epigrams on country ceremony:

> Up with the Quintill, that the Rout,
> May fart for joy, as well as shout:
> Either's welcome, Stinke or Civit,
> If we take it, as they give it.

These expressions of ambivalence about the power of wine and festival to transport us to a superior world remind us of "The Hock-cart" at the beginning of *Hesperides*. Toward the end of Herrick's volume we see glimpses of a different "Hesperides," a place reminiscent of the orgiastic "Land of Cockaigne" as Brueghel portrayed it (ca. 1567), where a knight kneels openmouthed under a table, and a soldier, a peasant, and a scholar lie replete to the point of stupor, even nausea, under a table that circles an ominous tree. The tree at the center of Brueghel's Land of Cockaigne seems to recall a pastoral vision, even Hesperides, but this leafless tree is the axis of a flattened garden of base pleasures. The figure of the scholar is particularly suggestive, incongruously dressed in rustic clothes that are covered by a sumptuous coat, lying spread-eagled on his own writing, his hands unable to move toward a book clasped shut, his face a stunned grimace as he waits for wine to pour itself into his open mouth. Wish fulfillment has become a nightmare of humiliation and incapacity.[20]

But if the bacchanalian aspect of *Hesperides* is also revealed to have its "common" aspect, it is not entirely clear that Herrick, once he has admitted this, can retain his own sense of social superiority. It is very rare in *Hesperides* that Herrick assumes another's persona. Late in *Hesperides*, however, is a rollicking song sung by tinkers (H-1051), which enunciates the voices that we did not hear in "The Hock-cart":

> Along, come along,
> Let's meet in a throng
>   Here of Tinkers;
> And quaffe up a Bowle
> As big as a Cowle
>   To Beer Drinkers.

The tinkers, far from envying the "smirking wine" associated in *Hesperides* with their social betters and with poetry, propose:

> The pole of the Hop
> Place in the Ale-shop
>   to Bethwack us;
> If ever we think

> So much as to drink
> > Unto *Bacchus.*

Their motivation for avoiding the Canary wine is simple economy:

> Who frolick will be,
> For little cost he
> > Must not vary,
> From Beer-broth at all,
> So much as to call
> > For Canary.

Among the very last poems in *Hesperides* is a mocking epigram un-usual for its gentleness and compassion, "Upon Flood, or a thankfull man" (H-1112):

> *Flood,* if he has for him and his a bit,
> He sayes his fore and after Grace for it:
> If meate he wants, then Grace he sayes to see
> His hungry belly borne by Legs *Jaile-free.*
> Thus have, or have not, all alike is good,
> To this our poore, yet ever patient *Flood.*

We might suspect in this poem a degree of identification between patient Flood and the poet whose own economic security was dramatically shat-tered in 1647. The identification becomes unmistakable, however, when we leave the conflicting impulses of *Hesperides* for the unified perspective of *Noble Numbers,* for there, expressed as an epigram addressed "To God, in time of plundering" (N-124), is an account of Herrick's own patience, gratitude, and willingness to say "Grace," even when his last "bit" has been taken away:

> Rapine has yet tooke nought from me;
> But if it please my God, I be
> Brought at the last to th'utmost bit,
> God make me thankfull still for it.
> I have been gratefull for my store:
> Let me say grace when there's no more.

⟡⟡⟡ Herrick's uneasy stance between the poems celebrating beauty, love, and inspiration and the interlayered poems spitting mockery and

171

contempt for women, for human passion, indeed, for poetry and even for himself, may perhaps be ascribed to his own doubts about his place in the culture of early Stuart England. Certainly Jonson in his books of collected poetry reveals self-doubt, even self-hatred. In his attack on his Muse for having "betray'd" him to a "worthlesse lord" at the center of *Epigrammes,* in his praise of Penshurst and its unbegrudged hospitality to everyone—even to him—at the beginning of *The Forrest,* in the self-despising charge, "Goe now, and tell out dayes summ'd up with feares," in the ode to Cary and Morison in *Under-wood,* Jonson exposes both the disparity between his ideals and the reality to which he had to conform, on the one hand, and, on the other, his profound unease with these compromises and with his own place in the world he corrects. Martial, too, had been both the poet who celebrated his age—virtually the only poet who could bring himself to do so—and the outside observer able to enunciate clearly the decadence and hypocrisy of first-century Rome.

Herrick's poetry spans the reigns of the first two Stuart kings. It reflects his attraction to the mystique of divine right monarchy, to the trappings and sensuous pleasures of a life of ease, and to the privileged position of wealth and title. In his bids for patronage and his impassioned deifications of the Stuarts in his poetry, he served as one of the perpetuators of that society. As a poet who articulated their values, he aspired to be one of the "Lords of Wine and Oile."

Yet, at the same time, he was drawn with both disgust and fascination to the ugly, the debased, and the anarchistic. Herrick's intense self-consciousness, his many poses—as old man, shepherd, impassioned lover, voice of wisdom, harsh jester, sardonic wit, friend, son, brother, professional poet, singer for court and country—may all be interpreted as symptoms of his disquiet. Amy Richlin has pointed out the isolated, socially ambiguous position of both the poet of obscenity and the teller of class-based jokes.[21] Similarly, Anthony Low has recently argued in *The Georgic Revolution* that between 1630 and 1660 there developed a sharp polarization between those poets (Puritan) who celebrated the georgic ideal of the worthy laborer and those poets (Cavalier / Royalist) who clung to idealized pastoral and "were inclined to see anything georgic as increasingly ugly, base, and threatening to what they valued." Low singles Herrick out, however, as a Cavalier poet who was curiously sensitive to the realities of rural labor and who "at his most cynical or bitter" perceives the country not as a pastoral but as "a place where one man exploits another, and where all struggle for advantage and survival."[22]

Certainly the mocking epigrams, Southey's vile weeds in the lovely garden, are powerful images from a dark view of the world. Their dissonance plays under the beauties of *Hesperides* and contributes to the power of the volume as a whole. When, at the very end of *Hesperides,* Herrick gives an anguished account of "His change" (H-1016), he articulates himself the frightening line he has walked and, finally, crossed:

> My many cares and much distress,
> Has made me like a wilderness:
> Or (discompos'd) I'm like a rude,
> And all confused multitude:
> Out of my comely manners worne;
> And as in meanes, in minde all torne.

CHAPTER NINE

The Epigrams of Advice

✿ In the center of *Hesperides* Herrick places a poem "Upon himself" (H-456), which makes explicit both the generic and the social tensions inherent in the volume, tensions that reach a crisis at midvolume. Among the series of poems which paradoxically yoke "loathed" Devonshire and poetic inspiration, "Upon himself" is the first that calls for a complete renunciation of that "pastoral" world:[1]

> Come, leave this loathed Country-life, and then
> Grow up to be a Roman *Citizen.*
> Those mites of Time, which yet remain unspent,
> Waste thou in that most Civill Government.
> Get their comportment, and the gliding tongue
> Of those mild Men, thou art to live among:
> Then being seated in that smoother *Sphere,*
> Decree thy everlasting *Topick* there.
> And to the Farm-house nere return at all;
> Though Granges do not love thee, Cities shall.

The explicit course that Herrick urges upon himself is a return to the sophistication of the city and the urbane voice of city poetry, the voice for which Martial is the classical prototype.[2] Once he has "grown up" to citizenship, Herrick advises himself to "Decree thy everlasting *Topick.*" In the Oxford edition of Herrick's poetry, L. C. Martin glossed "Topick" as "place," the meaning listed second in the *OED.* J. Max Patrick subsequently accepted this gloss in his edition.[3] But "place" makes little sense in the context of the poem. It is symptomatic of the way Herrick's poems have been read that both his editors ignore the primary seventeenth-century meaning of "Topick": "Pertaining to or of the nature of a commonplace or general rule." This meaning, however, accords not only with the sense of the poem but with the make-up of the entire *Hesperides*. Herrick tells himself here that he must assume the topical, aphoristic voice—the voice of the epigrammatist.

But the poem's diction undermines its statement. The men of the city are "mild"; they "waste" their time in "that most Civill Government." Theirs is a "smoother Sphere" of the "gliding tongue." There is something pointless and emasculated about these citizens that is the undesirable opposite of the "rude" Devonshire men. Herrick, who at the beginning of the volume had pleaded with his Muse to stay safely at home in the country because "for the Court, the Country wit / Is despicable unto it," now urges himself to become a city poet—but in terms that betray considerable skepticism. The tension between pastoral and epigrammatic remains taut through the end of this poem, just as it does in "To his Muse" at the beginning of *Hesperides*, where the poet urges the pastoral voice on his recalcitrant Muse. It is significant, though, that the poet's voice now pleads—however sarcastically—for the city and against the "Country-life." Although Herrick is clearly ambivalent, the terms of his equation have begun to shift away from the pastoral and toward the "Roman."

Interestingly, L. C. Martin has suggested that Herrick may here be echoing Ben Jonson's "Ode to Himselfe," which Jonson used to preface the published version of his poorly received play *The New Inn* in 1629.[4] Jonson's poem opens with an expostulation to himself to "Come leave the loathed Stage, / And the more loathsome Age" and to return to lyric poetry:

> Leave things so prostitute,
> And take th'Alcaike Lute;
> Or thine owne Horace, or Anacreons Lyre;
> Warme thee by Pindars fire:
> And though thy Nerves be shrunke, and blood be cold,
> Ere years have made thee old,
> Strike that disdainfull heat
> Throughout, to their defeat:
> As curious fooles, and envious of thy straine,
> May blushing sweare, no Palsi's in thy braine.

But if Herrick is imitating Jonson here, his poem is the mirror image of Jonson's address to himself. Rather than calling up the lyric voices of Horace, Anacreon, Alcaeus, and Pindar, Herrick urges himself to "Decree thy everlasting *Topick*" in the city. Part of the "Roman life" of the "gliding tongue" in the "smoother Sphere" or "most Civill Government" is the declamation of commonplaces, axioms, epigrams.

Characteristically, Herrick cannot regard his poetry without some ambivalence and sarcasm. If the pastoral can be mocked in "To his Muse" at the beginning of the volume, where it will predominate, so also here at the threshold of the latter half of the volume, which will be so decisively dominated by "topicks," Herrick calls himself to the epigrammatic, urbane role in a voice heavy with irony.

Further complicating Herrick's poem is the resolution of Jonson's prototypical "Ode to Himselfe." Jonson promises himself, in defiance of his detractors,

> But when they heare thee sing
>   The glories of thy King;
> His zeale to God, and his just awe of men,
>   They may be blood-shaken, then
> Feele such a flesh-quake to possesse their powers,
>   That no tun'd Harpe like ours,
>   In sound of Peace or Warres,
>   Shall truely hit the Starres
> When they shall read the Acts of *Charles* his Reigne,
> And see his Chariot triumph 'bove his *Waine.*

Jonson is calling himself to the role of lyric court poet who will immortalize "the Acts of *Charles* his Reigne." Herrick, on the other hand, urges himself to turn away from the lyric, pastoral mode, which he has used up to this point in *Hesperides* for, among other things, exuberant praise of the Stuarts. At midvolume he turns more and more decidedly to the aphoristic, sententious voice of indirect advice to the king.

Herrick's reversal of the generic order of Jonson's ode falls at a crucial place in *Hesperides,* part of the cluster of elegies for inspiration lost because of "our wasting Warre" that marks the fifth and sixth centuries: the pastoral lament for the departure of Henrietta Maria (H-421), the broken reed of "The Poet hath lost his pipe" (H-573), and "The troublesome times" (H-596). At the end of this sequence is the poem "The bad season makes the Poet sad" (H-612), in which Herrick laments that he is

> Dull to my selfe, and almost dead to these
> My many fresh and fragrant Mistresses:
> Lost to all Musick now; since every thing

> Puts on the semblance here of sorrowing.
> Sick is the Land to'th'heart. . . .

"The bad season" ends with a nostalgic dream of the kind of poetry he might write again if the old order were to be restored:

> But if that golden Age wo'd come again,
> And *Charles* here Rule, as he before did Raign;
> If smooth and unperplext the Seasons were,
> As when the *Sweet Maria* lived here:
> I sho'd delight to have my Curles halfe drown'd
> In *Tyrian Dewes,* and Head with Roses crown'd.
> And once more yet (ere I am laid out dead)
> *Knock at a Starre with my exalted Head.*[5]

Appropriately, Herrick here echoes closely Jonson's commitment in "Ode to Himselfe" to write of "The glories of thy King" in notes that "shall truely hit the Starres." In a movement directly opposite to that of Jonson's retreat from the public stage to the rarified atmosphere of court poetry, Herrick, in this heavily qualified passage, bids a reluctant farewell to lyric poetry, not only in praise of the king or in honor of Herrick's "many fresh and fragrant Mistresses," but even lyric poetry "to my selfe."

⁂ So little is known of Herrick's life that any use of these meager biographical facts as a context for *Hesperides* must be tentative. To discuss Herrick's political and social assumptions as they shift and resolve throughout *Hesperides,* however, necessitates at least a sense of Herrick's career and family. The organization and changing tenor of *Hesperides* come more clearly into focus if we remember when and under what circumstances the poems were written. We have dates or approximate dates for only a small fraction of Herrick's poems, but these poems, plus the strong evidence that Herrick composed more and more tightly compressed poems as he grew older so that most, if not all, of the two-line epigrams are from the second half of his poetic career, give us a strong sense of Herrick's position in 1648.

Except for his father's death, the first thing we know about Herrick's youth was his apprenticeship as a goldsmith at the age of sixteen in 1607, supposedly for a term of ten years, under the direction of his very successful uncle, Sir William Herrick. The Herrick family, many of them ironmongers, had been important figures in Leicester for generations; Herrick's uncle and godfather, Robert Herrick, was MP for Leicester and three times its mayor. Herrick's father, Nicholas, moved to London to be apprenticed to the Goldsmiths' Company, a guild that required both literacy and property ownership as a condition for apprenticeship and was often the choice of younger sons of the gentry. Nicholas Herrick later apprenticed his younger brother William. In 1605 William Herrick was knighted for his services to Elizabeth and James, chief among these apparently being judicious loans. Herrick's mother, Julian Stone, was from a prominent London family; in Herrick's generation several of his maternal cousins had strong Puritan leanings.

In 1613 Herrick was freed from his apprenticeship and enrolled at St. John's College, Cambridge (for reasons of economy, he completed his degree at Trinity Hall, BA 1617, MA 1620). In 1623, at the age of thirty-two, he was ordained deacon and then priest. But from 1617 until 1629 and his appointment to Dean Prior, very little is known of Herrick's life. Chute speculates that he was ordained in order to become a nobleman's chaplain; Croft speculates that before he was ordained, Herrick served as secretary to Bishop Williams.[6] Herrick addresses an intriguing poem to Williams, occasioned by Williams's imprisonment from 1637 to 1640 (H-146A). Herrick offers the hope that "Mighty *Cesar*" shall soon speak, "and then, / All bolts, all barres, all gates shall cleave." Herrick's poem ends on a personal note that does suggest a close relationship between the two:

> This, as I wish for, so I hope to see;
> Though you (my Lord) have been unkind to me:
> To wound my heart, and never to apply
> (When you had power) the meanest remedy:
> Well; though my griefe by you was gall'd, the more;
> Yet I bringe Balme and Oile to heal your sore.

Herrick's association with Williams, the only figure of ecclesiastical authority addressed in *Hesperides* except for Joseph Hall, Herrick's immediate superior, should remind us of the complex political and personal factions in the Anglican church. It has become a commonplace to call Herrick "Laudian" and to construct arguments based upon that association, but to assume that Herrick is only or simply "Laudian" is a very long leap to make with no hard evidence under foot. Certainly Bishop Williams represented a position very different from Laud's, and Laud regarded him as an enemy.

Herrick sailed on the Isle of Rhé expedition in 1627 as one of the chaplains to Buckingham. He certainly had some connection with the court. Several of the poems in *Hesperides* and *Noble Numbers* were "sung before the King," and Herrick writes poems to influential court figures such as Endymion Porter, William and Henry Lawes, John Crofts, and John Selden.

The poems we can definitely trace to this period in Herrick's life before he left London for Dean Prior are few: "A Country life" to his brother Thomas Herrick, two epigrams to other family members, epithalamia to Sir Thomas Southwell and Sir Clipseby Crewe, a cluster of poems apparently occasioned by his trepidation at setting sail on the Isle of Rhé expedition, including the belated farewell at the grave of his father and "His Sailing from Julia." The pastoral and religious poems "sung to the King" and the fairy court poems were probably written in the 1620s. There are only two poems with political implications assignable to this period: Herrick's careful epigram to Buckingham (H-245) and the "New-yeares gift" he sent to Sir Simeon Steward (H-319).[7]

"A New-yeares gift" is a characteristic celebration of Herrick's love of country festival, of lyric poetry, and of drunken escape from care. Herrick, writing from the country and addressing his friend in the city, begins by listing all the things his missive will *not* report:

> No newes of Navies burnt at Seas;
> No noise of late spawn'd *Tittyries:*
> No closset plot, or open vent,
> That frights men with a Parliament:
> No new devise, or late found trick,
> To read by th'Starres, the Kingdoms sick;
> No ginne to catch the State, or wring
> The free-born Nosthrills of the King,
> We send to you; but here a jolly
> Verse crown'd with *Yvie*, and with *Holly:*
> That tels of Winters Tales and Mirth . . .

Herrick's references to the "Tytere tues" brotherhood, to the rumors that the navy had been destroyed, and to an upcoming Parliament definitively date the poem as written at Christmas 1623.[8] These and the other pressing political concerns the poem names are, however, dismissed in favor of Christmas revelry. His friends are to think of Herrick in the country with his milkmaids and his Twelfth-day King and Queen elected by a lucky choice of cakes that have a bean or pea embedded in them. Steward and Herrick's other friends in the city are to

> Sit crown'd with Rose-buds, and carouse,
> Till *Liber Pater* twirles the house
> About your eares; and lay upon
> The yeare (your cares) that's fled and gon.
> . . . .
> And thus, throughout, with Christmas playes
> Frolick the full twelve Holy-dayes.
>
> (ll. 41–44, 49–50)

But the year that is fled and gone is not, of course, so easily forgotten. By opening the poem with a detailed list of the topics of the day, Herrick deliberately shadows the convivial wish for forgetfulness at the end.

Herrick may have succeeded in the 1620s and 1630s in immersing himself in "capring Wine" and "Lyrick Verse." And he would not have been alone, especially in the "halcyon days" of Charles's personal rule. There are, for example, no poems in *Hesperides* on the major political events of the 1620s such as Charles's wooing of the Spanish infanta, James's death, Charles's accession, and Buckingham's assassination, and from the late 1630s there is only the poem on Bishop Williams's imprisonment.[9] Herrick's abjuration of the "newes," the "noise," the "frights" that prefaces "A New-yeares gift" indicates not only that he wished to escape into happy revelry but that he was aware of the realities that impinge upon it. At the end of "the full twelve Holy-dayes," the year begins anew.

In 1630 Herrick left London and assumed the vicarship of Dean Prior, a small village located midway on the main road between Exeter and Plymouth, about twenty miles from each city. It is from this move that critics have traditionally dated a change in Herrick's poetry, a time of "ennobled numbers" in "loathed Devonshire." Anthony à Wood reports that Herrick "became much beloved by the Gentry in those parts for his florid and witty Discourse"; he wrote compliments and occasional poems on weddings and funerals for influential parish members such as the Lowman, Northleigh, and Yard families.[10] It is to this period that L. C. Martin tentatively assigns the poems "which are most highly valued today," that is, lyric poems like "To the Virgins," "The Lilly in a Christal," or "Corinna's going a Maying."[11] Herrick's situation must at times have been decidedly unsympathetic, however. Devonshire was staunchly Puritan in its sympathies, and an Anglican vicar who wrote poems about happy debauchery and old country rituals must have occasioned some resentment.

The last news we hear of Herrick before the publication of *Hesperides* is in 1640, when Archbishop Laud's secretary, William Dell, noted that Herrick was in London without leave of absence from his post.[12] Dell insinuated that Herrick had fathered the illegitimate child of Thomasin Parsons, a daughter of the Westminster organist. No official record of this has been found. Herrick addresses an epigram to Thomasin Parsons at the end of *Hesperides* and at the beginning places what seems to be an oblique defense, "The suspition upon his over-much familiarity with a Gentlewoman" (H-136).[13] But as far as concerns the 1640 visit to London, the Stationers' Register records that Andrew Crooke applied to publish "The seuerall Poems" of Herrick in 1640. This volume apparently never appeared, but Herrick might have been in London at that time in an attempt to arrange for such a publication.

Connections between Herrick's poetry and his life have usually been found in a kind of romantic recreation of his early life in Dean Prior. Actually, however, the clearest contemporary evidence in *Hesperides* is all from the 1640s, since Herrick includes a number of poems occasioned by the civil war. There are, for example, the lovely epitaph on William Lawes, who was killed in 1645 (H-907); the "Dirge upon the death of . . . Bernard Stuart," killed in 1645 (H-219), and a poem to one of Stuart's brothers, who survived the war (H-451); and a poem congratulating Charles "upon his taking of Leicester," the family seat of the Herrick family, in 1645.

Clearly, however, Herrick saw the war from the vantage of Devonshire. He praises Sir John Berkeley's heroic fortitude in holding Exeter against parliamentary siege (H-745); he praises Lady Ann Villiers (Lady Dalkeith), Buckingham's niece, who was appointed governess to Charles and Henrietta Maria's last child, born in Exeter in 1644 and left there with her governess until 1646, when Lady Dalkeith took her abroad (H-341); he encourages Ralph Hopton on his Cornwall campaigns (H-1002).[14] With the exception of the prefatory poem to Prince Charles, the first Stuart poem in *Hesperides* is the epigram "TO THE KING, Upon his comming with his Army into the West" (H-77).[15] Since "Hesperides" may, on one level, be taken to refer to the "West Country" of Devonshire and also, of course, to Herrick's poetry, this poem bravely opens the volume on several levels:

> Welcome, most welcome to our Vowes and us,
> Most great, and universall *Genius!*
> The Drooping West, which hitherto has stood
> As one, in long-lamented-widow-hood;
> Looks like a Bride now, or a bed of flowers,
> Newly refresh't, both by the Sun, and showers.
> War, which before was horrid, now appears
> Lovely in you, brave Prince of Cavaliers!
> A deale of courage in each bosome springs
> By your accesse; (*O you the best of Kings!*)
> Ride on with all white *Omens;* so, that where
> Your Standard's up, we fix a Conquest there.

Since the association of the king with pastoral and romantic imagery is characteristic of the early part of *Hesperides,* Herrick's early placement of this poem written in 1644 is a deliberate contribution to the mood of the first part of the volume.

Charles spent the last few days of July 1644 in Exeter on his way to Cornwall in pursuit of Essex. This was one of the most optimistic moments of the royalist campaign. Earlier in the summer the queen had fled Exeter in fear of her life as Essex marched into Devonshire in an attempt to capture her; by September, Charles had trapped Essex and could leave behind a peninsula completely under royalist control except for the city of Plymouth, which, at terrible cost, remained a staunch parliamentary stronghold throughout the war.[16] It was for Charles a rare instance of good fortune and successful military tactics and the high point of the war for any Devonshire royalist. Herrick's placement of his epigram on the occasion at the beginning of *Hesperides* was therefore appropriate.

The other notable moment for the royalist cause in Devonshire was the arrival of Prince Charles in January 1645. At this nearly hopeless point in the war, royalists throughout the western counties—Somerset, Dorset, Cornwall, and Devon—had urged on the king the strength of the Western Association, until he had finally agreed to send his fifteen-year-old son as its nominal head. In truth, the royalists of the Western Association hoped that its purported strength would be generated by the presence of the heir. Unfortunately, this was far from true. The armies of the west were the king's last hope, and there was little hope there. Endless internecine bickering and suspicion, personal aggrandizement, brutal ravaging of the countryside—all tore the royalist cause apart as effectively as the parliamentarians could.[17] And the parliamentarians themselves were approaching rapidly. Fairfax and the New Model Army advanced unchecked. In August 1645, when Fairfax decided to detour from his drive on Devon to take Bristol, Prince Charles moved to Exeter to organize a defense against the inevitable arrival of the New Model Army. His advisers also wished to still rumors that he was about to flee the country because the royalist cause was lost. Indeed, a number of desperate Devon gentry approached the prince in Exeter and asked him to negotiate peace with Parliament on his own authority.[18]

It was under these ominous circumstances that Herrick addressed to Charles the poem that begins,

> What Fate decreed, Time now ha's made us see
> A Renovation of the West by Thee.
> That Preternaturall Fever, which did threat
> Death to our Countrey, now hath lost his heat:
> And calmes succeeding, we perceive no more
> Th'unequall Pulse to beat, as heretofore.
>
> (H-756)

Herrick's praise is, in these lines, extravagant, as it always has been in his poems to the Stuarts, and his confidence may seem to be blindly foolhardy. But after offering his opening compliment, Herrick tempers this epigram of royal praise with advice and serious reservations:

> *Something there yet remaines for Thee to do;*
> Then reach those ends that thou wast destin'd to.
> Go on with Sylla's Fortune; let thy Fate
> Make Thee like Him, this, that way fortunate,
> Apollos Image side with Thee to blesse
> Thy Warre (discreetly made) with white successe.
> Meane time thy Prophets Watch by Watch shall pray;
> While young Charles fights, and fighting wins the day.
> *That done,* our smooth-pac't Poems all shall be
> Sung in the high Doxologie of Thee . . .
>
> (italics added)[19]

Charles can be a divine figure worthy of his poet-prophets' "Doxologie" of praise only if he succeeds in winning the war. And clustered close to

Herrick's poem of qualified praise of the prince are a group of epigrams urging the necessity of faithful friends in war and warning repeatedly against delay, warnings epitomized by "Consultation" (H-749):

> Consult ere thou begin'st, that done, go on
> With all wise speed for execution.

All this was particularly apt advice for a young prince surrounded by generals like Goring and Grenville who were so caught up in a struggle for jurisdiction and privileges that they missed every chance to aid the king. This Stuart poem late in *Hesperides*, written in praise of Prince Charles upon his arrival in Exeter but surrounded by its contingent epigrams, introduces us to several essential characteristics of Herrick's volume: the undercurrent of advice on ruling and on the course of the civil war; the shaping of Herrick's perception of the war by his vantage point in Devon; and the shift in Herrick's poetic stance in the 1640s from lyric celebration to a clearly epigrammatic mode of advice.

At this point, it is necessary to make a brief and tentative exploration of the dating of Herrick's poetry by style and by order of placement in *Hesperides*. At the end of the nineteenth century, Edward Everett Hale, Jr., suggested that as Herrick grew older his poetry tended to become more and more closed and epigrammatic, basing his theory on a stylistic analysis of the poems with established dates.[20] Since 348 of the poems in *Hesperides* are only two lines long and 222 four lines long, such a theory has large implications for our view of the volume as a whole. Hale's theory is corroborated, in general, by the rest of the hard evidence we have. First, not one of Herrick's brief epigrams appears in a manuscript before the publication of *Hesperides*, whereas 39 lyric poems, including song texts, "mistress" poems, and the Sack poems, appear over and over again. "The Curse" (H-138B), for example, occurs in eleven different manuscripts.[21] On the other hand, in the 1650 edition of Sir John Mynts and James Smith's *Wits Recreation*, 75 *Hesperides* poems are reprinted, 61 of them epigrams.[22] If Herrick's epigrams had been in circulation in the 1620s and 1630s, it seems likely that they would have found their way into commonplace books, since such brief, witty, and scurrilous poems were often collected – Herrick's significant representation among the epigrams of *Wits Recreation* in 1650 indicates the popularity of these poems.

Another intriguing piece of evidence for Herrick's turn to briefer and briefer epigrams late in his career is his use in *Noble Numbers* of John Gregory's 1646 *Notes and Observations upon some passages of Scripture*.

Herrick writes a number of two-line epigrams that are almost exact transcriptions from Gregory. This is our closest evidence for Herrick's actual mode of composition late in his career.

More important evidence, however, is the tenor of Herrick's epigrams. As we have seen, the epigrams of praise span Herrick's life as a writer and also span the entire textual space of *Hesperides;* the mocking epigrams, too, occur throughout the book, although they may be the product of Herrick's life in Devonshire in the 1630s and 1640s. But the terse epigrams of advice to the king appear to be largely the product of the decade of unrest and civil war preceding the publication of *Hesperides.* These important epigrams have been virtually ignored by critics. Although certainly no critic today would espouse Gosse's extreme position that Herrick was the "only one of the whole school [of Royalist lyricists who] was undisturbed by the political crisis" and "with imperturbable serenity, continued to pipe out his pastoral ditties, and crown his head with daffodils, when England was torn to pieces with the most momentous struggle for liberty in her annals," yet Herrick has not been credited with the specific involvement and commentary on his times that the epigrams of advice reveal.[23] Both DeNeef and Barbara Herrnstein Smith argue, for example, that the epigram form itself is reactionary and "definitive," and, on that basis, DeNeef finds Herrick's epigrams of advice uninteresting.[24] Smith and DeNeef can only come to these conclusions if they examine single epigrams alone. But the epigram is a form intended to be read as part of a whole. Woven throughout *Hesperides,* Herrick's political epigrams of advice form a subtle and mutable discourse. They echo against the poems of royal praise and complicate them with whispered cautions.

That Herrick took seriously his role not only as a poet of the cultural hegemony but also as an adviser to the king is clear in a number of epigrams. At the midpoint of *Hesperides,* linked by proximity to the crucial "The bad season makes the Poet sad" (H-612), is a free translation of Horace:

> No wrath of Men, or rage of Seas
> Can shake a just mans purposes:
> No threats of Tyrants, or the Grim
> Visage of them can alter him;
> But what he doth at first entend,
> That he holds firmly to the end.
> ("Purposes," H-615)

The threat the poet perceives here, whether it is from the parliamentarian forces or Charles himself, is clearly political.

Clustered around the "bad season" are other epigrams that reveal Herrick's "purposes" as he envisions them here at midvolume. In the poem preceding "The bad season" Herrick sends his Muse to Charles, Prince of Wales, the dedicatee of *Hesperides,* the subject of a series of poems in the volume, and the great hope of the West Country. But Herrick here speaks to Prince Charles, not as a court poet inspired by his Muse, but as a man:

> Go wooe young *Charles* no more to looke,
> Then but to read this in my Booke:
> How *Herrick* beggs, if that he can-
> Not like the Muse; to love the man,
> Who by the Shepheards, sung (long since)
> The Starre-led-birth of Charles the *Prince.*

The "golden Age" over, Herrick must now speak in a different voice. Between the "bad season" and "Purposes," for example, is an epigram, "Like Pattern, like People," that is typical of Herrick's aphoristic voice. It is italicized throughout to give it axiomatic weight:

> *This is the height of Justice, that to doe*
> *Thy selfe, which thou put'st other men unto.*
> *As great men lead; the meaner follow on,*
> *Or to the good, or evill action.*

A prince must redeem himself; his own stature will earn him a just reward. "Like Pattern, like People" is characteristic of Herrick's use of apparent flattery to make a point. If a prince is truly brave, the epigram implies, he will do himself what he asks of others; if he is truly great, he will be emulated.

In the final century of *Hesperides,* Herrick outlines an ideal poet who seems to match Grosart's description of the oblivious songster:

> Give me a man that is not dull,
> When all the world with rifts is full:
> But unamaz'd dares clearely sing,
> When as the roof's a tottering:
> And, though it falls, continues still
> Tickling the *Citterne* with his quill.
>
> (H-1036)

Herrick might be condemned, on the grounds of this poem, of frivolity in the face of a tragic situation. But it requires enormous belief in poetry and in himself for a poet to keep singing as the world falls apart around him. The special poignancy of this poem is that Herrick, at least, did not seem to sustain his lyric voice in the face of radical change. The poem is a wish only; poem after poem has already asserted that the lyric voice is lost. Placed so near the end of the volume, surrounded almost completely by epigrams, "His desire" seems poignant at best. And directly following it, "Caution in Councell" (H-1037) expresses more accurately the role of the poet in the latter half of *Hesperides:*

> Know when to speake; for many times it brings
> Danger to give the best advice to Kings.

Indeed, Herrick seems to have believed that he would be liable for punishment for his poems. For a late epigram, "Wit punisht, prospers most" (H-1034), Herrick borrows a sentence originally found in Tacitus's *Annals,* although Herrick's direct source was probably Jonson's *Sejanus:*[25]

> Dread not the shackles: on with thine intent;
> *Good wits get more fame by their punishment.*

The context in *Sejanus* was a comment on the fate of Cremutius Cordus, the historian whose annals Tiberius burned because he saw them as an indirect commentary on his own reign:

> . . . the punishment
> Of wit, doth make th'authority increase.
> Nor do they aught, that use this cruelty
> Of interdiction, and this rage of burning;
> But purchase to themselves rebuke, and shame,
> And to the writers an eternal name.
>
> (3.1.475–80)[26]

The whole scene of Cordus's defense and condemnation seems, in fact, to have had a special relevance for Herrick. Cordus had defended his history by naming previous Roman leaders who had tolerated, even praised, artistic works critical of their policies—or had condemned them to their own detriment. Among these Cordus names the example of "The epigrams of Bibaculus, and Catullus," which

> Are read, full stuffed with spite of both the Caesars;
> Yet deified Julius, and no less Augustus!

> Both bore them, and contemned them: (I not know
> Promptly to speak it, whether done with more
> Temper, or wisdom) for such obloquies
> If they despisèd be, they die suppressed,
> But, if with rage acknowledged, they are confessed.
>
> $(3.1.434-41)^{27}$

Not only do the last two lines supply Herrick with the basis for his epigram on "Anger" (H-776),

> Wrongs if neglected, vanish in short time;
> But heard with anger, we confesse the crime,

but the echo opens up the whole discussion by Cordus of the state's relationship to writers, especially the writers of epigrams.

Indeed, in the final moments of *Hesperides,* the possibility of the poet's violent death is foregrounded dramatically. Herrick's last poem "On Himselfe" (H-1128)—the last poem spoken in "Herrick's" voice and the poem that directly precedes "The pillar of Fame"—prepares the poet for the death that may result from the publication of his book:

> The worke is done: young men, and maidens set
> Upon my curles the *Mirtle Coronet,*
> Washt with sweet ointments; Thus at last I come
> To suffer in the Muses *Martyrdome:*
> But with this comfort, if my blood be shed,
> The Muses will weare blackes, when I am dead.

Herrick's strategy of advice in *Hesperides* will be carefully indirect, partly out of discretion but partly too out of a diplomatic sensitivity to the best way to catch the ear of a king. It is the strategy made possible by the epigram book's deliberate proximities, but it is open to the same attack as base flattery that was leveled at earlier epigrammatists. A decade after *Hesperides* appeared, for instance, Thomas Pecke published his important collection of classical and modern epigrams, *Parnassi Puerperium* (1659).[28] In Pecke's own *Century of Heroick Epigrams* appended to the collection, there appears a poem startling in its cynicism. It is at first glance a highly typical epigram of biblical and political wisdom, employing, as was conventional, the metaphor of the good shepherd; an epigram of Herrick's, for example, had argued:

In things a moderation keepe,
Kings ought to sheare, not skin their sheepe.

(H-780)

Pecke's epigram, however, is ambivalent even in its title, "A good Shepherd onely shears his Sheep, &":

None could persuade Tiberius to play
The Tyrant, for a while; nor would He lay
Taxations on the Provinces. The Wool,
A carefull Shepherd clips; Kings must not pull
Their Subjects skin over their Eares.
But, who Complements thus? An Hypocrite.

(32)

More telling than the cynical attitude toward Tiberius in Pecke's epigram is the blow that the last line of the epigram directs at the first five. It serves as a critique of epigrammatists who flatter or are otherwise subservient, and hence reflects also on another of Herrick's more infamous poems, "Duty to Tyrants" (H-97), often cited by later critics as a demonstration of Herrick's simple-minded royalism:

Good Princes must be pray'd for: for the bad
They must be borne with, and in rev'rence had.
Doe they first pill thee, next, pluck off thy skin?
Good children kisse the Rods, that punish sin.
Touch not the Tyrant; Let the Gods alone
To strike him dead, that but usurps a Throne.

Indeed, it is possible that in "A good Shepherd onely shears his Sheep, &" Pecke may be speaking to Herrick, echoing the anger with which Harington had attacked Bastard for including compliments to Elizabeth among his criticisms of Elizabethan society. An examination of Herrick's procedures in *Hesperides,* however, reveals both how complex and agonized is Herrick's position, and how honest.

In the early, lyrical half of *Hesperides* there are only a few epigrams of political advice, but they cluster meaningfully around the Stuart poems. For example, following the important sequence of epigrams to Charles, Henrietta Maria, and the duke of York, which hymn their place in "This *great Realme of Poetry,*" "*This Sacred Grove,*" this "*Hellicon*" (H-264, -265, -266) — marked typographically and thematically as central to *Hesperides* —

is a corresponding sequence of sharply italicized epigrams. These epigrams gather together in three poems Herrick's conflicting impulses in his attitude to the king throughout the rest of *Hesperides*. The first (H-268), borrowed from the advice of Suetonius Paulinus that Tacitus records in his *Histories* (2.25), seems directly applicable to the civil war:

> *That Prince takes soone enough the Victors roome,*
> *Who first provides, not to be overcome.*

This may perhaps have been occasioned by Charles's divided command, lack of coherent strategy, or, of course, by devastating defeats like Naseby and the loss of Bristol, both in 1645. It stands in chillingly pragmatic contrast to the fanciful and glorifying poems of praise that precede it.

The next epigram in the sequence (H-269) has frequently been cited as a "definition" of Herrick's extreme royalism, his apparent support for the Stuart theory of monarchy as a divinely constituted institution, subject to no human controls:

> *The Gods to Kings the Judgement give to sway:*
> *The Subjects onely glory to obay.*

Certainly it seems to agree with the poet's attitude in "TO THE KING" and "QUEENE." But Herrick again found this sentence in Tacitus's *Annals*, spoken by Terentius to Tiberius, the classical byword for tyranny. Its source, therefore, adds a grave complication to the epigram's import. Herrick's attitude toward the nature of kingship and its potential for corruption is much more complex than "Obedience in Subjects," at face value, suggests.

The final epigram of the three (H-270) is a gentle reminder that harsh legality, suspicion, and punishment breed exactly what they attempt to repress: *"Leave to transgresse / Enfeebles much the seeds of wickednesse."*

As there is in all of Herrick's poetry, there is a hint of dry humor and irony in the poems of advice to the king. They puncture with sensible advice the royal poems of praise that they surround, casting doubt on the practical value of kingdoms of flowers and wood-nymph queens. At mid-volume, for instance, there is a disconcerting pair of poems—lyric and epigram—that carries a level of mockery for both the pomp of kingship and the rhetoric of court poetry. The first poem is a two-line epigram (H-682) offering a piece of dry Machiavellian advice:

Kings must not oft be seen by publike eyes;
State at a distance adds to dignities.

This epigram is a curious preparation for the lyric that closely follows it (H-685), a poem of extravagant praise for Charles I that ends:

Princes, and such like Publike Lights as these,
Must not be lookt on, but at distances:
For, if we gaze on These brave Lamps too neer,
Our eyes they'l blind, or if not blind, they'l bleer.

"We" are engaged in an enthusiastic encomium to the king, even though we know (because the poet has just told us) that the blazing glory of the king's appearance is merely a show intended to impress us. The lyric becomes a game consciously played by king and poet, and observed by the reader.

The advice that Herrick offers often grates against the Stuart poems in this way and, in a wider sense, intrudes upon the volume as a whole until it finally dominates the end of *Hesperides*. One further example of Herrick's painful juxtapositions is occasioned by Charles's storming of Leicester on May 31, 1645 (H-823). Herrick congratulates the king with a fulsome celebration of his good fortune:

This Day is Yours *Great* CHARLES! and in this War
Your Fate, and Ours, alike Victorious are.
In her white Stole; now Victory do's rest
Enspher'd with Palm on Your Triumphant Crest.
Fortune is now Your Captive; other Kings
Hold but her hands; You hold both hands and wings.

Following this panegyric is an epigram that punctures the triumph of that moment and has implications for the purposes of *Hesperides* itself:

'Twas *Cesars* saying: *Kings no lesse Conquerors are*
By their wise Counsell, then they be by Warre.
                            ("Counsell," H-825)

In light of contemporary events, this epigram had stinging relevance. Within weeks of the taking of Leicester, Charles was defeated at Naseby, the crucial battle of the war, which doomed the rest of his struggle to futility. His defeat at Naseby was largely the fault of poor planning and poor advice. Caught off guard by Fairfax's rapid approach with the New

Model Army, Charles refused to retreat as Rupert urged, but followed instead the reckless advice of Digby and John Ashburnham to stand his ground.²⁹ As a result, he was utterly crushed. Two epigrams after "Counsell" Herrick says dryly,

> In desp'rate cases, all, or most are known
> Commanders, *few for execution.*

On June 18, two and a half weeks after its capture, the king surrendered Leicester again to the parliamentarians. Herrick's epigram is at once a sad gloss on the civil war and on his own flamboyant poetry of praise.

Herrick's analysis of advice extends beyond the poet himself to the king who must choose his counselors wisely and heed their advice with discretion. He warns against sycophants and false praise, for example, warnings that are part of his acute awareness that the king's position is vulnerable to other men's ambition. Up until the end of the civil war, the parliamentary leaders had argued that they were not fighting against the king but were trying to rescue him from bad advisers who had poisoned his mind and gained excessive control over him. Charles's advisers were frequently the source of his unpopularity, from Buckingham and Henrietta Maria through Laud and Strafford. Clarendon observed at the beginning of his *History of the Rebellion*

that the most signal parts of [Charles's] misfortunes proceeded chiefly from the modesty of his nature, which kept him from trusting himself enough, and made him believe that others discerned better, who were much inferior to him in those faculties; and so to depart often from his own reason, to follow the opinions of more unskilled men, whose affections he believed to be unquestionable to his service.³⁰

This analysis helps to explain the theme of distrust which appears both in political epigrams like "Pollicie in Princes" (H-438):

> That Princes may possesse a surer seat,
> 'Tis fit they make no One with them too great,

and in more generally gnomic epigrams, such as the early sententia (H-177):

> To safe-guard Man from wrongs, there nothing must
> Be truer to him, then a wise Distrust.
> And to thy selfe be best this sentence knowne,
> *Heare all men speak; but credit few or none.*

~~🙰~~. In *Hesperides*, Herrick offers advice about a number of key problems that plagued Charles during the last decade of his reign. Underlying his specific advice is his concept of the nature of kingship. It has been assumed, based on a few epigrams, that Herrick was an unquestioning monarchist who accepted the principle of absolute monarchy by divine right. This position, however, is an oversimplification that results from taking out of context a few apparently extremist statements. A case in point is "The Difference Betwixt Kings and Subjects" (H-25):

> Twixt Kings and Subjects ther's this mighty odds,
> Subjects are taught by *Men;* Kings by the *Gods.*

This is the first epigram on kings in *Hesperides.* It complements the Stuart poems of the beginnings of the volume, and it is the one political epigram that critics have usually quoted to seal their views of Herrick's politics. Yet *Hesperides* has a number of epigrams that are frankly realistic about how men become kings. Also within the first century, for example, are two epigrams that may reflect the political situation in the 1640s. In contrast to the divine right doctrine of "The Difference Betwixt Kings and Subjects" is the pragmatic observation of "Ambition" (H-58):

> In Man, Ambition is the common'st thing;
> Each one, by nature, loves to be a King.

More specifically threatening is the aphorism that Herrick borrows from Seneca's *Hercules in Aetna* (ll. 614–15):

> As oft as Night is banish'd by the Morne,
> So oft, we'll think, we see a King new born.
> (H-80)

Entitled "Dangers wait on Kings," this epigram is placed immediately after the poem "TO THE KING AND QUEENE, UPON THEIR UNHAPPY DISTANCES," which mourns either the temporary separation of Henrietta Maria and Charles by the civil war in 1642 or their permanent separation in 1644, when the queen sailed for France.[31] In "Ambition"'s allusion to a constantly shifting pattern of sovereignty, J. Max Patrick suggests that Herrick may have been referring to the power struggles between the different parliamentary leaders during the civil war, most notably Cromwell's replacement of Fairfax as head of the army.[32] But it seems equally possible that Herrick is here referring to the surges of hope and ensuing despair that plagued the royalist cause, especially in the long downward spiral after Henrietta Maria's departure. Herrick rarely if ever refers to the parliamentarians in *Hesperides*, and, as we have seen, he usually places epigrams of advice and comment to the king in close proximity to those that praise him. Another epigram on the treacherous condition of kingship, for example,

> Empires of Kings, are now, and ever were,
> (As *Salust* saith) co-incident to feare
>
> (H-430)

follows closely on Herrick's lament for Henrietta Maria's departure, "A Pastorall sung to the King" (H-421).

Late in *Hesperides*, Herrick seems fascinated with the idea that a man could actually elevate himself to kingship through ambition and talent. "Kings" (H-707) seems to be philosophically in direct contrast with "The Difference Betwixt Kings and Subjects":

> Men are not born Kings, but are men renown'd;
> Chose first, confirm'd next, and at last are crown'd;

as does "Beginning, difficult" (H-259):

> *Hard are the two first staires unto a Crowne;*
> *Which got, the third, bids him a King come downe.*

But the position that Herrick seems to have reached in general is that kingship must be seized and held by strength of character. This is not to say that "The Difference Betwixt Kings and Subjects" is the only place in *Hesperides* where Herrick espouses the theory of divine right. But by the end of the volume, Herrick acknowledges this contractual aspect of kingship, a position that brings him closer to Sir Thomas More than, say, to Robert Filmer. The early epigram "The power in the people" (H-345), for example, is sour with disapproval:

> Let Kings Command, and doe the best they may,
> The saucie Subjects still will beare the sway.

But at the other end of *Hesperides* the epigram "Obedience" (H-1073) calls to mind the early divine right epigram "Obedience in Subjects" (H-269) and answers it from the perspective of the civil war:

> The Power of Princes rests in the Consent
> Of onely those, who are obedient:
> Which if away, proud Scepters then will lye
> Low, and of Thrones the Ancient *Majesty.*[33]

Again, in the first century there occurs the bitter epigram "Duty to Ty-rants" (H-97), which I have already noted in connection with Thomas Pecke, counseling that the people have no right to rise up against even the cruelest ruler:

> Good Princes must be pray'd for: for the bad
> They must be borne with, and in rev'rence had.
> Doe they first pill thee, next, pluck off thy skin?
> *Good children kisse the Rods, that punish sin.*
> Touch not the Tyrant; Let the Gods alone
> To strike him dead, that but usurps a Throne.

Past the midpoint of the volume, however, is the epigram "Bad Princes pill their People" (H-826), which echoes "Duty to Tyrants" but emphasizes only the resentment of the first poem and neglects its counsel of submission:

> Like those infernall Deities which eate
> The best of all the sacrificed meate;
> And leave their servants, but the smoak and sweat:
> So many *Kings,* and *Primates* too there are,
> Who claim the Fat, and Fleshie for their share,
> And leave their Subjects but the starved ware.

Typical of Herrick's strategies, this poem follows the epigram of praise "TO THE KING, upon his taking of *Leicester.*" Aptly, the royalist behavior in Leicester was perhaps the most extreme and infamous of a general pattern of plundering that the royalist forces perpetrated throughout the war (and especially in Devon). One hundred forty carts filled with plunder left Leicester the day it fell.[34]

Like More, Herrick draws Aristotle's distinction between "Kings and Tyrants" (H-861), *"Kings seek their Subjects good: Tyrants their owne."* Clear-ly, Herrick has mixed feelings about the power and inherent vices of kingship.

The complexity of Herrick's position is evidenced by the epigram to his first cousin, Sir Thomas Soame (H-466), written sometime after 1641:

> Seeing Thee *Soame,* I see a Goodly man,
> And to that Good, a great *Patrician.*
> Next to which Two; among the City-Powers,
> And Thrones, thy selfe one of Those Senatours:
> Not wearing Purple only for the show;
> (As many Conscripts of the Citie do)
> But for True Service, worthy of that Gowne,
> The *Golden* chaine too, and the *Civick* Crown.

Soame was a prominent London merchant and the leading candidate for Lord Mayor of London in 1640; he was excluded from the office, however, because of the king's disfavor. In 1640 he had been imprisoned for refusing, as alderman, to list men in his ward who would be financially capable of advancing money for a forced loan to Charles. Before the Star Chamber, Soame said simply that he thought the duty unjust. A member of Parliament, he sided with the parliamentary side through the civil war but in 1648 was removed from his aldermanship and secluded from the House of Commons. The dignified Roman terms of this poem reveal Herrick's admiration for Soame's position as "a great Patrician" and a "Senatour" "among the City-Powers."

Nevertheless, Herrick's faith seems ultimately to lie, not in fallible men, but in the rules and traditions of society. Just as he celebrates rituals in his lyric poetry, an epigram like "Lawes" (H-1041):

> Who violates the Customes, hurts the Health,
> Not of one man, but all the Common-wealth

celebrates continuity and traditions and warns of the dangers threatened by their violation. Herrick's use of the code word "Common-wealth" seems to direct this epigram against the parliamentarians, whose attacks against "one man," the king, hurt the very realm they claimed to serve. On the other hand, another epigram of the same title (H-608) urges the force of law to contain the power of kings:

> When Lawes full power have to sway, we see
> Little or no part there of Tyrannie.

A root issue in the civil war was the supremacy of law over authoritarianism. The first sermon that John Donne preached to Charles upon his succession to the throne initiated Charles's reign with a theme that would haunt the king until his death: "Dispute not the Lawes, but obey them when they are made. . . . Let the Law bee sacred to thee, and the Dispensers of the Lawe, reverend. Keepe the Lawe, and the Lawe shall keepe thee."[35] For twenty years Charles was charged by his opposition with undervaluing the weight of law; ironically, Charles's trial for his life was a travesty of English law.

In *Hesperides* Herrick affirms law and custom as liberating forces. "Conformity," for example, is a wall between freedom and "Dissolution," "Whose crack gives crushing unto all" (H-76). Although "conformity" did not carry in 1648 the clearly Anglican connotation it would after the Restoration, Herrick may here be thinking, at least in part, of the conformity of the Church of England's rituals and rules upon which Laud had insisted.[36] When in the epigram "Liberty" (H-395) Herrick speaks of freedom he certainly means the freedom that honored traditions and respected laws, both religious and civil, guarantee:

> Those ills that mortall men endure,
> So long are capable of cure,
> As they of freedome may be sure:
> But that deni'd; a griefe, though small,
> Shakes the whole Roofe, or ruines all.

Charles's perennial problem in his effort to do without Parliament was lack of money. During the years of personal rule, Sir Richard Weston's creative resurrection of old feudal statutes and levies such as ship-money and knighthood fines gained Charles enough money to get by until the First Bishops' War with Scotland, but these taxes also earned Charles a fair degree of resentment. After Weston's death in 1635 and during the civil war, Charles's demands were constant and became insatiable. In Devon, for example, during the years of royalist administration the constables had the thankless job of collecting from all citizens an assessment of money and supplies every week. As soon as the royalists began their Devonian offensive against the occupying parliamentarian forces in 1642, they implemented the king's Commission of Array, an unprecedented demand that the county forces be turned over to royalist leaders and that the county then provide the funds to arm and train them. Even among those loyal to the king, the Commission of Array caused tremendous resentment, which the parliamentarians inflamed by arguing that the commission was evidence that the king was the aggressor and that he acted outside the law.[37] In 1642, Herrick's friend Thomas Shapcott read before Quarter Sessions Devon's agonized petition to the king:

Your Majesty commands our Obedience to the Commission of Array; whilst both Houses of Parliament adjudgeth us Betrayers of our Liberty and Property if we do so. . . . How unhappy are we here, made Judges in apparent Contraries! In how hard a Condition are we, whilst a Twofold Obedience, like Twins in the Womb, strives to be borne to both! We cannot choose but look upon the Privileges of Parliament with a natural Affection; from our Father's Loins, we desire a Touch that leads thither, as the Needle to the Load-stone; we desire to preserve them, because the Death of Liberty, without the Support, is inevitable.[38]

By the time Fairfax arrived, the county had been wrung dry and was desperately sick of the war, no matter where individual sympathies had lain.[39]

Herrick's epigrams on immoderate taxation should be read in the context of this important civil war issue. Of course, the burdens of taxation are the subject of complaint in all societies, but in Caroline England the right of taxation became a crucial point of contention, especially after Charles's conflict with Parliament over tonnage and poundage in 1629 and later the trial of John Hampden in 1637 for his refusal to pay ship-money. I have already mentioned Herrick's epigram "Moderation," *"Kings ought to sheare, not skin their sheepe"* (H-780), a statement most clearly applicable to the issue of taxation. Later he states that a healthy society stands on two things: "The first *Commerce* is, and the next *Command*" (H-847). Since Charles's heavy taxation was seen as a crippling yoke on commerce, the epigram obliquely warns the king while reiterating Herrick's belief that a king must truly lead his people. Another epigram, "Rest Refreshes" (H-922), is typical of the careful generality of Herrick's epigrams. Its last line is borrowed from Ovid's *Ars Amatoria;* it can be read as advice on love, or simply on good farming practice:

> Lay by the good a while; a resting field
> Will, after ease, a richer harvest yeild:
> Trees this year beare; next, they their wealth with-hold:
> *Continuall reaping makes a land wax old.*

But "Rest Refreshes" is part of a long series of fourteen epigrams, several of which are specifically directed to the king, several more of which can be easily so construed. The georgic advice to let the land rest might, therefore, be taken as criticism of Charles's policies. But if he were brought to the mark, Herrick could always plead the generality and innocence of his axiom.

Charles's troubles with Parliament in the early years of his reign stemmed in part from his series of disastrous and expensive military campaigns. Once he decided to do without Parliament, he could no longer afford the expense of interference abroad, even in the affairs of his sister and her husband, the Elector Palatine. Charles's enforced policy of international pacifism was, however, extremely unpopular. The English people grew restive under the policy of noninvolvement with Protestant affairs abroad. Court poets celebrated the blessings of peace during the 1630s, but after the death in 1632 of Gustavus Adolphus, the great Protestant hero, the English court's pastoral idyll became increasingly difficult to defend with conviction.[40]

Herrick's epigram "Power and Peace" (H-788) is both counsel and prophecy:

> 'Tis never, or but seldome knowne,
> Power and Peace to keep one Throne.

Herrick here echoes Thomas Bastard's sonnet of praise and hinted counsel, "Eliza, thou has spread a golden peace," where Bastard, after calling Elizabeth's reign a Golden Age, ends with an epigram puncturing this idyll:

> But who did heare, or who did ever read,
> Peace without wars, or something else instead.

At the very end of *Hesperides* Herrick emphatically acknowledges the political folly of trying to balance English bellicosity. "On Love" (H-1083), for example, is actually an astute political observation:

> That love 'twixt men do's ever longest last
> Where War and Peace the Dice by turns doe cast.

And "Peace not Permanent" (H-1030) is more pointed. The epigram probably refers to London, the center of parliamentary power and the beginning of all of Charles's problems:

> Great Cities seldome rest: If there be none
> T'invade from far: They'l finde worse foes at home.

During the late 1630s and the 1640s, Charles himself contributed to his ultimate "martyrdom." He could be absolutely rigid about principles he held and absolutely unforgiving of those he perceived as his enemies. At the same time, he frequently lost his advantage during the war by being too lenient and too generous in his peace terms. Increasingly, he was seen by his enemies as a dangerously untrustworthy man, willing to promise almost anything by the end of the war, while at the same time actively plotting to betray his promises.

Curiously, Herrick's advice to the king on these crucial issues seems almost to be a mirror of the conflicting actions of Charles himself. Yet although there are epigrams that urge moderation and clemency and others that urge a sterner, more authoritarian rule, it seems unlikely that Herrick would be advocating such inconsistency. Sir Philip Warwick, who was secretary to and the intimate of Charles during the last years of the king's life, attributed the disastrous conclusion of the civil war to the weakness and vacillation in Charles's character:

A little sharpness of temper of body, and uncommunicableness in society or council (by seeming on a pish to neglect all another said and he approved not), made him less grateful than his friends wished. And indeed had . . . the king more vigorously interposed therein, and been master of both parties, his armies had probably been more prosperous than they were, yet neither of them stood in awe of him, and so the consequence was fatal.[41]

Warwick's character sketch reveals not only Charles's inability to accept advice, his distance, and his coldness but also his ineffectual presence as king, the position on whose inherent advantage of power Charles never seemed able to capitalize. From the disaster of Charles's fumbled attempts to arrest the Five Members of Parliament early in 1642, which left him looking not only like a fool but dangerously outside the law, to his alteration between cold dismissal of parliamentary peace envoys and futile begging for negotiations, Charles never seemed able either to seize power completely or to seize public opinion.

Herrick's position on how a king should rule is largely indebted to Ben Jonson. The plays, especially *Sejanus,* were an important source for Herrick's epigrams. And clearly too, *Discoveries,* with its gathering of political axioms, was, for Herrick, a crucial text. *Timber or the Discoveries Made upon Men and Matter as They Have Flowed out of His Daily Readings,* probably collected by Jonson out of his commonplace book, and published in the posthumous 1640 folio, is a casual collection of comments

on art and politics, many of them garnered from Jonson's wide reading in
the classics, but many others Jonson's own reflections on what he had
read and observed.

We find in *Discoveries* the source for Herrick's epigram on taxation,
"Kings ought to sheare, not skin their sheepe."[42] But Jonson's influence may
also partly account for a series of epigrams in which Herrick considers
the Machiavellian doctrines of power, force, and necessary cruelty. Jonson
quotes Machiavelli, for example, on the sagacity of a prince using his min-
isters as the instrument of his cruelty, but Jonson goes on:

But I say, he puts off man, and goes into a beast, that is cruell. No vertue is
Princes owne; or becomes him more, then his *Clemency:* And no glory is
greater, then to be able to save with his power. Many punishments sometimes, and in some cases, as much discredit a Prince, as many Funerals a *Physi-
cian.* The state of things is secur'd by Clemency; Severity represseth a few, but
it irritates more. The lopping of trees makes the boughes shoote out thicker;
And the taking away of some kind of enemies, increaseth the number. It is
then, most gracious in a Prince to pardon, when many about him would
make him cruell; to thinke then, how much he can save, when others tell
him, how much he can destroy: not to consider, what the impotence of
others hath demolish'd; but what his owne greatnesse can sustaine. These are
a *Princes* vertues; And they that give him other counsels, are but the *Hang-
mans* Factors.[43]

In words and phrases sometimes borrowed directly from Jonson, Herrick counsels in *Hesperides*, "For punishment in warre, it will suffice, / If
the chiefe author of the faction dyes" (H-335); "Nothing can be more
loathsome, then to see / *Power* conjoyn'd with Natures *Crueltie*" (H-597);
*"Kings must not use the Axe for each offence: / Princes cure some faults by
their patience"* (H-998); or *"That Prince must govern with a gentle hand, /
Who will have love comply with his command"* (H-1067). Over and over
again Herrick urges "Clemency in Kings" (H-775); *"Kings ought to be more
lov'd, then fear'd"* (H-672). In a completely italicized, unusually forthright
epigram on "Cruelty" (H-929), Herrick restates Jonson's position with
powerful concision:

> *Tis but a dog-like madnesse in bad Kings,*
> *For to delight in wounds and murderings.*
> *As some plants prosper best by cuts and blowes;*
> *So Kings by killing doe encrease their foes.*

But Herrick's insistence on the importance of clemency may also have stemmed from his perspective in Devonshire. Herrick's village of Dean Prior lies halfway on the road between Exeter and Plymouth, twenty miles from each city. Plymouth was the only parliamentary outpost in the west to remain firm throughout the war, in spite of the siege the royalists laid from January 1644 to January 1646. Exeter repulsed the royalists in heavy fighting in 1642 but fell later in the year to become the royalist stronghold until the end of the war. Throughout the war, battles raged within ten miles of Dean Prior and, perhaps even more disturbing, the royalist forces roamed the countryside, desperately seeking supplies and plundering without restraint from their superiors. In parliamentarian propaganda, Devonshire became a symbol for royalist rapaciousness.[44] Devonshire was strongly Puritan in sympathy already, and by the end of the war the royalist forces had alienated even the gentry who had remained loyal to the king. The county turned willingly to Fairfax in 1646, if only for the sake of stability. In light of the situation in Devonshire during the civil war, Herrick's epigrams on moderation take on a special significance.

The eventual outcome of the war must have been increasingly evident to Herrick. His poem of high praise to Sir John Berkeley (H-745) for his governorship of Exeter, for example, uses the ominous metaphor of Berkeley as Hector holding a doomed Troy. A number of epigrams were probably written after 1646, when Devon was under the control of the New Model Army and Herrick must have been prepared to leave. Epigrams like "Pitie to the prostrate" (H-550),

> Tis worse then barbarous cruelty to show
> No part of pitie on a conquer'd foe

or "The credit of the Conquerer" (H-553),

> He who commends the vanquisht, speaks the Power,
> And glorifies the worthy Conquerer

may be addressed to the actual victors of the civil war. At the very end of *Hesperides* is an epigram (H-1029) that could be addressed to either side; again both as counsel and as prophecy:

> *Those ends in War the best contentment bring,*
> *Whose Peace is made up with a Pardoning.*

While most of Herrick's political epigrams advise moderation and clemency, increasingly toward the end of *Hesperides* there seems to be an edge of ruthlessness to Herrick's counsel. Perhaps as the situation grew more desperate, Herrick grew skeptical of ideal kingship and impatient with Charles's vacillations. But the meaning of these Machiavellian sentences must be considered in the context of their sources. At midvolume, for example, is one of Herrick's most aggressive pieces of advice (H-488):

> Shame is a bad attendant to a State:
> *He rents his Crown, That feares the Peoples hate.*

This, like other dark epigrams in *Hesperides*, is an adage from Jonson's *Sejanus*;[45] when Tiberius asks:

> Are rites
> Of faith, love, piety, to be trod down?
> Forgotten? and made vain?

Sejanus replies:

> All for a crown.
> The prince who shames a tyrant's name to bear,
> Shall never dare do anything, but fear.
> (2.175–79)

The source of Herrick's epigram makes this profoundly suspect advice. When here and elsewhere Herrick advises a tyrannic power, advice that runs directly counter to his position that a "King ought to be more lov'd, then fear'd," his advice is weighted heavily with bitterness and resignation. Among the final poems of *Hesperides* is an epigram (H-1097) that must certainly register disappointment in Charles's performance:

> *Kings must be dauntlesse: Subjects will contemne*
> *Those, who want Hearts, and weare a Diadem.*

But Herrick does not here suggest an equation between courage and ruthlessness. Six epigrams later, however, as part of the final series of political advice, is a bitterly sarcastic epigram entitled "A King and no King" (H-1103):

> *That Prince, who may doe nothing but what's just,*
> *Rules but by leave, and takes his Crowne on trust.*

This harsh epigram placing the king above the law has been taken as final confirmation of Herrick's "militant royalism."[46] But again, its source makes complicated any attempt to pin down Herrick's intentions. "A

King and no King" is borrowed from Seneca's *Thyestes*, a play about revenge and civil war, brother pitted against brother. In a dialogue that has
reverberations throughout *Hesperides*, the axiom of "A King and no King"
is spoken by Atreus, the classical prototype of a cruel tyrant:

> Atreus: Herein is greatest good of royal power:
> The populace not only must endure
> Their master's deeds, but praise them.
> Attendant: Fear shall make
> Those hostile who were first compelled to praise;
> But he who seeks the fame of true applause
> Would rather by the heart than voice be praised.
> Atreus: The lowly oft enjoy praise truly meant,
> The mighty ne'er know aught but flattery.
> The people oft must will what they would not.
> Attendant: The king should wish for honesty and right;
> Then there is none who does not wish with him.
> Atreus: When he who rules must wish for right alone
> He hardly rules, except on sufferance.
> Attendant: When reverence is not, nor love of law,
> Nor loyalty, integrity, nor truth,
> The realm is insecure.
> Atreus: Integrity,
> Truth, loyalty, are private virtues; kings
> Do as they will.[47]

It is the nature of epigrams that they are often ambiguous. Alone, they
seem to stand as clear pronouncements, unquestioned beliefs. But placed
together, they shift in a mutable and unstable dialogue. Whether Herrick
quotes Atreus with approval or whether his sympathies lie with the Attendant cannot be argued with absolute certainty. But throughout *Hesperides*, in the political epigrams and in the rest of his poetry, Herrick
honors "reverence," "love of law," "loyalty, integrity, truth." "A King and
no King" may be, not so much advice, but confirmation that indeed by
1648 "the realm is insecure." The title itself, borrowed from Beaumont
and Fletcher's play, had currency in the political discourse of the critical
year between the end of the war and Charles's execution. In 1647, for example, the royalist journal *Mercurius Aulicus* reported, with bitter sarcasm, that the parliamentarians were rehearsing for their own "revival" of
the play.[48]

In *Hesperides*, "A King and no King" is followed by an epigram, "Plots not still prosperous" (H-1104), that may refer to Charles's failed attempt in 1647 to escape his imprisonment by the parliamentarians:

> All are not ill Plots, that doe sometimes faile;
> Nor those false vows, which oft times don't prevaile.

It is a poem that explicitly rejects blame, but nevertheless it is a poem full of regret. That regret sounds very clearly in our ears because "A King and no King" is preceded by an epigram that acknowledges the terms of the war and its outcome:

> If Kings and kingdomes, once distracted be,
> The sword of war must trie the Soveraignty.

For by 1648, sovereignty had passed to the kingdom; all plots had failed, and the king's crown rested on his head "but by leave." This frank epigram casts a mocking shadow back through the volume and across the "divine right" epigrams, mocking Charles I, perhaps, but certainly mocking, with painful and humiliating irony, Herrick's own ideals. Earlier the Tacitean epigram "Strength to Support Soveraignty" (H-971) made explicit the poet's role as adviser and baldly stated the reality behind the theory of divine right:

> Let Kings and Rulers, learne this line from me;
> *Where power is weake, unsafe is Majestie.*

After the last Stuart poem in *Hesperides*, the extremely conditional and elegiac "TO THE KING, Upon his welcome to Hampton-Court" (H-961), epigrams predominate and are almost completely stripped of the ceremonial reverence for the king which Herrick had maintained, at least in part, earlier in the volume.

And by the very end, *Hesperides* is heavily epigrammatic. In the final one hundred poems, for example, eighty-seven are epigrams and most of the thirteen lyric poems are farewells. By this final century, Herrick's role as counselor to kings is predominant. In his essay "On Great Place," Francis Bacon said that "the vices of authority are four: delays, corruption, roughnesse, and facility [easiness to be led]"; each of these vices is pointedly attacked by Herrick by the end of *Hesperides*.

The very last epigram on kings in *Hesperides* casts a darker shadow not only on the pride of kings but, implicitly, on their poets as well. "Flatterie" (H-1105) asks:

> What is't that wasts a Prince? example showes,
> 'Tis flatterie spends a King, more then his foes.

The wise counsel of "Flatterie" is ironic and self-mocking, since, in the beginning of *Hesperides*, the poet contributed to the kind of flattery that "spent" Charles, the isolating, idealizing praise that blinded him to the shifting dangers beneath his façade of authoritarian kingship. The epigram stands as a corrective to *Hesperides* itself.

In the address "To the Readers" prefacing *Sejanus*, Jonson argues that he has "discharged the . . . offices of a tragic writer" by including in his play "truth of argument, dignity of persons, gravity and height of elocution" and *"fulness and frequency of sentence"* (italics added). It may be argued that there is a strain of tragedy in *Hesperides* as well. It reflects the events of Herrick's time, the reign and fall of Charles I and the war that sundered the country, events that Herrick would surely have seen as tragic. It is full, as well, of wise sentence and sharp correction, which surround the lyric and pastoral world of Stuart England. Tragic inevitability is fostered by the fact that none of the poet's advice is heeded, nor did Herrick expect it would be. Early in *Hesperides* he had predicted:

> By Time, and Counsell, doe the best we can,
> Th'event is never in the power of man.
>
> (H-294)

CONCLUSION

"With my Lines, my Life must full-stop here"
("His charge to Julia at his death")

۶۶۶۶. At midvolume, Herrick's turn from the country to the city, its voice, and its concerns was, as we have seen, overlaid with mocking reservations. But in the second half of *Hesperides,* Herrick's choice seems no longer to be blurred by ambivalence. "His returne to London" (H-713) opens with an impassioned embrace of his earlier home in heavily erotic imagery:

> From the dull confines of the drooping West,
> To see the day spring from the pregnant East,
> Ravisht in spirit, I come, nay more, I flie
> To thee, blest place of my Nativitie!

It is tempting to associate "His return to London" with Herrick's expulsion from Devonshire in 1647; indeed, whether or not the poem was written under those circumstances, Herrick deliberately arranges the volume to give the impression that it suggests his own life. When he greets London with reverence, we are intended to remember how in *Hesperides'* first century he reviles the river Dean-bourn and the people who live near it: "O men, O manners; Now, and ever knowne / To be *A Rockie Genera-tion!*" But London offers the very opposite of Devon's "warty incivility":

> Thus, thus with hallowed foot I touch the ground,
> With thousand blessings by thy Fortune crown'd.
> O fruitfull Genius! that bestowest here
> An everlasting plenty, yeere by yeere.
> O *Place!* O *People!* Manners! fram'd to please
> All *Nations, Customes, Kindreds, Languages!*

The remainder of the poem is a plea for return and acceptance, an affirmation of his own identity, and an assertion that he has indeed "grown up to be a Roman *Citizen*":

207

> I am a free-born *Roman;* suffer then,
> That I amongst you live a Citizen.
> London my home is: though by hard fate sent
> Into a long and irksome banishment;
> Yet since cal'd back; henceforward let me be,
> O native countrey, repossest by thee!
> For, rather then I'le to the West return,
> I'le beg of thee first here to have mine Urn.
> Weak I am grown, and must in short time fall;
> Give thou my sacred Reliques Buriall.

"His returne to London" seems to resolve completely Herrick's ambivalence between Devonshire (and "ennobled numbers") and London (and "everlasting Topicks"). But his jubilant return to London is a return to die. Claude Summers has traced in this poem a "counterplot," another story told by the poem's "ambiguity of statement and contradictory tone."[1] Because of the sadness Summers hears in this apparently triumphant poem, he argues that it is actually a poem about exile rather than return. There is, as we have seen, a tension maintained in *Hesperides* between lyric inspiration and its attendant otherworldliness, on the one hand, and epigrammatic advice and crude mockery, on the other. By the end of *Hesperides*, however, the voice of the "Roman citizen" is clearly predominant. The grief and anger that Summers identifies in "His returne to London" do not invalidate Herrick's stance as a "Roman citizen" but underline the choice Herrick must make, a choice that will resolve the tension that maintains Herrick's characteristic poetic stance.

Part of this change must mean the end of Herrick's lighter personae, both the poet who had styled himself the "Lyrick Prophet" and the Anacreontic old man petted by his mistresses, poses that had increasingly been qualified and mocked throughout *Hesperides* and that are ultimately resolved in the poet's projection of his own death. But as the culmination of the elegiac and epigrammatic movement of the volume, Herrick's imagery of his own death achieves a sense of dignity and sorrow that is a profound advance on the early poems. In the first century, placed between the flirtatious "To his Mistresse objecting to him neither Toying or Talking" (H-38) and the Anacreontic "Dream" (H-40) of Love whipping him with myrtle twigs, we read "Upon the losse of his Mistresses":

> I have lost, and lately, these
> Many dainty Mistresses:

Stately *Julia*, prime of all;
Sapho next, a principall:
Smooth *Anthea*, for a skin
White, and Heaven-like Chrystalline:
Sweet *Electra*, and the choice
Myrha, for the Lute, and Voice.
Next, *Corinna*, for her wit,
And the graceful use of it:
With *Perilla:* All are gone;
Onely *Herrick's* left alone,
For to number sorrow by
Their departures hence, and die.

Here, death seems only a bathetic pose. But by the end of *Hesperides,* after
we have seen the collapse of the "golden Age," the "shepherds feast," after
the epigrams have questioned and then engulfed the lyric poems, the
poet's anticipation of death is indeed affecting. Throughout *Hesperides*
Herrick seeks not to escape death, not to transcend it, as critics have
argued, but to embrace it. The rituals that surround death have an almost
erotic attraction for Herrick. Herrick's obsession with ritual farewell,
with tombs, and with proper homage paid in memory of the dead must
bring us back to the early poem at his father's grave. There is a sense in
which *Hesperides* may be understood as a restless search for forgiveness for
Herrick's abandonment of his father's grave and a search for a way to return to London, his symbolic home. Directly following the early "Discontents in Devon" (H-51), for example, is a brief and passionate epigram
"To his Paternall Countrey" (H-52):

O Earth! Earth! Earth heare thou my voice, and be
Loving, and gentle for to cover me:
Banish'd from thee I live; ne'r to return,
Unlesse thou giv'st my small Remains an Urne.

This sense of radical dispossession, this plea for return and acceptance, is
to be repeated much later in "His returne to London." And in an epigram
"On himselfe" (H-860), Herrick makes clear the attraction of the "Paternall grave":

If that my Fate has now fulfill'd my yeere,
And so soone stopt my longer living here;
What was't (ye Gods!) a dying man to save,

But while he met with his Paternall grave;
Though while we living 'bout the world do roame,
We love to rest in peacefull Urnes at home,
Where we may snug, and close together lye
By the dead bones of our deare Ancestrie.

(italics added)

At the tomb of his father, "seven *Lusters*" after Nicholas Herrick's death and just before Herrick left London for Devonshire, Herrick had offered, almost desperately, the symbolic gestures of his very personal kind of lyric poetry:

. . . Behold; behold, I bring
Unto thy Ghost, th'Effused Offering:
And look, what Smallage, Night-shade, Cypresse, Yew,
Unto the shades have been, or now are due,
Here I devote; And something more then so;
I come to pay a Debt of Birth I owe.

Lyric poetry is to buy Herrick freedom from this haunting shade by giving his father poetic immortality, and Herrick will indeed fulfill his promise. But there is never a time in *Hesperides* when Herrick rests easy with his bargain. Devon and inspiration are always fraught with reservations and dissatisfaction. Herrick both mourns his expulsion from Devon and rejoices at his return: to London, and home; to death, and the calm sanctuary of the grave.[2]

Threatened by "Plunder" (H-460) and "dejection" (H-993) throughout the 1640s and driven out of Devonshire at last in 1647, Herrick is driven metaphorically from the source of his inspiration. As the sententious epigrams gradually replace the ceremonial lyrics in *Hesperides*, Herrick seems to be portraying a shift in his own mind, a shift in symbolic place, from Devon to London; and a shift in purpose, from a singer of country festivals and pretty girls to a serious but futile role as a voice of sense in a senseless time. Epigrams are placed throughout the first half of *Hesperides* and lyrics throughout the latter half; the tension between the two modes creates the integrity of *Hesperides*. But the shift in dominant voice as the volume progresses is striking and powerful.

Herrick's choice of generic structure for his collected poems makes possible his creation of this semiautobiographical persona and the submerged narrative thread he suggests. The strongest identifying characteristic of the *Hesperides*' persona, which binds his character and the volume together and which links themes as different as the political reality of Stuart England, immortalizing praise, gross mockery, and idealized love, is his obsession with death. Death was the first topic of this, the most ancient of poetic forms, originally graven on monuments. In earlier epigram books, death may be an implicit topic. Martial's and Harington's epigram books reflect their daily lives and, therefore, their aging as the years pass.[3] Ben Jonson, in the more self-consciously crafted volumes, *Epigrammes* and *Under-wood*, is tormented by what he sees as personal failures at the end of his life. But Herrick fashions the semiautobiographical epigrammatic persona into a fictional character, "Herrick," the "lyrick Prophet," whose death concludes *Hesperides*. *Hesperides* may be seen emblematically as resembling Poussin's painting (ca. 1635) of shepherds in a scene of pastoral beauty gathered at a grave upon which is carved the epitaph "Et in Arcadia ego."[4] The shepherds in Poussin's painting seem filled with a calm joy as they trace the graven words. Similarly, we too must finally recognize, graven throughout *Hesperides*, the epitaph of the poet.

Hesperides is, in many ways, a memorial volume. Epitaphs for named and unnamed children, for mothers, virgins, hopeful youths felled in their prime, heroes lost in battle, are everywhere throughout the centuries of Herrick's epigram book. Meditation on the evanescent beauty and early death of flowers is one of Herrick's most successful themes, resulting in celebrated lyrics like "To Daffadills" (H-316) and "The Funerall Rites of the Rose" (H-686). Even poems that are not explicitly about death nevertheless gain their power from death's implicit threat. "To the Virgins, to make much of Time," for example, and "Corinna's going a Maying" are the most masterful of a number of poems that in their final lines remind a mistress, a friend, or himself that:

> . . . when or you or I are made
> A fable, song, or fleeting shade;
> All love, all liking, all delight
> Lies drown'd with us in endlesse night.
> ("Corinna's going a Maying," H-178)

It may be argued that in Herrick's epigram book, death is the major structural device; the poet's obsession with death becomes the recurring motif of the book until his death literally ends "his Story."

In *Hesperides*, named for the islands of the dead at the western edge of the world, death seems to offer a special refinement of living pleasure, a final peace, safety, and the attainment of a kind of accepting love which must remain elusive in life. "All love, all liking, all delight" have less and less attraction for the poet as he makes his volume imply his own evolution. To become "a fable, song, or fleeting shade" is the ultimate achievement of the poet, the realization of Herrick's ideal of endless life in the world's memory.

In the central sixth century, for instance, the macabre poem "His Winding-sheet" (H-515) makes very clear the interconnection of Eros and Thanatos in *Hesperides*. With more passion than Herrick woos any "mistress" (except perhaps for his feminized Sack and her oblivion), Herrick summons his cerements:

> Come thou, who art the Wine, and wit
> Of all I've writ:
> The Grace, the Glorie, and the best
> Piece of the rest.
> Thou art of what I did intend
> The All, and End.
> And what was made, was made to meet
> Thee, thee my sheet.
> Come then, and be to my chast side
> Both Bed, and Bride.
> We two (as Reliques left) will have
> One Rest, one Grave.
> And, hugging close, we will not feare
> Lust entring here:
> Where all Desires are dead, or cold
> As is the mould:
> And all Affections are forgot,
> Or Trouble not.

The echo of Ben Jonson's epigram "On my first Sonne" in the third and fourth lines points up painfully the sterility of a desire that is always turned toward death.[5] Lying in the grave, wrapped in a winding sheet, nothing will trouble him. No lust, no poverty, or legal wranglings:

> All wise; all equall; and all just
> Alike i'th'dust.
> Nor need we here to feare the frowne
> Of Court, or Crown.

Where Fortune bears no sway o're things,
There all are Kings.

It is not only the press of desire that Herrick yearns to escape but the "noise," the "fright," the "newes" of the outside world, the "frowne / Of Court, or Crown." Even as he assumes the voice of epigrammatic counsel in *Hesperides,* he begins the movement toward death. Forced by circumstances and his own sense of responsibility to turn to "London" and to citizenship, Herrick the "Lyrick Prophet" begins the path to his "martyrdom."

Just as *Hesperides* is prefaced by a formal opening, so too it closes with a sequence of eight final poems. Indeed, the whole last century has a sense of closure, beginning with "His tears to Thamasis" (H-1028), his *"fare-ye-well for ever"* to the river Thames and its environs, and with two poems on the final festival days of the Christmas season, "Twelfe night" (H-1035) and "Saint Distaffs day" (H-1026). "Twelfe night, or KING and QUEENE" recalls Herrick's "New-yeares gift" sent to Sir Simeon Steward bidding him forget the problems of the world during "the full twelve Holy-dayes" of Christmas. But here, late in *Hesperides,* after Twelfth Night is over, the book becomes a farewell to poetry and a preparation for death. Placed between "Saint Distaffs day" and "His tears to Thamasis" is the epigram "Sufferance" (H-1027), which expresses the poet's readiness to end his life:

> In hope of ease to come,
> Let's endure one Martyrdome.

In this final century, almost every poem is an epigram, most of them epigrams of advice to the king, including several of the epigrams on the dangers of offering advice to kings. The epigram "Obedience" (H-1073) lies in the last century as well and is profoundly disturbing at the end of a volume that at times has defended so passionately "The Power of Princes":

> The Power of Princes rests in the Consent
> Of onely those, who are obedient:
> Which if away, proud Scepters then will lye
> Low, and of Thrones the Ancient *Majesty.*

Hesperides

Among the longer poems here at the very end of *Hesperides* are "The Tinkers Song," sung in the beery voices of the tinkers themselves; the poem to Weeks, filled with Herrick's fear that his friend will turn him away in his moment of desperation; the dialogue with Elizabeth Wheeler, written so many years before, urging her to stay in the city with him; and the epigram on his brother, Nicholas, praising him for his adventurous and worldly life. The last poem before the sequence of eight concluding epigrams, "The Hagg" (H-1122), is tellingly uncharacteristic of Herrick's usual procedures. Written in a singsong meter borrowed from Jonson's *Masque of Queenes*, divided into lyric stanzas, "The Hagg" "sings" of the nightmares and stench of the mocking epigrams:[6]

> The staffe is now greas'd,
> And very well pleas'd,
> She cockes out her Arse at the parting,
> To an old Ram Goat,
> That rattles i'th'throat,
> Halfe choakt with the stink of her farting.
>
> In a dirtie Haire-lace
> She leads on a brace
> Of black-bore-cats to attend her;
> Who scratch at the Moone,
> And threaten at noone
> Of night from Heaven for to rend her.
>
> A hunting she goes;
> A crackt horne she blowes;
> At which the hounds fall a bounding;
> While th'Moone in her sphere
> Peepes trembling for feare,
> And night's afraid of the sounding.

Its combination of epigrammatic content and lyric form is a fitting conclusion to the body of *Hesperides*, where the "sweet" of love poetry, the "salt" of correction, and the "gall" of mockery maintain an uneasy and dynamic tension. Here at the end, however, they come together in a final dark song of ugliness.

Of the final eight poems in *Hesperides*, the first six epigrams are farewells to poetry and to his book; he will "write no more of Love," "no more of life; but wish twas ended, / And that my dust was to the earth commended" (H-1124); "The Haven [is] reacht to which I first was bound" (H-1127). "Herrick" speaks for the last time in the third poem from the end of *Hesperides:*

> The worke is done: young men, and maidens set
> Upon my curles the *Mirtle Coronet,*
> Washt with sweet ointments; Thus at last I come
> To suffer in the Muses *Martyrdome:*
> But with this comfort, if my blood be shed,
> The Muses will weare blackes, when I am dead.

Now, when the "worke is done," he appeals to two very different sets of mourners: the "young men, and maidens," who should set the "Mirtle Coronet," symbolic of love, upon his head; and the Muses, who will witness his "martyrdome" and mourn his "blood."

As John Kimmey has demonstrated, the penultimate poem in *Hesperides*, "The pillar of Fame" (H-1129), is shaped in the form of Herrick's grave monument and is spoken by a new, plural voice, perhaps the "young men, and maidens," perhaps the Muses.[7] It is a testimony to the survival of Herrick's poetry "Tho Kingdoms fal":

> Fames pillar here, at last, we set,
> Out-during *Marble, Brasse,* or *Jet,*
> Charm'd and enchanted so,
> As to withstand the blow
> Of   overthrow:
> Nor shall the seas,
> Or O U T R A G E S
> Of storms orebear
> What we up-rear,
> Tho Kingdoms fal,
> This pillar never shall
> Decline or waste at all;
> But stand for ever by his owne
> Firme and well fixt foundation.[8]

At midvolume Herrick had already left directions "To his Tomb-maker" (H-546):

> Go I must; when I am gone,
> Write but this upon my Stone;

> *Chaste I liv'd, without a wife,*
> *That's the Story of my life.*
> Strewings need none, every flower
> Is in this word, Batchelour.
>   (italics added)

And so, appropriately, written at the base of "The pillar of Fame," his "stone," is the only untitled poem and the final poem in *Hesperides*, the epitaph:

> To his Book's end this last line he'd have plac't,
> *Jocond his Muse was; but his Life was chast.*

The epitaph's last line is a translation of a line from Ovid's *Tristia*, "Vita verecunda est; Musa iocasa mea" (2.354), and echoes as well the conclusion of one of Martial's epigrams to Caesar:

> innocuos censura potest permittere lusus:
> lasciva est nobis pagina, vita proba.
>   (1.4)

> [A censor can permit harmless trifling: wanton is my page; my life is good.]

Notes

ONE "Read'st my Booke unto the end": The Integrity of *Hesperides*

1. Leavis first enunciated this argument in a book review in *Scrutiny* 4 (1935): 236–56. He incorporated an expanded version of it the next year in *Revaluation: Tradition and Development in English Poetry* (London: Chatto & Windus, 1936), pp. 36, 40, from which I cite.

2. T. S. Eliot, "What Is Minor Poetry?" *Sewanee Review* 54 (1946): 9–10. Originally published in *Welsh Review* 3 (1944): 256–67.

3. The ritual or "ceremonial" aspect of his poetry has dominated Herrick criticism. See the two most recent books on Herrick: A. Leigh DeNeef, *"This Poetick Liturgie": Robert Herrick's Ceremonial Mode* (Durham, N.C.: Duke University Press, 1974), and Robert H. Deming, *Ceremony and Art: Robert Herrick's Poetry*, De Proprietatibus Litterarum, Series Practica, 64 (The Hague: Mouton, 1974). I am indebted throughout to the studies by Claude J. Summers and Leah Marcus on Herrick as a Stuart poet. See Claude J. Summers, "Herrick's Political Poetry: The Strategies of His Art," in *"Trust to Good Verses": Herrick Tercentenary Essays*, ed. Roger Rollin and J. Max Patrick (Pittsburgh: University of Pittsburgh Press, 1978), pp. 171–83, and "Herrick's Political Counterplots," *SEL* 25 (1985): 165–82; Leah Sinanoglou Marcus, "Herrick's *Noble Numbers* and the Politics of Playfulness," *English Literary Renaissance* 7 (1977):108–26, *Childhood and Cultural Despair: A Theme and Variations in Seventeenth-Century Literature* (Pittsburgh: University of Pittsburgh Press, 1978), pp. 94–152, and "Herrick's *Hesperides* and the 'Proclamation made for May,'" *Studies in Philology* 76 (1979): 49–74. Marcus has expanded the argument of "Herrick's *Hesperides* and the 'Proclamation made for May'" in a chapter of her recent book, *The Politics of Mirth: Jonson, Herrick, Milton, Marvell, and the Defense of the Old Holiday Pastimes* (Chicago: University of Chicago Press, 1986), pp. 140–68. Unfortunately, I saw this version of Marcus's argument too late to take full cognizance of it in my study.

4. Cleanth Brooks, "What Does Poetry Communicate?" in *The Well*

Wrought Urn: Studies in the Structure of Poetry (New York: Reynall & Hitchcock, 1947), pp. 67–79.

5. John L. Kimmey, "Order and Form in Herrick's *Hesperides*," *JEGP* 70 (1971): 268.

6. Edmund W. Gosse, "Robert Herrick," *Cornhill Magazine* 32 (1875): 189. Gosse also dismisses the "foolish statement that all editors of Herrick have repeated, sheeplike, from one another, namely, that Catullus was his great example and model."

7. For theoretical discussions of titling, see Theodor W. Adorno, "Titel," in *Noten zur Literatur* (Frankfurt: Suhrkamp, 1965), 3:7–18; Jacques Derrida, "TITLE (to be specified)," *Sub-stance* 31 (1981): 5–22; Alastair Fowler, "Generic Signals," in *Kinds of Literature: An Introduction to the Theory of Genres and Modes* (Cambridge: Harvard University Press, 1982), pp. 88–105; John Hollander, "'Haddock Eyes': A Note on the Theory of Titles," in *Vision and Resonance: Two Senses of Poetic Form* (New York: Oxford University Press, 1975), pp. 212–26; Stephen G. Kellman, "Dropping Names: The Poetics of Titles," *Criticism* 17 (1975): 152–67; Harry Levin, "The Title as Literary Genre," *Modern Language Review* 72 (1977): xxiii–xxxvi; and Peter J. Rabinowitz, *Before Reading: Narrative Conventions and the Politics of Interpretation* (Ithaca: Cornell University Press, 1987), pp. 58–62, 113–14.

8. G. C. Moore Smith, "Herrick's 'Hesperides,'" *Modern Language Review* 9 (1914): 373–74; F. W. Moorman, *Robert Herrick: A Biographical and Critical Study* (1910; reprint, New York: Russell & Russell, 1962), p. 141; and *The Complete Poetry of Robert Herrick,* ed. J. Max Patrick (New York: New York University Press, 1963), p. 5. Heather Asals has stressed the importance of the epigram and the proverb in *Hesperides* and has suggested that the golden apples may be those of Proverbs 25:11–"A word fitly spoken is like apples of gold in pictures of silver" (see "King Solomon in the Land of the Hesperides," *Texas Studies in Literature and Language* 18 [1976]: 365).

9. John L. Kimmey, "Robert Herrick's Persona," *Studies in Philology* 67 (1970): 221–36.

10. See my "Herrick's 'Julia' Poems," *John Donne Journal* 6 (1987): 65–87.

11. In Jonson's 1616 *Works* he added to the end of *Poetaster* the "Apologetical Dialogue," which had been suppressed by authority in the 1602 edition. The whole "Dialogue" is an explicit and ironically exaggerated disclaimer of political and satiric intent, which, in explaining in detail how the author does *not* want his text read, makes very clear how he does. The author includes within his explanation an epigram whose title he points to with exaggerated care:

> . . . I will onely speake
> An *Epigramme* I here have made: It is
> *Vnto true Souldiers.* That's the *lemma.* Marke it.

(*Works,* ed. C. H. Herford and P. and E. Simpson [Oxford: Clarendon Press, 1941], 4: 321.)

12. For example, T. G. S. Cain, "'Times trans-shifting': Herrick in Meditation," in Rollin and Patrick, *"Trust to Good Verses,"* pp. 103–23, bases his argument on the idea of the Hesperides as an enclosed garden.

13. All quotations and the numbering of the poems are from *The Complete Poetry of Robert Herrick,* ed. J. Max Patrick (New York: New York University Press, 1963). All italics are Herrick's unless otherwise noted. I am also deeply indebted to L. C. Martin's scholarly notes in his edition of Herrick, *The Poetical Works* (Oxford: Clarendon Press, 1956).

14. See Gordon Braden, "Robert Herrick and Classical Lyric Poetry," in *The Classics and English Renaissance Poetry: Three Case Studies* (New Haven: Yale University Press, 1978), especially pp. 180–232.

15. Abraham Cowley, *The Complete Works,* ed. Alexander Grosart, 2 vols. (1881; reprint, New York: AMS Press, 1967), 1:18.

16. See Josephine Waters Bennett, "Britain among the Fortunate Isles," *Studies in Philology* 53 (1956): 114–40; and Frances A. Yates, *Astraea* (London: Routledge & Kegan Paul, 1975).

17. Dewitt T. Starnes and Ernest William Talbert, *Classical Myth and Legend in Renaissance Dictionaries* (Chapel Hill: University of North Carolina Press, 1955), pp. 309–12.

18. D. J. Gordon, "The Imagery of Ben Jonson's *Masques of Blacknesse and Beautie,*" in *The Renaissance Imagination,* ed. Stephen Orgel (Berkeley and Los Angeles: University of California Press, 1975), p. 135.

19. Starnes and Talbert, *Classical Myth and Legend,* pp. 310–11.

20. Kimmey, "Order and Form," p. 259. "Here the number of two-line epigrams rises sharply in number from twenty-three in H-500 through H-600 to forty-one in H-600 through H-700. More ominous strings of these epigrams appear." Among the critics who have also noted changes in the volume are Alfred Pollard, ed., *The Hesperides and Noble Numbers,* 2 vols., Muses' Library (New York: Scribner; London: Lawrence & Bullen, 1891); Floris Delattre, *Robert Herrick: Contribution à l'étude de la poésie lyrique en Angleterre au dix-septième siècle* (Paris: Felix Alcan, 1911); Richard J. Ross, "'A Wild Civility': Robert Herrick's Poetic Solution of the Paradox of Art and Nature" (Ph.D. diss., University of Michigan, 1958); and Deming, *Ceremony and Art.*

Twenty-one percent (125) of the first six hundred poems are two-line epigrams; that percentage exactly doubles in the second half of the volume, to 42 percent.

21. For dates, both positive and speculative, see Martin, pp. xxxvi–xl; Patrick, passim; and Mark L. Reed, "Herrick among the Maypoles: Dean Prior and the *Hesperides,*" *SEL* 5 (1965): 133–50.

The most detailed consideration of the order of *Hesperides* is Edward

Everett Hale, Jr., *Die Chronologische Anordnung der Dichtungen Robert Herricks* (Halle: C. A. Kaemmerer, 1892). Essentially, Hale concludes that as Herrick's career progressed, his verse tended to become more and more closed and epigrammatic and that, therefore, we may surmise that *Hesperides* is arranged chronologically. I agree that Herrick's poetry became increasingly epigrammatic in later years, but I do not believe that we can posit a simple chronological arrangement.

The first consideration in discussing the arrangement of Herrick's poetry is that very few of the poems can be assigned firm dates (L. C. Martin assigns dates to forty-five). Beyond this, one enters a relatively subjective area of probable dates based on topic (e.g., old age) or style (e.g., epigrammatic) or inclusion in a commonplace book (based on the assumption that Herrick's poetry stopped circulating in manuscript when he left London). The impression of chronological arrangement which *Hesperides* gives is blurred by an analysis of what little data we have. Using only Martin's very conservative list of dated poems and considering poem H-565 as the mathematical center of the volume, there are thirteen poems datable before 1630, when Herrick left London for Devonshire, and thirty-two poems written in the 1630s and 1640s. Of the thirteen early poems, nine fall in the first half of the volume, but four come later, including "His tears to Thamasis" (H-1028), probably written in 1630 but placed at the end of the volume as part of its elegiac mood. Of the thirty-two poems written after 1630, seventeen fall in the first half of the volume and fifteen in the second. It can perhaps be safely said that many of Herrick's early poems are in the first half of the volume, but that the later poems are distributed throughout *Hesperides*.

22. Poems to Cupid are distributed fairly evenly throughout *Hesperides* (seventeen in the first half, eleven in the second), but the persona assumes a growing animosity to Love as the volume progresses. The final poem "To Cupid" (H-1120) is the culmination of this growing tension:

> I have a leaden, thou a shaft of gold;
> Thou kil'st with heate, and I strike dead with cold.
> Let's trie of us who shall the first expire;
> Or thou by frost, or I by quenchlesse fire:
> *Extreames are fatall, where they once doe strike,*
> *And bring to'th'heart destruction both alike.*

The poems dedicated to flowers or built entirely upon a conceit of flowers almost disappear later in *Hesperides*. There are forty-one in the first half, eight in the second.

23. Court poets made much of the appearance of a bright star in the noon sky at Charles's birth. In poems of Richard Corbett, Henry King, Thomas Randolph, John Hoskyns, and in the 1630 volume *Britanniae Natalis*, for

example, the future Charles II was linked inexorably to the star imagery of his birth. Although Herrick's prefatory poem is superior as poetry, it is conventional in its imagery and sentiments.

24. Patrick, p. 38.

25. Ibid., p. 9.

26. For further corroboration of the ominous timeliness of Herrick's poetry, see Claude Summers's compelling argument that "Rex Tragicus," at the end of *Noble Numbers* (N-263), is not only a poem on the crucifixion of Christ but a powerful and deliberate foreshadowing of Charles's execution ("Herrick's Political Counterplots," pp. 174–82).

27. I am indebted to Annabel Patterson for pointing out the importance of the pastoral tree as political symbol in Stuart England.

28. Herford and Simpson, 7:687. *Neptune's Triumph* was to have been performed on Twelfth Night, 1624, but, because of a diplomatic imbroglio over precedence between the French and Spanish ambassadors, the masque was not performed. Jonson rewrote it for the next year as *The Fortunate Isles and their Union.*

29. See Roy Strong, *Van Dyck: Charles I on Horseback* (New York: Viking Press, 1972), pp. 45–47.

30. James Howell, *Dodona's Grove, or the Vocall Forest.* Quoted from the third edition (Cambridge: Printed by R.P., for H. Moseley, 1645), p. 41.

31. Compare Jonson's epigram "To K. Charles for 100. pounds he sent me in my sicknesse," in which Jonson thanks Charles for curing the poet's evil, poverty, as he does the King's Evil, scrofula. The epigram is complicated by the suggestion that the king cure the "Peoples Evill" as well, a probable reference to the dissolution of Parliament in 1629 (Herford and Simpson, 8:235 and 11:92). See, too, Thomas Campion's Jacobean masque on the occasion of the marriage of Somerset and Frances Howard, where the queen is presented with a "Tree of Golde":

> . . . this Tree of Grace and Bountie heere,
> From which for our enchaunted Knights we craue
> A branche, pull'd by your Sacred Hand, to haue;
> That we may beare it as the Fates direct,
> And manifest your glory in th' effect.
> In vertues fauour then, and Pittie now,
> (Great Queene) vouchsafe vs a diuine touch't bough.

The squire who receives this bough is to go forth "like th' Euening Starre," that is, like Hesperides (Campion, *Works,* ed. Percival Vivian [Oxford: Clarendon Press, 1909], p. 153).

32. Summers, "Herrick's Political Poetry," pp. 176–77.

33. In Marvell's "Upon Appleton House," a hewel chooses a hollow oak:

And through the tainted side he mines.
Who could have thought the tallest oak
Should fall by such a feeble stroke!

Nor would it, had the tree not fed
A traitor-worm, within it bred,
(As first our flesh corrupt within
Tempts impotent and bashful sin).
And yet that worm triumphs not long,
But serves to feed the hewel's young,
While the oak seems to fall content,
Viewing the treason's punishment.

The Complete Poems, ed. Elizabeth Story Donno (Penguin Books: 1972), p. 92.

34. Braden, "Herrick and Lyric Poetry," pp. 218–32. The poet refers to himself in Herculean terms in H-197, -304, -849, -1123, S-6, and N-73. William L. Trogden argues in "Classical Mythology in the Poetry of Robert Herrick" (Ph.D. diss., University of Missouri-Columbia, 1973), p. 255, that "the partially stylized portrait of Herrick in profile" by William Marshall on the frontispiece is meant to suggest Hercules.

35. Alexander Ross, *Mystagogus Poeticus, or the Muses Interpreter.* Quoted from the third edition (London: Printed by R.P. for Joshua Kirton, 1653), p. 168, and John Dryden, *Works,* ed. Earl Miner (Berkeley and Los Angeles: University of California Press, 1969), 3:305.

36. Vivanti Corrado, "Henry IV, the Gallic Hercules," *Journal of the Warburg and Courtauld Institutes* 30 (1967): 176–97.

37. See D. J. Gordon, "Rubens and the Whitehall Ceiling," in *The Renaissance Imagination,* pp. 24–50.

38. Thomas Carew, *The Poems . . . with his Masque* Coelum Britannicum, ed. Rhodes Dunlap (Oxford: Clarendon Press, 1949), ll. 933–34 and 944–46. Further references to Carew will be to this edition.

39. See Michael P. Parker, "Carew's Politic Pastoral: Virgilian Pretexts in the 'Answer to Aurelian Townsend,'" *John Donne Journal* 1 (1982): 101–16.

40. Leah Sinanoglou Marcus, "The Occasion of Ben Jonson's *Pleasure Reconciled to Virtue,*" *SEL* 19 (1979): 286–90.

41. Sir Philip Sidney, *Works,* ed. Albert Feuillerat (Cambridge: Cambridge University Press, 1923), 3:40.

42. See Eugene M. Waith, *The Herculean Hero in Marlowe, Chapman, Shakespeare, and Dryden* (New York: Columbia University Press, 1962); G. Karl Galinsky, *The Herakles Theme* (Oxford: Basil Blackwell, 1972); Jeff Shulman, "At the Crossroads of Myth: The Hermeneutics of Hercules, from Ovid to Shakespeare," *ELH* 50 (1983): 83–105.

43. Herford and Simpson, 7:486.

44. See *The Entertainment at Highgate, The Masques of Blacknesse and Beautie, Pleasure Reconciled to Virtue,* and *The Fortunate Isles.*

45. John Milton, *Complete Poems and Major Prose,* ed. Merritt Y. Hughes (New York: Odyssey, 1957), p. 113.

46. See *The King's Arcadia—Inigo Jones and the Stuart Court: A Quatercentenary Exhibition Held at the Banqueting House, Whitehall, from July 12th to September 2nd, 1973,* catalogued by John Harris, Stephen Orgel, and Roy Strong (Arts Council of Great Britain, 1973); Stephen Orgel, *The Illusion of Power* (Berkeley and Los Angeles: University of California Press, 1975) and *The Jonsonian Masque* (Cambridge: Harvard University Press, 1965); Gordon Parry, *The Golden Age Restor'd: The Culture of the Stuart Court, 1603–1642* (Manchester: Manchester University Press, 1981); and Roy Strong, *Splendour at Court* (London: Weidenfeld & Nicolson, 1973).

47. The verb is Leah Marcus's. See her article "Herrick's *Hesperides* and the 'Proclamation made for May'" for a discussion of Herrick's use of the traditional "merrie England" as Stuart propaganda.

48. Herford and Simpson, 7:735.

49. Stephen Orgel and Roy Strong, *Inigo Jones: The Theatre of the Stuart Court,* 2 vols. (London: Sotheby Parke Bernet; Berkeley and Los Angeles: University of California Press, 1973), 1:2.

50. David Lindley, "Embarrassing Ben: The Masques for Frances Howard," *English Literary Renaissance* 16 (1986): 343–59, has demonstrated Jonson's embarrassment at having to work into art questionable political propaganda. Indeed, Lindley suggests that "it is precisely in registering the complexity of the struggle within the poet's work to sustain the transmutation of the circumstances of the Jacobean court and its politics into self-sufficient myth that the true fascination of the [masque] genre lies" (358–59).

51. Orgel, *Illusion of Power,* pp. 40, 49–52.

52. Orgel and Strong, *Inigo Jones,* 1:74. All quotations from *Salmacida Spolia* are from this edition, 2:729–34.

53. Alexander Ross, *Mystagogus Poeticus,* cited in Starnes and Talbert, *Classical Myth and Legend,* p. 403.

54. The witch poems are H-643, -888, -890, -891, and -1122. The fairy poems are H-223, -293, -299, -443, -556, and -638. The king's masques were almost without exception performed during the Christmas and New Year's revels, usually on Twelfth Night. Interestingly, Herrick has a series of Christmas and Twelfth Night poems toward the end of *Hesperides:* H-784, -785, -786, -787, -892, -893, -894, -980, -1026, and -1035.

55. The final line refers to a nursery rhyme about a little man named Moss who caught his runaway mare when he found her sleeping in a tree (D. H.

Woodward, ed., *The Poems and Translations of Robert Fletcher* [Gainesville: University of Florida Press, 1970], pp. 139, 200).

56. Horace, *Complete Works*, trans. Charles E. Passage (New York: Ungar, 1983), p. 118.

57. Hesiod, *The Works and Days; Theogony; the Shield of Herakles*, trans. Richmond Lattimore (Ann Arbor: University of Michigan Press, 1959), ll. 212–30.

58. Manfred Weidhorn, *Dreams in Seventeenth-Century Literature* (The Hague: Mouton, 1970), p. 95.

TWO "The Argument of his Book"

1. Algernon C. Swinburne, "Preface," *The Hesperides and Noble Numbers*, ed. Alfred Pollard, 2 vols. (New York: Scribner; London: Lawrence & Bullen, 1891) 1:xi. John Masefield used the idea of Herrick as a songwriter to damn him with faint praise: Herrick "is never more, as he is never less, than a consummate song-writer. . . . His interest is not so much in life, as in the adornment and luxurious refinements of life" ("Introduction," *The Poems of Robert Herrick*, The Chapbooks [London: E. Grant Richard, 1906], p. xiii). Among the few substantive discussions of Herrick's nonlyric poetry are A. Leigh DeNeef, *"This Poetick Liturgie": Robert Herrick's Ceremonial Mode* (Durham, N.C.: Duke University Press, 1974), pp. 109–41; Floris Delattre, "Les Paysans du Devonshire," in *Robert Herrick: Contribution à l'étude de la poésie lyrique en Angleterre au dix-septième siècle* (Paris: Felix Alcan, 1911), pp. 147–60; Robert W. Halli, Jr., "Robert Herrick's Epigrams on Commoners," *South Atlantic Bulletin* 43 (1978): 30–41; John L. Kimmey, "Robert Herrick's Satirical Epigrams," *English Studies* 51 (1970): 312–23; Helen Marlborough, "Herrick's Epigrams of Praise," in *"Trust to Good Verses": Herrick Tercentenary Essays*, ed. Roger Rollin and J. Max Patrick (Pittsburgh: University of Pittsburgh Press, 1978), pp. 159–69; and Claude Summers, "Herrick's Political Poetry: The Strategies of His Art," in *"Trust to Good Verses,"* pp. 171–83.

2. Rosalie Colie, *The Resources of Kind: Genre-Theory in the Renaissance*, ed. Barbara K. Lewalski (Berkeley and Los Angeles: University of California Press, 1973), pp. 25–26. See also Alastair Fowler's amplification of Colie's reading of the "Argument," *Kinds of Literature: An Introduction to the Theory of Genres and Modes* (Cambridge: Harvard University Press, 1982), p. 196.

3. James Hutton, *The Greek Anthology in Italy to the Year 1800* (Ithaca: Cornell University Press; London: Humphrey Milford, 1935), p. 56. On the close relationship between epigram and sonnet, see also Mario Praz, *The Flaming Heart* (1958; reprint, Gloucester, Mass.: Peter Smith, 1966), pp. 208–20; 267.

4. Thomas Sébillet, *Art Poétique françoyse* (Paris, 1548), quoted by Rosalie

L. Colie, *Shakespeare's Living Art* (Princeton: Princeton University Press, 1974), p. 83.

5. Colie, *Shakespeare's Living Art*, p. 76.

6. Fowler, *Kinds of Literature*, p. 138. In the introduction to his sonnets in the second (1797) edition of *Poems on Various Subjects*, Coleridge suggests: "Perhaps, if the Sonnet were comprized in less than fourteen lines, it would become a serious epigram. . . . The greater part of Warton's Sonnets are severe and masterly likenesses of the style of the Greek *epigrammata*" (quoted by Geoffrey H. Hartman, "Wordsworth, Inscription, and Romantic Nature Poetry," in *Beyond Formalism: Literary Essays, 1958–1970* [New Haven: Yale University Press, 1970], p. 212).

7. See, for example, Ben Jonson's fourteen-line epigrams of praise: *Epigrammes*, 14, 89, 103, 111, 128, 131, and 132 and *Under-wood*, 60, 64, 65, 68, and 70. Jonson has only one fourteen-line epigram that is not an epigram of praise, "On Poet-Ape" (*Epigrammes* 56), but there the form can be read as part of the poem's satire.

8. Sir John Harington, 1.37; *The Letters and Epigrams*, ed. Norman Egbert McClure (Philadelphia: University of Pennsylvania Press, 1930), pp. 162–63. Further references to Harington's epigrams will be to this edition and will use both the double integer numeration of the 1618 edition and the numbers McClure assigned. Numbers 347 and higher are from BL Addit. MS. 12049 and were not included in the 1618 edition.

9. Colie, *Shakespeare's Living Art*, p. 79.

10. Thomas Bastard, *Chrestoleros. Seuen Bookes of Epigrames* (Spenser Society, 1888; reprint, New York: Burt Franklin, 1967), p. 7. Further references to Bastard's poetry will use his own double integer numbering. References in text are to book and number.

11. Alexander Grosart, in his edition of Bastard's poetry, was the first to note the similarity: "The opening Epigram of *Chrestoleros* (Lib.i.I) seems to me to be echoed in the opening of the *Hesperides*, though of course there is really no comparison between Bastard and Herrick" (*The Poems English and Latin*, Occasional Issues [Printed for the Subscribers, 1880], p. xvi). See also Hoyt Hopewell Hudson, *The Epigram in the English Renaissance* (Princeton: Princeton University Press, 1947), p. 20; Robert Herrick, *The Poetical Works*, ed. L. C. Martin (Oxford: Clarendon Press, 1956), p. 498; A. Leigh DeNeef, "Herrick's 'Argument' and Thomas Bastard," *Seventeenth-Century News* 29 (1971): 9–10.

12. See Jean McMahon Humez, "The Manners of Epigram: A Study of the Epigram Volumes of Martial, Harington, and Jonson," (Ph.D. diss., Yale University, 1971), pp. 216–20.

13. Samuel Sheppard, *Epigrams Theological, Philosophical, and Romantick* (London, 1651), pp. 1–2. In his prefatory address "To the Reader," Sheppard

says that there are few true epigrammatists "and in English none but Bastard and Harrington" (A₃v).

14. See Hyder E. Rollins, "Samuel Sheppard and His Praise of Poets," *Studies in Philology* 24 (1927): 509–55, and Joseph Frank, *The Beginnings of the English Newspapers, 1620–1660* (Cambridge: Harvard University Press, 1961), passim.

15. DeNeef, "Herrick's 'Argument,'" pp. 9–10.

16. On the "Argument" see, for example, DeNeef, *"This Poetick Liturgie,"* pp. 4–11; Robert H. Deming, *Ceremony and Art: Robert Herrick's Poetry*, De Proprietatibus Litterarum, Series Practica, 64 (The Hague: Mouton, 1974), pp. 59–61; Jay A. Gertzman, "Robert Herrick's Recreative Pastoral," *Genre* 7 (1974): 183–95; John L. Kimmey, "Studies in Cavalier Poetry," *English Studies Collection* 2 (1977): 1–25; and Sydney Musgrove, *The Universe of Robert Herrick*, Auckland University College Bulletin no. 38; English Series no. 4 (Auckland: Pelorus Press, 1951), pp. 5–6.

17. Quoted in Thomas Pecke, *Parnassi Puerperium* (London: F. Cottrel for Tho. Bassett, 1659), pp. 137–38. More's poem was originally published in his *Epigrammata* (1518); the first English edition of More's poems was published by Humphrey Moseley in 1638.

18. See, for example, Ben Jonson's "Epithalamion" (*Under-wood*, 77, ll. 57–58) and his epigram "To My L. the King, on the Christning His Second Sonne James" (*Under-wood*, 84, ll. 15–16).

19. Joan Ozark [Holmer], "Fairy Poetry of the Early Seventeenth Century" (Ph.D. diss., Princeton University, 1973).

20. If the "Argument" is meant to embrace both *Hesperides* and *His Noble Numbers*, then the concluding couplet would refer to the sacred portion of the work, especially the poems about the Harrowing of Hell. But the "Argument" is placed within the clearly defined borders of *Hesperides* itself.

THREE The Classical Models

1. Alastair Fowler, for example, has called *Hesperides* "this greatest of English epigram sequences" (*Kinds of Literature: An Introduction to the Theory of Genres and Modes* [Cambridge: Harvard University Press, 1982], p. 197).

2. Thomas Pecke, *Parnassi Puerperium* (London: F. Cottrel for Tho. Bassett, 1659), p. A₃; *Works*, ed. C. H. Herford and P. and E. Simpson (Oxford: Clarendon Press, 1947), 8:635.

3. Bacon, for example, in *De Augmentis Scientiarum* discusses as a separate branch of learning the poetry he considers "feigned history," "Poesy *Narrative, Dramatic,* and *Parabolical.*" Bacon dismisses from this discussion "Satires, Elegies, Epigrams, Odes, and the like; and refer[s] them to philosophy and the arts of speech. And under the name of Poesy, I treat only of feigned

history." Quoted in Wesley Trimpi, *Ben Jonson's Poems: A Study of the Plain Style* (Stanford: Stanford University Press, 1962), p. 191.

4. Cited by Hoyt Hopewell Hudson, *The Epigram in the English Renaissance* (Princeton: Princeton University Press, 1947), pp. 9–10.

5. Quoted in James Hutton, *The Greek Anthology in Italy to the Year 1800* (Ithaca: Cornell University Press; London: Humphrey Milford, 1935), p. 62.

6. Rosalie Colie's paraphrase of Minturno, *Shakespeare's Living Art* (Princeton: Princeton University Press, 1974), p. 84.

7. Quoted in Hutton, *Greek Anthology in Italy*, pp. 19–20.

8. Hudson, *English Renaissance*, p. 14, and Colie, *Shakespeare's Living Art*, pp. 86–89.

9. See Hudson, "The Epigram in Schools and Colleges," in *English Renaissance*, pp. 145–69, and Fowler, *Kinds of Literature*, p. 200.

10. Pecke, *Parnassi Puerperium*, p. A₃. He continues, "And not onely Verse, but Prose, is dull, and languishing, unlesse the sparkling Genius of the Epigrammatist, be artificially interwoven."

11. Mario Praz, *The Flaming Heart* (1958; reprint, Gloucester, Mass.: Peter Smith, 1966), p. 207.

12. Fowler, *Kinds of Literature*, p. 196. He points out that the epigram effectively eradicated the sonnet from English literature until the end of the eighteenth century.

13. Quoted in Fowler, *Kinds of Literature*, p. 196.

14. No. 409, Thursday, June 19, 1712, *The Spectator*, ed. Donald F. Bond, 5 vols. (Oxford: Clarendon Press, 1965), 3:530. Earlier, Addison had declared that "mixt wit" was the province of epigrams: "a Composition of Punn and true Wit, . . . more or less perfect as the Resemblance lies in the Ideas or in the Words: Its Foundations are laid partly in Falsehood and partly in Truth: Reason puts in her Claim for one Half of it, and Extravagance for the other" (No. 62, Friday, May 11, 1711), 1:267. See also essay no. 70.

15. Geoffrey Hartman, "Wordsworth, Inscriptions, and Romantic Nature Poetry," in *Beyond Formalism: Literary Essays, 1958–1970* (New Haven: Yale University Press, 1970), pp. 206–30. Hartman goes on, "The general change from Neoclassical to Romantic style parallels curiously the difference between the brief, witty, pointed epigram of the Latin tradition, influential on the development of the heroic couplet, and the simpler, more descriptive, anecdotal epigram which is a staple of the Greek Anthology" (pp. 216–17).

16. Scholarly work on the English epigram is surprisingly meager. Hoyt Hopewell Hudson's *Epigram in the English Renaissance* (1947) would surely have been a major contribution, but he died after writing only the beginning. James Hutton, too, planned to write an exhaustive study of the influence, specifically, of the Greek Anthology on English literature. He felt, however, that he needed to explain the continental tradition first as essential

background. He completed *The Greek Anthology in Italy* (1935) and *The Greek Anthology in France* (Ithaca: Cornell University Press, 1946) but never published his proposed volume on the English tradition.

In Albert C. Baugh, ed., *A Literary History of England*, 2d ed. (New York: Appleton-Century Crofts, 1967), the English epigram is discussed in a footnote that offers pity to any future historian of the form for his "sad task" but doubts that the distasteful job will ever be undertaken (p. 394). C. S. Lewis, in *English Literature in the Sixteenth Century* (Oxford: Clarendon Press, 1954), admits frankly that he cannot bear to read any epigrams (pp. 477–78). Of Heywood's epigrams he declares, "Served cold in print, and in such quantity, they are (at least to my taste) unendurable" (p. 146). For more on Heywood's reputation, see John Heywood, *Works*, ed. Burton D. Milligan (Urbana: University of Illinois Press, 1956), pp. 10–13.

Sir John Harington has suffered perhaps the most remarkable and undeserved neglect of any of the English epigrammatists. Mandell Creighton concluded his 1890 *DNB* entry for Harington, "His epigrams, disfigured by coarseness, are forgotten" (quoted by D. H. Craig, *Sir John Harington* [Boston: Twayne, 1985], p. 132). T. S. Eliot, in a 1927 review of McClure's edition of Harington's epigrams, commented that they "illustrate well the mentality of a cultivated and wholly uninspired country gentleman of the time" (Craig, *Harington*, p. 109; for more on Harington's reputation, see Craig, p. 152, n. 35).

17. Judith Scherer Herz, "Epigrams and Sonnets: Milton in the Manner of Jonson," *Milton Studies* 20 (1984): 29–41.

18. Hutton, *Greek Anthology in Italy*, pp. 64–65.

19. References and translations from Martial will be to the Loeb edition, trans. and ed. Walter C. A. Ker, 2 vols. (London: Heinemann; New York: Putnam, 1925), unless otherwise noted. References and translations from Catullus will be to *The Poems of Catullus: A Bilingual Edition*, trans. Peter Whigham (Berkeley and Los Angeles: University of California Press, 1966).

20. See the preface to book 1, 1.7, 1.109, 4.14, 7.99, and 10.103 and the "Lesbia" poems.

21. Kenneth Quinn, *Catullus: An Interpretation* (New York: Barnes & Noble, 1973), p. 129.

22. T. P. Wiseman, *Catullan Questions* (Leicester: Leicester University Press, 1969), pp. 4–6. Wiseman has expanded this study in his recent book *Catullus and His World: A Reappraisal* (Cambridge: Cambridge University Press, 1985). About one central poem, for example, he argues: "Like most of the poems in the collection, poem 63 probably had a life of its own before the collection was put together. But in its setting next to the wedding-songs and the epic tale, in the central position between the two blocks of personal and occasional poetry, it acquires an extra resonance, echoing in another genre the preoccupations of the poet-lover. The collection is in itself a work of art.

Catullus wrote for people who took poetry seriously—for re-readers, who would come back to Attis, Peleus and Ariadne with the whole cycle of Lesbia poems in their minds. For such readers, the collection is more than the sum of its parts" (pp. 181–82).

23. David O. Ross, *Style and Tradition in Catullus* (Cambridge: Harvard University Press, 1969), argues that the poems in the first part of the book are Hellenistic and that the poems in the second half are Roman epigrams.

24. It is possible that poem 116 is either spurious or an early Catullan poem that he himself did not include in the arrangement of the "liber Catulli," in which case the attack on Mentula is the final poem. Catullus's attacks on both Mentula and Mamurra can be read as attacks on Caesar himself, especially since Caesar read them that way. Suetonius records: "As for Valerius Catullus, by whose verses concerning Mamurra [Caesar] could not choose but take knowledge that he was noted and branded with perpetual infamy, when he excused himself unto him and was ready to make satisfaction, he bade him to supper that very day; and, as he used before time, so he continued still to make his father's house his lodging" (*History of Twelve Caesars*, trans. Philemon Holland, ed. J. H. Freese [London: Routledge; Dutton, 1923], pp. 45–46).

25. The phrase is James Lowell's from *Among My Books* (Boston, 1870), p. 341. Gordon Braden has rightly observed that classical source hunting has long constituted a large part of Herrick criticism ("Robert Herrick and Classical Lyric Poetry," in *The Classics and English Renaissance Poetry: Three Case Studies* [New Haven: Yale University Press, 1978], p. 173). One of the first serious readings of Herrick during his nineteenth-century rediscovery was Nathaniel Drake's in *Literary Hours* (1804); Drake postulated that "perhaps there is no collection of poetry in our language which, in some respects, more nearly resembles the *Carmina* of Catullus" than *Hesperides* (quoted by Braden, p. 177). Elizabeth Hageman, *Robert Herrick: A Reference Guide* (Boston: G. K. Hall, 1983), lists 31 works on Herrick and Catullus.

26. James McPeek, *Catullus in Strange and Distant Britain* (Cambridge: Harvard University Press, 1939), passim. McPeek concludes that Herrick seems so "Catullan" because his poetry frequently recalls Catullus's two most famous poems, "vivamus, mea Lesbia," and "Lugete, o Veneres." It is difficult to find any direct influence, however, even in the case of these two poems. Where Herrick does seem to go directly to Catullus is for details for his epithalamia.

27. Herrick, *The Poetical Works*, ed. L. C. Martin (Oxford: Clarendon Press, 1956), pp. 514–15. Another, rather maddening application of Catullus to Herrick is Braden's comparison of counting kisses in "vivamus, mea Lesbia" with "To Anthea" (H-74). Braden scornfully disparages Herrick because in "To Anthea" he "touched but not really imitated" Catullus, "the old story of

decontextualization, but with a special vengeance." Herrick "needs to dis-
member the Catullan poem before he can safely introduce it into his world"
("Herrick and Lyric Poetry," pp. 178, 180). In a note, Braden cites the "curiously close parallel to Herrick's dismemberment of the poem" with Jonson's two
songs to Celia (*The Forrest*, 5, 6) and Campion's "My sweetest Lesbia." It
seems reasonable to wonder whether Herrick was imitating Jonson or
Campion, not Catullus.

28. I am indebted to Jean McMahon Humez, "The Manners of Epigram:
A Study of the Epigram Volumes of Martial, Harington, and Jonson" (Ph.D.
diss., Yale University, 1971), for her detailed description of the Martialian epigram book. See also Bruce R. Smith, "Ben Jonson's *Epigrammes:* Portrait-
Gallery, Theater, Commonwealth," *SEL* 14 (1974): 91–109.

29. The best-known example of the urbanity of Martial's epigrams is his
poem on the neighbor he watches from his window every day but has never
met (1.86).

30. For all references to the preface to book 1, I refer to Peter Howell, *A
Commentary on Book One of the Epigrams of Martial* (London: Athlone Press,
1980).

31. Humez, "Manners of Epigram," pp. 38–57, and Amy Richlin, *The Garden of Priapus: Sexuality and Aggression in Roman Humor* (New Haven: Yale
University Press, 1983), pp. 9–10, 228–29.

32. See Frederick M. Ahl, *Lucan: An Introduction* (Ithaca: Cornell University Press, 1976), p. 29, and John Garthwaite, "Domitian and the Court Poets
Martial and Statius" (Ph.D. diss., Cornell University, 1979), p. 170.

33. For a list of Domitian's victims and their alleged crimes, see Suetonius,
Domitian, p. 10.

34. Ahl, *Lucan*, pp. 20, 26–27, 32–35.

35. Garthwaite, "Domitian and the Court Poets," p. 3.

36. *Institutio Oratoria*, 9.2.67. The translation is Annabel Patterson's in
*Censorship and Interpretation: The Conditions of Writing and Reading in Early
Modern England* (Madison: University of Wisconsin Press, 1984), pp. 14–15.

37. Garthwaite examines, for example, Martial's sixth book and demonstrates how it mocks the poems to Domitian which praise Domitian's moral
reforms as "censor in perpetuity" of Roman life. Martial's ninth book is his
most thoroughly imperial volume; yet Garthwaite argues that it is "a carefully
fashioned, coherent sequence of interrelated motifs" which creates an invidi-
ous comparison between the emperor's lavish temple-building program and
the poet's poverty ("Domitian and the Court Poets," p. 62).

38. Ahl, *Lucan*, pp. 30–33, and Garthwaite, "Domitian and the Court
Poets," p. 174.

39. 1.6, 14, 22, 44, 48, 51, 60, 104.

40. By the time Martial addressed this epigram to him, Domitian himself was the censor.

41. The original epigram reads:

> Qui gravis es nimium, potes hinc iam, lector, abire
>   quo libet: urbanae scripsimus ista togae;
> iam mea Lampsacio lascivit pagina versu
>   et Tartesiaca concrepat aera manu.
> o quotiens rigida pulsabis pallia vena,
>   sis gravior Curio Fabricioque licet!
> tu quoque nequitias nostri lususque libelli
>   uda, puella, leges, sis Patavina licet.
> erubuit posuitque meum Lucretia librum,
>   sed coram Bruto; Brute, recede: leget.

That translation is an act of interpretation and creation is particularly clear in versions of Martial's epigrams. Walter Ker's translation of this epigram for the Loeb Classical Library, for example, is scholarly and restrained:

You, reader, who are too strait-laced, can now go away from here whither you will: I wrote these verses for the citizens of wit; now my page wantons in verse of Lampsacus, and beats the timbrel with the hand of a figurante of Tartessus. Oh, how often will you with your stiff poker beat at your garb, though you may be more strait-laced than Curius and Fabricius! You also, O girl, may, when in your cups, read the naughtiness and sportive sallies of my little book, though you may be from Patavium. Lucretia blushed and laid down my volume; but Brutus was present. Brutus, go away: she will read it.

Compare Anthony Reid's translation in *Epigrams of Martial Englished by Divers Hands*, ed. J. P. Sullivan and Peter Whigham (Berkeley and Los Angeles: University of California Press, 1987), a selection of translations that are, in the editors' terms, frankly "modern":

> Let every prudish reader use his feet
> And bugger off—I write for the elite.
> My verses gambol with Priapic verve
> As dancing harlots' patter starts a nerve.
> Though stern as Curius or like Fabricius,
> Your prick will stiffen and grow vicious.
> Girls while they drink—even the chastest folk—
> Will read each naughty word and dirty joke.
> Lucretia blushes, throws away my book.
> Her husband goes. She takes another look.

42. The best discussion of Herrick's royalist poems is Claude J. Summers in "Herrick's Political Counterplots," *SEL* 25 (1985): 165–82, and "Herrick's

Political Poetry: The Strategies of His Art," in *"Trust to Good Verses": Herrick Tercentenary Essays*, ed. Roger Rollin and J. Max Patrick (Pittsburgh: University of Pittsburgh Press, 1978), pp. 171–83.

43. *Harper's Classical Dictionary*, ed. Harry Thurston Peck (New York: Harper & Bros., 1897), 2:1416.

44. Leah Sinanoglou Marcus, "Herrick's *Hesperides* and the 'Proclamation made for May,'" *Studies in Philology* 76 (1979): 60–69.

45. See Hutton, *Greek Anthology in Italy;* Robert Ralson Cawley, "The History and Nature of the Early Epigram," *Journal of Historical Studies* 1 (1968): 311–25; Kathryn McEuen, *Classical Influence upon the Tribe of Ben* (Cedar Rapids, Ia.: Torch Press, 1939), pp. 204–50; Fowler, *Kinds of Literature*, p. 138; Colie, *Shakespeare's Living Art*, p. 81; and Hudson, *English Renaissance*, passim.

46. Grotius translated the entire Planudean Anthology in 1631, but, although it was well known in manuscript, his translation was not published until 1795. The Palatine manuscript was not published until 1772–76.

47. See Hutton, *Greek Anthology in Italy* and *Greek Anthology in France*.

48. See Braden, "Herrick and Lyric Poetry," pp. 196–213.

49. See Richlin, *Garden of Priapus*, pp. 47–52.

50. Hudson wryly observed, "To put the matter bluntly, the moment an epigram becomes very good—if it is not funny or too obviously ingenious—it is now in danger of being classed as a lyric" (*English Renaissance*, pp. 8–9). See also Paul Nixon, *Martial and the Modern Epigram* (New York: Longmans, Green, 1927), pp. 24–28.

51. See McEuen, *Tribe of Ben*, pp. 204–9, 218–20, 228, 233, 234–39, 243, 245–50, and Nixon, *Martial and the Modern Epigram*, p. 19.

52. The classical source for "To the Virgins" may be the closing distich of Ausonius's *Rosae:*

> Collige virgo rosas, dum flos noves, & novas pubes,
> Et memor esto aevum sic properare tuum.

Hudson suggests that Herrick may have been familiar with one of three Renaissance sources: Parkhurst's Latin poem "In Quasdam Eximia Forma Puellas, Nive Lusitantes," Kendall's translation "Of Certaine Faire Maydens Plaiying with Snowe" in *Flowers of epigrammes* (1577), or Edward May's free adaptation in his *Epigrams* (1633):

> You tender Virgins, fairer than the Snow
> with which you play.
> Note how it melts, thinke how the Roses grow,
> and how decay.

Just so does beauty fade, and age draw on,
Winter makes hast, and summer's quickly gone.
(Hudson, *English Renaissance*, pp. 101–2)

53. Hutton, *Greek Anthology in Italy*, p. 57; Colie, *Shakespeare's Living Art*, p. 81.

54. See Charles Clay Doyle, "Appendix D, Reprints, Translations, and Adaptations of More's Latin Poems in the Sixteenth and Seventeenth Centuries," in *The Complete Works of Saint Thomas More*, ed. Clarence H. Miller et al., vol. 3, pt. 2 (New Haven: Yale University Press, 1984), pp. 695–744. For a detailed discussion of the role of the Greek Anthology and of Thomas More in the sententious epigram tradition in the sixteenth century, see Mary Thomas Crane, "*Intret Cato:* Authority and the Epigram in Sixteenth-Century England," in *Renaissance Genres: Essays on Theory, History, and Interpretation*, ed. Barbara Kiefer Lewalski, Harvard English Studies, 14 (Cambridge: Harvard University Press, 1986), pp. 158–86. Furthermore, James A. Riddell has noted the influence of Thomas More's *Epigrammata* on Jonson in "The Arrangement of Ben Jonson's *Epigrammes*," *SEL* 27 (1987): 53–70.

55. All references to and translations of More's Latin epigrams will be to the Yale edition, vol. 3, pt. 2.

56.   Nos uelet instabiles uentus quatit omnis aristas,
         Quolibet impellunt spes, dolor, ira, metus.
         Nil habet in rebus pondus mortalibus ullum,
         Momento pudor est, si moueare leui.

[As every wind strikes and bends ears of grain, so hope and grief and wrath and fear drive us where they will. In the affairs of mortals nothing has real weight. You should be ashamed if you are moved by a light touch.]

57. Four of these (nos. 259, 263–65) are personal epigrams, probably written after 1518; four are replies to Brixius's *Antimorus* (nos. 266–69); and the remaining three are on a variety of topics (nos. 260–62).

58. In the Yale edition, the numeration of the *Epigrammata* begins with nineteen, since the *Progymnasmata* precedes the *Epigrammata*. For a discussion of the coronation poem, see Clarence H. Miller, "The Epigrams of More and Erasmus," in *Works*, vol. 3, pt. 2:42–46.

59. Three of More's political epigrams are translations from the Greek Anthology: Epigrams 25, 39, and 142.

60. The editors of the Yale edition count 23 political epigrams (*Works*, vol. 3, pt. 2:62). Damian Grace, "Thomas More's *Epigrammata:* Political Theory in a Poetic Idiom," *Parergon* 3 (1985): 115–29, counts 31. Grace's article examines More's decision to collect the epigrams and publish them as one work. He reaches a conclusion about the *Epigrammata* as a consciously political and

consciously integrated text that is very close to mine. Of particular interest is his tracing of ironic echoes of the coronation epigram throughout the rest of the epigrams.

61. Richard Marius, *Thomas More: A Biography* (New York: Knopf, 1985), p. 246.

62. Fowler dated the poem by its title, "D. Thomae Mori Tetrastichon ab ipso conscriptum, triennio antequam mortem oppeteret." The poem appears in three manuscripts, including Nicholas Harpsfield's biography of More, which he presented to Roper in 1557 or 1558, and in each case is attributed to More. See *Works*, vol. 3, pt. 2:67, 424.

63. See *Works*, vol. 3, pt. 2:424.

64. *The Metamorphosis of Ajax*, ed. Elizabeth Story Donno (London: Routledge & Kegan Paul, 1962), pp. 99–101. "The first was, when the King sent to him to know if he had chaunged his mind; he answered, yea: the King sent straight a counseller to him, to take his subscription to the sixe Articles. Oh sayd he, I have not changed my mind in that matter, but onely in this; I thought to have sent for a Barber, to have bene shaven ere I had died, but now if it please the King, he shal cut off head, and beard, and all together. But the other was milder, and pretier; for after this, one coming to him as of good will, to tell him he must prepare him to die, for he could not live: he called for his urinall, and having made water in it, he cast it, & viewed it (as Physicians do) a pretie while; at last he sware soberly, that he saw nothing in that mans water, but that he might live, if it pleased the King; a pretie saying, both to note his owne innocencie, and move the Prince to mercie."

65. Leicester Bradner, Charles A. Lynch, and Revilo P. Oliver, "Subjects and Themes," in *Works* vol. 3, pt. 2:62.

66. Epigrams 109, 114, 115, 201, and 243.

67. Epigrams 21, 23, 112, and 115.

FOUR The English Models

1. Gabriel Harvey, *Marginalia*, ed. G. C. Moore Smith (Stratford upon Avon: Shakespeare Head Press, 1913), pp. 233–34. The same point was made in the mid-seventeenth century by Anthony à Wood, *Atheniae Oxonienses*, ed. Philip Bliss, 4 vols., 3d ed. (1813; reprint, New York: Burt Franklin, 1967), 1: 351. See also Robert Carl Johnson, *John Heywood* (New York: Twayne, 1976), p. 17.

Heywood was also the grandfather of John Donne, another epigrammatist. On Donne's nineteen epigrams, see M. Thomas Hester, "Reading Donne's Epigrams: 'Raderus'/'Ralphius,'" *Papers on Language and Literature* 21 (1985): 324–30.

2. Francis Meres is quoted in the introduction to Heywood, *Works and*

Miscellaneous Short Poems, ed. Burton A. Milligan (Urbana: University of Illinois Press, 1956), pp. 3, 5. The rest of Meres' short list runs "Drante, Kendal, Bastard, Dauies." Further references to Heywood's poems will be to this edition.

3. Sir John Davies, *The Poems,* ed. Robert Krueger (Oxford: Clarendon Press, 1975). Further references to Davies' poems will be to this edition.

4. Sir John Harington, *The Metamorphosis of Ajax,* ed. Elizabeth Story Donno (London: Routledge & Kegan Paul, 1962), pp. 102–3.

5. John Davies of Hereford's epigram "To olde Iohn Heywood the Epigrammatist, wheresoeuer," included in his *Scourge of Folly* (1611), begins:

> Olde Heywood, haue with thee in His od vaine
> That yet with Booke-sellers, as new doth remaine.
> New poets sing riming, but thy Rymes aduance
> Themselues in light measures: for thus they doe dance.
>
> (p. 137)

6. Compare Herrick's "The Tythe. To the Bride" (H-581) with Heywood's "The account of a mans children" (5.27). See A. Leigh DeNeef, "Herrick and John Heywood," *Notes and Queries* 17 (1970): 408.

7. According to Johnson, Heywood probably remained in England for about five years after Mary's death in 1558.

8. Puttenham in *The Arte of English Poesie* (1589) said that "Iohn Heywood the Epigrammatist who for myrth and quicknesse of his conceits more then for any good learning [that] was in him came to be well benefited by the king" (quoted in Milligan, *Works,* p. 4). Jean McMahon Humez in "The Manners of Epigram: A Study of the Epigram Volumes of Martial, Harington, and Jonson" (Ph.D. diss., Yale University, 1971), pp. 177–200, argues that the persona of the jester is the defining characteristic of the English epigram tradition, but that Jonson made the jester the focus of *attack* in his *Epigrammes.*

9. In a discussion of George Herbert's "Outlandish Proverbs," James Thorpe has remarked that "we are dealing with a genre that has had, despite its importance, surprisingly little scholarly attention." "Lines of inquiry" which Thorpe suggests that would be particularly applicable to Heywood are the Old Testament Book of Proverbs and the *Adagia* of Erasmus: "Reflections and Self-Reflections: 'Outlandish Proverbs' as a Context for George Herbert's Other Writings," in *Illustrious Evidence: Approaches to English Literature of the Early Seventeenth Century,* ed. Earl Miner (Berkeley and Los Angeles: University of California Press, 1975), p. 27.

10. Heywood also wrote a long allegorical poem, *The Spider and the Fly,* which he considered his masterpiece. Although it was not published until 1556, after Mary became queen, it may have been inspired by "The Pilgrimage of Grace" (September 1536), an armed protest in the North against the dissolu-

235

tion of the monasteries. It also deals allegorically with civil unrest, especially attacking enclosure and rising rents. In the allegory, the flies are probably the Catholics, the spiders are probably the Protestants, but Mary is certainly the Maid who solves their disputes. See Johnson, *John Heywood*, pp. 26–28, 58–68.

11. John Heath, *Two Centuries of Epigrams* (London, 1610), p. B₈. According to Drummond of Hawthornden, Jonson classed Heath's poems with John Taylor the Water Poet's in the category of popular trash (*Works*, ed. C. H. Herford and P. and E. Simpson [Oxford: Clarendon Press, 1947], 8:582).

12. James Gairdner, *Lollardy and the Reformation in England: An Historical Survey*, 4 vols. (London: Macmillan, 1908), 2:411.

13. Jack D. Winner, "Ben Jonson's *Epigrammes* and the Conventions of Formal Verse Satire," *SEL* 23 (1983): 61–76.

14. Joseph Hall, *The Collected Poems*, ed. A. Davenport (Liverpool: University Press of Liverpool, 1949).

15. *A Transcript of the Registers of the Company of Stationers of London between 1554–1640*, ed. Edward Arber, 5 vols. (London: Priv. print., 1875–77), 3: 677–78.

16. George Puttenham, *Arte of English Poesie* (Menston, England: Scolar Press, 1968), bk. 1, chap. xxvii, p. 43.

17. See Amy Richlin, *The Garden of Priapus: Sexuality and Aggression in Roman Humor* (New Haven: Yale University Press, 1983), pp. 81–104, and Antoinette B. Dauber, "Herrick's Foul Epigrams," *Genre* 9 (1976–77): 87–102, on the "anality" of epigrams.

18. Such epigrams were attached to priapic statues and were widely attributed to Vergil in the seventeenth century. See John Penkethman, *The epigrams of P. Virgilius Maro* (London, 1624).

19. Hoyt Hopewell Hudson, *The Epigram in the English Renaissance* (Princeton: Princeton University Press, 1947), p. 163.

20. Epigram collections were often arranged as calendars, an association that has interesting connotations for *Hesperides*.

21. This "timeliness" is a distant relation of the "timeliness" that More felt the epigrams should have for the king.

22. See John Owen, *Epigrammatum*, ed. John R. C. Martyn, Textus minores, 49 (Leiden: E. J. Brill, 1976), and Leicester Bradner, *Musae Anglicanae: A History of Anglo-Latin Poetry (1500–1925)* (New York: MLA; London: Oxford University Press, 1940), pp. 86–90.

23. Herford and Simpson, 1:138.

24. Everard Guilpin called Davies "our English Martiall" in *Skialetheia* (1598), epigram 20.

25. Thomas May prefaced his translation of *Selected Epigrams of Martial* (1629) by saying, "The Translation of these Epigramms is a thing (Reader) which I confess for divers Reasons I was loath to publish. . . . because it is

more than probable, that divers Gentlemen have exercised or pleased them-
selues in translating some of these, and may therefore peruse mine with a
more rigid censure."

26. Davies, *Poems*, p. ix.

27. As a member of the Society of Antiquarians, Davies gave a learned
paper on the epitaph, arguing for a broad latitude in its composition and
comparing the epitaph to its closely related form, the epigram: "the only
Rule that is observ'd in them is that which is Required in an Epigrame, Witt
and brevitie" (*Poems*, p. xliii). Davies' own epigrams were usually composed
of quatrains, often joined together to form loose sonnets. An interesting companion piece to Davies' epigrams are his Gulling Sonnets that mock by indi-
rection the "sweet" member of the twinned forms. Rosalie Colie remarked
that in Davies' *Epigrams* "we see that the sonnet-form and sonnet-language
have fused remarkably with epigrammatic and satiric modes. Davies was
officially a sonneteer and an epigrammatist; in his book of epigrams, the first
poem . . . is on the epigram, and is a quatorzain" (*Shakespeare's Living Art*
[Princeton: Princeton University Press, 1974], p. 90).

28. In this, too, Bastard may have been imitating Martial, since Martial
mentions in epigram 7.5 that his first seven books were published as a single
volume.

29. See, for example, John Heath, *Two Centuries*, 1.15; and John Davies of
Hereford, *Scourge of Folly* (London, 1611), epigram 106.

30. Harington said in 1607 that he intended Queen Elizabeth to be a special audience for his epigrams against married clergy, since he knew her dis-
like of the practice. Her agreement made him bolder in attacking "somwhat
unhappily, but rather plesantly than maliciously against preists marriages."
In 1607 Harington engaged in a controversy with Bishop Hall over the
marriage of clergy. See D. H. Craig, *Sir John Harington* (Boston: Twayne,
1985), p. 92, and M. H. M. MacKinnon, "Sir John Harington and Bishop
Hall," *Philological Quarterly* 37 (1958): 80–94.

31. Harington's running argument with Bastard is continued in other
poems. See *The Letters and Epigrams*, ed. Norman E. McClure (Philadelphia:
University of Pennsylvania Press, 1930), no. 359, and *Chrestoleros* 1.16.

32. Thomas Bastard, *The Poems English and Latin*, ed. Alexander B. Grosart, Occasional Issues (Printed for the Subscribers, 1880), p. xli.

33. See McClure no. 61; see also nos. 15, 22, 79, 110, 122, 126, 134, 257, 315, 386,
and 410.

34. Craig, *Sir John Harington*, p. 89. See McClure nos. 30, 182, 198, 326, and
388.

35. Humez, "Manners of Epigram," p. 177.

36. In 1602 Harington sent his epigrams as a Christmas present to James in
Scotland, along with an ingenious lantern of gold, silver, brass, and iron.

There is a watercolor of this lantern at the end of Folger MS Va. 249. See Craig, *Sir John Harington*, p. 25.

37. Harington's letter to Sir Hugh Portman (Oct. 9, 1601), McClure, p. 90.

38. Norman McClure discovered a rough draft of the manuscript at the British Library in 1929 (Addit. MS 12049). He conjectured that Harington had prepared it for presentation to Prince Henry. (A fair copy of the presentation manuscript has since been identified at the Folger Library [Va. 249].) McClure did not, however, use the manuscript as the basis for his edition but relied instead on the posthumous 1618 edition of Harington's epigrams. McClure's edition, then, the only modern edition of Harington's poems, does not reflect Harington's own arrangement of his epigrams into four complete centuries. Instead, McClure included almost all of the poems found only in the manuscript but not in the 1618 edition in a group at the end of his edition. See McClure, pp. 37, 126, 404–5; Humez, "Manners of Epigram," pp. 201–9; Craig, *Sir John Harington*, pp. 94–95.

McClure omitted four poems in the Prince Henry manuscript altogether. For these and for the differences between the mock-up and fair copies, see R. H. Miller, "Unpublished Poems by Sir John Harington," *English Literary Renaissance* 14 (1984): 148–58.

39. Harington presented Henry with a number of his works. In 1604 he sent James a translation of book 6 of the *Aeneid* with a commentary for Henry's use. He also sent Henry a series of entertaining letters about the adventures of his remarkable dog, Bungey. In 1608 Harington presented Henry with *A Supplie or Addicion to the Catalogue of Bishops* and in 1609 sent him his translation of *Orlando Furioso* accompanied by another amusing letter. See Craig, *Sir John Harington*, pp. 27–29.

40. I am indebted to Humez, "Manners of Epigram," pp. 227–29 and to Craig, *Sir John Harington*, pp. 94–95, for pointing out that "Of Treason" and "Of Monsters" precede "A Tragicall Epigram" in Folger MS Va. 249.

41. See Peter Beal, *Index of English Literary Manuscripts*, vol. 1, pt. 2 (London: Mansell; New York: Bowker, 1980). Beal lists, for example, fourteen appearances of "A Tragicall Epigram."

42. Joan Ozark [Holmer], "Fairy Poetry in the Early Seventeenth Century" (Ph.D. diss., Princeton University, 1973); Alfred Pollard, ed., *The Hesperides and Noble Numbers*, 2 vols., Muses' Library (New York: Scribner; London: Lawrence & Bullen, 1891), 2:305–11; W. J. Courthope, *A History of English Poetry* (1903; reprint, New York: Russell & Russell, 1962), 3:262–65; F. W. Moorman, *Robert Herrick: A Biographical and Critical Study* (1910; reprint, New York: Russell & Russell, 1962), pt. 2, chap. 3; Floris Delattre, *English Fairy Poetry from the Origins to the Seventeenth Century* (London: Henry Frowde; Paris: Henri Didier, 1912), pp. 147–87; K. M. Briggs, *The Anatomy of Puck* (London: Routledge & Kegan Paul, 1959), pp. 56–70; and

Norman K. Farmer, Jr., "Robert Herrick and 'King Oberon's Clothing': New Evidence for Attribution," *Yearbook of English Studies* 1 (1971): 68–77.

An interesting comparison could be made, too, of Drayton's *Muses' Elisium* (1630) and Herrick's "The Apparition of his Mistresse calling him to Elizium" (publ. 1640). Drayton's "Elisium" is a portrayal of retreat from an Iron Age in "Once faire *Felicia*, . . . now quite defac'd" (10.5) into pure poetry. Herrick's poem dramatizes a failure to escape—or the impossibility of escape.

Jonathan Post has traced in the 1651 *Olor Iscanus* of Herrick's younger contemporary Henry Vaughan a deconstruction of the pastoral stance similar to Herrick's. Post finds in Vaughan's career a pattern of crisis and change—as disturbing political realities shocked Vaughan into lyric poetry—that is almost a reverse image of Herrick's volume. See Jonathan F. S. Post, *Henry Vaughan: The Unfolding Vision* (Princeton: Princeton University Press, 1982).

43. Michael Drayton, *Works*, ed. J. William Hebel, 5 vols. (Oxford: Shakespeare Head Press, 1941), 5: 137–38.

44. I am indebted to Alastair Fowler in *Kinds of Literature: An Introduction to the Theory of Genres and Modes* (Cambridge: Harvard University Press, 1982), p. 185, for drawing my attention to Drayton's liminal poem.

45. Drayton, *Works*, 2:310.

46. According to the *OED*, in the seventeenth century "libertine" could mean "one who goes his own way."

47. Arthur Marotti, in "'Love is not Love': Elizabethan Sonnet Sequences and the Social Order," *ELH* 49 (1982): 396–428, has proposed a social theory of sonnet sequences that sheds a significant light on Drayton's shifting stance away from the sonnet and toward the epigram, and that has important implications as well for the epigram book as a genre.

FIVE "Father Ben": Jonson's *Epigrammes, The Forrest,* and *Under-wood*

1. Ben Jonson, *Works*, ed. C. H. Herford and P. and E. Simpson (Oxford: Clarendon Press, 1925), 1:133.

2. Herford and Simpson, 8:16.

3. I am indebted to Jean McMahon Humez, "The Manners of Epigram: A Study of the Epigram Volumes of Martial, Harington, and Jonson" (Ph.D. diss., Yale University, 1971), p. 263, for pointing out the proximity of these publication dates and Jonson's possible sense of rivalry.

4. See Harington's "A Preface, or rather a Briefe Apologie of Poetrie," the preface to his translation of *Orlando Furioso* (1591). He says there, "as for the Pastorall with the Sonnet or Epigramme, though many times they sauour of wantonnesse and loue and toying, and now and then breaking the rules of Poetrie, go into plaine scurrilitie, yet euen the worst of them may be not ill applied, and are, I must confesse, too delightfull, in so much as *Martial* saith,

Laudant illa, sed ista legunt.

[Those they praise, but they read the others.]

and in another place,

> *Erubuit posuitque meum Lucrecia librum:*
> *Sed coram Bruto. Brute recede, leget.*

[Lucretia blushed and laid down my volume; but Brutus was present. Brutus, go away: she will read it.]

(Ludovico Ariosto, *Orlando Furioso in English heroical verse* by John Harington, 2d imprint [London: R. Field for J. Norton and S. Waterson, 1607], [vi_r].)

5. See, for example, Jonson's epigram "On Court-Parrat," (*Epigrammes*, 71):

> To plucke downe mine, *Poll* sets up new wits still,
> Still, 'tis his lucke to praise me 'gainst his will.

Jonson probably intended this as a gibe against Henry Parrot, author of a number of epigram books. See Mark Eccles, "Jonson and the Spies," *Review of English Studies* 13 (1937): 388, and Joseph Loewenstein, "The Jonsonian Corpulence, or The Poet as Mouthpiece," *ELH* 53 (1986): 500–504.

6. All citations from Jonson's poetry will be from *The Complete Poetry*, ed. William B. Hunter, Jr. (New York: Norton, 1963).

7. Several times in *Under-wood* Jonson makes this strategy explicit. In an epigram in honor of "Lord Bacons Birth-day" (53), for example, Jonson concludes:

> Give me a deep-crown'd-Bowle, that I may sing
> In raysing him the wisdome of my King.

or in the "Epithalamion" for Jerome Weston:

> All is a story of the King and Queene!
> And what of Dignitie, and Honour may
> Be duly done to those
> Whom they have chose,
> And set the marke upon
> To give a greater Name, and Title to! Their owne!
>
> . . . .
>
> . . . for when a noble Nature's rais'd,
> It brings Friends Joy, Foes Griefe, Posteritie Fame;
> In him the times, no lesse then Prince, are prais'd.
> (77, ll. 91–96, 113–15)

8. On Jonson and classical imitation, including imitations specifically of Martial, see Richard S. Peterson, *Imitation and Praise in the Poems of Ben Jonson* (New Haven: Yale University Press, 1981); Thomas M. Greene, *The Light in Troy: Imitation and Discovery in Renaissance Poetry* (New Haven: Yale University Press, 1982); and Loewenstein, "The Poet as Mouthpiece," pp. 491–518.

9. Herford and Simpson, 2:348.

10. Hunter, pp. 3–4.

11. The final lines of "The Famous Voyage" make clear that Jonson has been thinking of Harington:

> In memorie of which most liquid deed,
> The citie since hath rais'd a Pyramide.
> And I could wish for their eterniz'd sakes,
> My *Muse* had plough'd with his, that sung *A-jax*.
>   (ll. 193–96)

12. See David Wykes, "Ben Jonson's 'Chaste Booke'–The *Epigrammes*," *Renaissance and Modern Studies* 13 (1969): 76–98.

13. Edward Partridge, "Jonson's *Epigrammes:* The Named and the Nameless," *Studies in the Literary Imagination* 6 (1973): 153–98.

14. But in his copy of Martial, Jonson penned in next to Martial's epigram "In Gallam" (9.37) the notation, "vel Lu. Co: B." David McPherson in his "Ben Jonson's Library and Marginalia: An Annotated Catalogue," *Studies in Philology*, Texts and Studies 1974, 71, no. 5 (1974): 11, comments: "In the epigram the speaker insultingly refuses the lascivious advances of an aging lady. Could Jonson possibly be implying that he had enjoyed Lucy's favors but is now refusing them? The letters are not formed very clearly, and I could easily be mistaken in my reading. Furthermore, 'Lu. Co: B' could mean many things besides 'Lucy, Countess of Bedford.'" See also Arthur Marotti, "Donne, Lady Bedford, and the Poetry of Compliment," in *John Donne: Coterie Poet* (Madison: University of Wisconsin Press, 1986), pp. 202–32, 334–39.

15. Certainly any discussion of poetic influence and literary sonship must be indebted to Harold Bloom's *The Anxiety of Influence* (New York: Oxford University Press, 1973).

16. "The Silva Tradition in Jonson's *The Forrest*," in *Poetic Traditions of the English Renaissance,* ed. Maynard Mack and George deForest Lord (New Haven: Yale University Press, 1982), p. 176.

17. The general pattern of *Under-wood* also resembles *Hesperides.* Almost all of the lyric poems are in the first third of the book. The remaining two-thirds are made up primarily of epigrams, elegies, and epistles.

18. Annabel Patterson, *Censorship and Interpretation* (Madison: University of Wisconsin Press, 1984), p. 126.

19. See "An Epistle to Master John Selden," 16, ll. 19–28, and "An Epistle to a Friend," 39, ll. 19–33.

20. Patterson, *Censorship and Interpretation*, p. 135. I am deeply indebted throughout my discussion of *Under-wood* to Annabel Patterson's "Cries and Whispers: Self-expression in Jonson's *Under-wood*," in *Censorship and Interpretation*, pp. 126–44.

21. Thomas Campion, *The Works*, ed. Walter R. Davis (Garden City, N.Y.: Doubleday, 1967), p. 12. In the early Renaissance the madrigal was associated with the epigram, especially with the Greek Anthology. See Mario Praz, *The Flaming Heart* (1958; reprint, Gloucester, Mass.: Peter Smith, 1966), p. 208.

22. Again, in the preface "To the Reader" of *Two Bookes of Ayres* (n.d.; ca. 1612–13) Campion insists on the similarity of song and epigram: "Short Ayres, if they be skilfully framed, and naturally exprest, are like quicke and good Epigrammes in Poesie, many of them shewing as much artifice, and breeding as great difficultie, as a larger Poeme. . . . To conclude: mine owne opinion of these Songs I deliver thus:

> Omnia nec nostris bona sunt, sed nec mala libris;
> Si placet hac contes, hac quoque lege legas.
>   Farewell."

Campion's "owne opinion" is a version of Martial, 1.16 (*Works,* 55).

23. "A Critical Dissertation of Epigrams," *A Collection of Epigrams* (London: 1727), p. ix. The anonymous author is probably William Oldys.

24. Louise Schleiner, "Herrick's Songs and the Character of *Hesperides,*" *English Literary Renaissance* 6 (1976): 89.

25. See, for example, the Neo-Latin epigrams of Richard Bruch, *Epigrammatvm Hecatontades Dvae* (1627); Huntingdon Plumptre, *Epigrammaton Opvscvlvm Dvobvs Libellis Distinctvm* (1629); Arthur Johnson, *Epigrammata* (1632). An especially grand example is William Cheeke, *Anagrammata, et Chron-Anagrammata Regia* (1613).

26. John Davies, *The Scourge of Folly, Consisting of satyricall Epigramms, and others in honour of many noble and worthy Persons of our Land* (1611).

27. The author justifies his choice of the epigram by asking, "Why may I not then . . . iustly make a tryal if by the help at least of this tune, this manner of writing I meane, they may recouer their senses, especially since it is not the skilfulnesse of the Musitian, but the direct hitting the patients vayne, which workes the cure?" (p. 8). The conflation of the contradictory imagery of song with the images of satire ("the direct hitting the patients vayne") is indicative of the wider range of the epigram in the Caroline period.

28. Frank Livingston Huntley, "King James as Solomon, The Book of Proverbs, and Hall's *Characters,*" in *Essays in Persuasion: On Seventeenth-Century English Literature* (Chicago: University of Chicago Press, 1981), pp. 49–53.

29. *The Latin Poetry*, trans. Mark McCloskey and Paul R. Murphy (Athens: Ohio University Press, 1965), pp. 6–7.

SIX *Hesperides* and the Classical Epigram: Martial or Anacreon?

1. *The Complete Poems of Robert Herrick*, 3 vols., ed. Alexander Grosart, Early English Poets (London: Chatto & Windus, 1876), 1: cxxii.

2. Floris Delattre, "L'ordre et la chronologie des *Hespérides*," in *Robert Herrick: Contribution à l'étude de la poésie lyrique en Angleterre au dix-septième siècle* (Paris: Felix Alcan, 1911), pp. 482–91; Herrick, *The Poetical Works*, ed. L. C. Martin (Oxford: Clarendon Press, 1956), pp. xxxvii–xl. Martin is very tentative in suggesting a chronological ordering because the arrangement is so inconsistent; "nevertheless that order, intentionally or not, seems to have had some effect on the arrangement" (p. xxxvii).

3. See Richard Capwell, "Herrick and the Aesthetic Principle of Variety and Contrast," *South Atlantic Quarterly* 71 (1972): 488–95; Leah Jonas, "Robert Herrick and Thomas Carew," in *The Divine Science: The Aesthetic of Some Representative Seventeenth-Century Poets*, Columbia University Studies in English and Comparative Literature, no. 151 (New York: Columbia University Press, 1940), pp. 237–38; Camille Chemin, "Robert Herrick (1591–1674)," *Revue pédagogique* 63 (1913): 54–72; and Emile Legouis, "Robert Herrick (1591–1674)," *Revue des cours et conférences* (14 and 25 January 1912), 361–67, 490–501.

4. See Antoinette B. Dauber, "Herrick's Foul Epigrams," *Genre* 9 (1976): 87–102; A. Leigh DeNeef on the "sportive voice" and the "gnomic voice" in *"This Poetick Liturgie": Robert Herrick's Ceremonial Mode* (Durham, N.C.: Duke University Press, 1974), pp. 109–41; Robert W. Halli, Jr., "Robert Herrick's Epigrams on Commoners," *South Atlantic Bulletin* 43 (1978): 30–41; John L. Kimmey, "Robert Herrick's Satirical Epigrams," *English Studies* 2 (1970): 312–23; Helen Marlborough, "Herrick's Epigrams of Praise," in *"Trust to Good Verses": Herrick Tercentenary Essays*, ed. Roger Rollin and J. Max Patrick (Pittsburgh: University of Pittsburgh Press, 1978), pp. 159–69; and Claude Summers, "Herrick's Political Poetry: The Strategies of His Art," in *"Trust to Good Verses,"* pp. 171–83.

5. Dorothy Matthis Huson, "Robert Herrick's *Hesperides* Considered as an Organized Work" (Ph.D. diss., Michigan State University, 1972), argued that the various type sizes of titles in *Hesperides* signal the division of the book into seven sections, which, along with *Noble Numbers*, are meant to correspond to the eight books of Augustine's *Confessions*. Although her conclusion is unconvincing, the idea of the bold-faced titles as markers is intriguing. In every case, these poems are dedicated to the Stuarts.

6. As Braden himself points out, Martial did not number his poems. The double integer reference was a contribution of the Renaissance epigram book tradition.

7. Braden does recognize the continuing tradition within which Herrick is working: "Standing between Herrick and Martial is the huge corpus of Renaissance epigrams, in which the Roman form is generalized to purposes that do not have much to do with the original specimens—purposes that, for example, Herrick's sententious epigrams, which have little precedent in Martial, are intended to serve. It is in terms of other traditions than the Roman that Herrick's epigrammatic practice is best, or at least most charitably understood" (*The Classics and English Renaissance Poetry: Three Case Studies* [New Haven: Yale University Press, 1978], p. 193). It is clear, however, that he does not place much value on that tradition.

8. Herrick's epigram "To his Booke" (H-7), for example,

> Come thou not neere those men, who art like *Bread*
> O're-leven'd; or like *Cheese* o're-renetted

is indebted to Harington's epigram comparing a book with cheese (4.72), an epigram that he, in turn, borrowed from Heywood (1.92).

9. Braden does not note this borrowing. Martin notes the parallels between three lines of Martial's poem and three lines of Herrick's (p. 498).

10. DeNeef, "*This Poetick Liturgie*," pp. 24–26, and Roger B. Rollin, *Robert Herrick* (New York: Twayne, 1966), p. 27. But Rosalie Colie has recognized the generic tension that the poem establishes: "Herrick's pastoral muse is conceived as yearning for her generic and dialectic opposite, the city, even as the poet, discontented occasionally in Devon, has settled for Devon and its natural beauty" (*The Resources of Kind: Genre-Theory in the Renaissance*, ed. Barbara K. Lewalski [Berkeley and Los Angeles: University of California Press, 1973], p. 26).

11. Peter Howell's translation, *A Commentary on Book One of the Epigrams of Martial* (London: Athlone Press, 1980).

12. See Norman K. Farmer, Jr., "Herrick's Hesperidean Garden: 'ut pictura poesis' Applied," in "*Trust to Good Verses*," pp. 15–52, where he discusses the frontispiece at length. He argues that it signals the "uniquely iconic quality" of Herrick's poetry, a quality he attributes to his theory that Herrick "consciously developed a poetic technique compatible with the operation of [the visual] imaginative faculties" (pp. 22, 47). I would argue that the iconic quality of Herrick's poems results more from their genre than from a theory of the visual arts. On the Renaissance frontispiece in general, see Margery Corbett and Ronald Lightbown, *The Comely Frontispiece: The Emblematic Title-Page in England, 1550–1660* (London: Henly; Boston: Routledge & Kegan Paul, 1979).

The seventeenth century saw a new interest in statuary, monuments, and their inscriptions. Thomas Howard, earl of Arundel, whose collection of marble statues was legendary, was particularly interested in the meaning of their inscriptions. These were deciphered by Sir Robert Cotton and John Selden, among others, and published in Selden's *Marmora Arundelliana* (1628). See Graham Parry, *The Golden Age Restor'd: The Culture of the Stuart Court, 1603–1642* (Manchester: Manchester University Press, 1981), pp. 108–36. Farmer suggested (p. 34) that Herrick saw the Arundel marbles and modeled some of his poems on them, and that the phrase "the white temple of my heroes" specifically refers to the marbles.

13.   Tempora cinxisset Foliorum densior umbra:
          Debetur Genio Laurea Sylva tuo.
        Tempora et Illa Tibi mollis redimîsset Olivia;
          Scilicet excludis Versibus Arma tuis.
        Admisces Antiqua Novis, Jocunda Severis:
          Hinc Juvenis discat, Foemina, Virgo, Senex
        Ut solo minores Phoebo, sic majores Unus
          Omnibus Ingenio, Mente Lepore, Stylo.

        [A denser shade of leaves thy brows should bind;
        A laurel grove is due to such a mind.
        The peaceful olive should those brows entwine,
        For arms are banished from such verse as thine.
        Old things with new thou blendest, grave with gay:
        Hence young and old, mother and maid may say,
        Phoebus except, all else thou dost outvie
        In style and beauty, and capacity.]

(Grosart's translation, cited in *The Complete Poetry of Robert Herrick*, ed. J. Max Patrick [New York: New York University Press, 1963], p. 8.) The poem is signed I.H.C.W.M. Martin, p. 498, and Patrick agree that it is almost certainly by John Harmar of the College of Westminster (c. 1594–1670), who became Professor of Greek at Oxford during the Commonwealth. Among his numerous works is an apology for Bishop Williams. He is also credited by Thomas Philipot (*Poems*, 1646, ed. L. C. Martin [Liverpool: University Press of Liverpool, 1950], p. 34) with knowledge of medicine.

    Herrick wrote an epigram late in *Hesperides* (H-966) "To his learned friend Master John Harmar, Phisitian to the Colledge of Westminster," comparing Harmar's skill in the Latin epigram with Martial's:

        When first I find those Numbers thou do'st write;
        To be most soft, terce, sweet, and perpolite:
        Next, when I see Thee towring in the skie,
        In an expansion no less large, then high;
        Then, in that compass, sayling here and there,
        And with Circumgyration every where;
        Following with love and active heate thy game,

> And then at last to truss the Epigram;
> I must confess, distinction none I see
> Between *Domitians Martiall* then, and Thee.
> But this I know, should *Jupiter* agen
> Descend from heaven, to re-converse with men;
> The Romane Language full, and superfine,
> If *Iove* wo'd speake, he wo'd accept of thine.

For the engraver, William Marshall, see *DNB*; Farmer, "Herrick's Hesperidean Garden," pp. 17–33; and *A Milton Encyclopedia*, ed. William B. Hunter, Jr., 9 vols. (Lewisburg: Bucknell University Press; London: Associated University Presses, 1978–83), 4: 96–97, 6: 204–6.

14. Martial, 11.16, ll. 9–10:

> erubuit posuitque meum Lucretia librum,
> sed corum Bruto; Brute, recede: leget.

[Lucretia blushed and laid down my volume; but Brutus was present. Brutus, go away: she will read it.]

15. Herrick does not quote Ovid exactly. Ovid's line reads, "defugiunt avidos carmina sola rogos."

16. See Robert Halli, Jr., "Vitalizing Immortality: Robert Herrick's '*His Age,*'" *Renaissance Papers 1984*, ed. Dale B. J. Randall and Joseph A. Porter (Durham, N.C.: Southeastern Renaissance Conference, 1985), pp. 47–55, and Achsah Guibbory, "'*No lust theres like to Poetry*': Herrick's Passion for Poetry," in "*Trust to Good Verses,*" pp. 79–87.

17. See Earl Miner, *The Cavalier Mode from Jonson to Cotton* (Princeton: Princeton University Press, 1971), pp. 250–305, on the importance of friendship in Cavalier poetry.

SEVEN The *Hesperides* of Herrick's "Saints" and "Heroes"

1. A notable exception is Roger Rollin's discussion in *Robert Herrick* (New York: Twayne, 1966), pp. 35–37, which stresses the pagan nature of this ceremony at Herrick's father's grave. Herrick's paganism is always disturbing and always requires some adjustment on the reader's part. It is particularly disturbing and revealing here at the grave of his father, dead by his own hand.

2. Rollin uses "This Sacred Grove," a phrase from the epigram "TO THE QUEENE" (H-265), as the running subtitle for all his chapters but does not discuss the epigrams of praise specifically. DeNeef treats them briefly in "*This Poetick Liturgie*": *Robert Herrick's Ceremonial Mode* (Durham, N.C.: Duke University Press, 1974), pp. 100–108, under the rubric of "The Functionary Voice." An interesting exception to the neglect of the epigrams of praise is Avon Jack Murphy's use of some of them, particularly the poems to Jonson,

as evidence that the persona of *Hesperides* is a "sound literary critic as well as a successful poet" who gains confidence in his own ability as the volume progresses: "Robert Herrick: The Self-conscious Critic in *Hesperides*," in *"Trust to Good Verses": Herrick Tercentenary Essays,* ed. Roger Rollin and J. Max Patrick (Pittsburgh: University of Pittsburgh Press, 1978), pp. 53–63.

3. Helen Marlborough, "Herrick's Epigrams of Praise," in *"Trust to Good Verses,"* pp. 159–69.

4. The metaphor of the "Hesperides" constellation as symbolic of the "Immortalls" who will *"circumspangle this my spacious Sphere"* is initiated in the prefatory poem to Prince Charles (who is styled there as the star of Hesperus) and appears frequently throughout the book. See, for example, H-146, -444, and -804, and see John L. Kimmey's close reading of "To the Most Illustrious, and Most Hopefull Prince, Prince CHARLES, Prince of Wales" in "Studies in Cavalier Poetry," *English Studies Collection* 2 (1977): 1–25.

5. In 1974, for instance, the three-hundredth anniversary of Herrick's death, two book-length studies of Herrick appeared, both of which emphasized the ceremonial aspects of *Hesperides:* A. Leigh DeNeef's *"This Poetick Liturgie": Robert Herrick's Ceremonial Mode* and Robert H. Deming's *Ceremony and Art: Robert Herrick's Poetry,* De Proprietatibus Litterarum, Series Practica, 64 (The Hague: Mouton, 1974).

6. Deming discusses "love's religion" in *Ceremony and Art,* pp. 90–98. See also H. M. Richmond, *The School of Love: The Evolution of the Stuart Love Lyric* (Princeton: Princeton University Press, 1964). The best example of "love's religion" in *Hesperides* is "To Groves" (H-499), a "Legend of those Saints / That di'd for love." Herrick's choice of saints is entirely pagan.

7. Leah Sinanoglou Marcus, *Childhood and Cultural Despair: A Theme and Variations in Seventeenth-Century Literature* (Pittsburgh: University of Pittsburgh Press, 1978); "Herrick's *Hesperides* and the 'Proclamation made for May,'" *Studies in Philology* 76 (1979): 49–74; "Herrick's *Noble Numbers* and the Politics of Playfulness," *English Literary Renaissance* 7 (1977): 108–26.

8. See Annabel Patterson, *Censorship and Interpretation: The Conditions of Writing and Reading in Early Modern England* (Madison: University of Wisconsin Press, 1984), pp. 45–46, 105–7, 171–72.

9. *The Complete Poems of Robert Herrick,* 3 vols., ed. Alexander Grosart, Early English Poets (London: Chatto & Windus, 1876), 1: xvi–xx.

10. See Floris Delattre, "L'ordre et la chronologie des *Hesperides*," in *Robert Herrick: Contribution à l'étude de la poésie lyrique en Angleterre au dix-septième siècle* (Paris: Felix Alcan, 1911), pp. 482–91; Herrick, *The Poetical Works,* ed. L. C. Martin (Oxford: Clarendon Press, 1956), pp. xxxvi–xl; and Richard L. Capwell, "Herrick and the Aesthetic Principle of Variety and Contrast," *South Atlantic Quarterly* 71 (1972): 488–95.

11. See Clarendon, *The History of the Rebellion and the Civil Wars in En-*

gland, ed. W. Dunn Macray, 6 vols. (Oxford: Clarendon Press, 1888), 3:214; 6:399–401, and Oldisworth in the *DNB.*

12. Herrick addresses an epigram earlier in *Hesperides* to the earl of Pembroke, and Montgomerie (H-359) praising his generosity to poets:

> Others there be, who righteously will swear
> Those smooth-pac't Numbers, amble every where;
> And these brave Measures go a stately trot;
> Love those, like these; regard, reward them not.
> But you my Lord, are One, whose hand along
> Goes with your mouth, or do's outrun your tongue;
> Paying before you praise; and cockring wit,
> Give both the Gold and Garland unto it.

Herrick's terms of praise are actually rather audacious, since Pembroke was infamous for his violent language, which necessitated the king's interference on several occasions and, during the civil war, added fuel to the royalists' attempts to discredit him.

13. See Marchette Chute, *Two Gentle Men: The Lives of George Herbert and Robert Herrick* (New York: Dutton, 1959), passim, and Martin, p. 528.

14. I am indebted to Annabel Patterson for this observation.

15. F. W. Moorman, *Robert Herrick: A Biographical and Critical Study* (1910; reprint, New York: Russell & Russell, 1962), p. 88, believed the poem was written on the occasion of Porter's brother's death. An anonymous review of Moorman's book in *Athenaeum,* 14 May 1910, p. 576, points this out as Moorman's one error of fact. Both L. C. Martin and J. Max Patrick in their editions of Herrick are "almost certain" that the poem was occasioned by William Herrick's death (pp. 515 and 104, respectively).

16. Noted by Patrick, p. 104.

17. See James S. Tillman, "Herrick's Georgic Encomia," in *"Trust to Good Verses,"* pp. 149–57; DeNeef, *"This Poetick Liturgie,"* pp. 31–35; Paul Jenkins, "Rethinking What Moderation Means to Robert Herrick," *ELH* 39 (1972): 49–65; Rollin, *Robert Herrick,* pp. 70–76; Maren-Sofie Røstvig, *The Happy Man: Studies in the Metamorphosis of a Classical Ideal,* rev. ed., Oslo Studies in English, 2 (Oslo: Norwegian University Press, 1962), vol. 1, *1600–1700,* passim; G. R. Hibbard, "The Country House Poem of the Seventeenth Century," *Journal of the Warburg and Courtauld Institutes* 19 (1956): 159–74.

18. See Karl Josef Höltgren, "Herrick, the Wheeler Family, and Quarles," *Review of English Studies* 16 (1965): 399–405. Patrick (p. 65) repeats Martin's speculation that Elizabeth Wheeler was a cousin of Herrick's and does not note Höltgren's discovery.

EIGHT The Mocking Epigrams

1. See, for example, Robert Southey, *Southey's Commonplace Book*, ed. John Wood Warter, Fourth Series (London: Longman, Brown, Green, & Longmans, 1851), pp. 303–5; Edmund W. Gosse, "Robert Herrick," *Cornhill Magazine* 32 (1875): 190–91; Alexander Grosart, ed., "Memorial-Introduction," to *The Complete Poems of Robert Herrick*, 3 vols., Early English Poets (London: Chatto & Windus, 1876), 1: cxx–cxxiii and cxxviii; Floris Delattre, *Robert Herrick: Contribution à l'étude de la poésie lyrique en Angleterre au dix-septième siècle* (Paris: Felix Alcan, 1911), pp. 148–49; M. L. S. Lossing, "Herrick: His Epigrams and Lyrics," *University of Toronto Quarterly* 2 (1933): 239–54.

2. Robert Southey, *Lives of the Uneducated Poets* (London: John Murray, 1831), p. 83.

3. Richard J. Ross, "'A Wild Civility': Robert Herrick's Poetic Solution of the Paradox of Art and Nature" (Ph.D. diss., University of Michigan, 1958).

4. John L. Kimmey, "Robert Herrick's Satirical Epigrams," *English Studies* 51 (1970): 312–23.

5. A. Leigh DeNeef, *"This Poetick Liturgie": Robert Herrick's Ceremonial Mode* (Durham, N.C.: Duke University Press, 1974), pp. 109–25.

6. Antoinette B. Dauber, "Herrick's Foul Epigrams," *Genre* 9 (1976–77): 87–102.

7. Robert W. Halli, Jr., "Robert Herrick's Epigrams on Commoners," *South Atlantic Bulletin* 43 (1978): 30–41.

8. Floris Delattre, "Les Paysans du Devonshire," in *Robert Herrick*, pp. 146–53.

9. Patrick's gloss, in *The Complete Poetry of Robert Herrick* (New York: New York University Press, 1963), p. 306.

10. Peter Stallybrass, "'Wee feaste in our Defense': Patrician Carnival in Early Modern England and Robert Herrick's 'Hesperides,'" *English Literary Renaissance* 53 (1986): 247. Stallybrass's use of Herrick in his argument is partial in other ways as well. He discusses at length, for example, the way that the Saint Distaffs Day and Candlemas Day poems "balance" "Twelfe night" (H-1035). But he does not make it clear that "Twelfe night" is the last of the ceremonial poems in *Hesperides*, so that the book ends not with an assertion of proper order but with misrule. In another instance, Stallybrass asserts that "Herrick's 'Ceremonies' are not innocent. He wants ceremony for the sake of conformity," but Stallybrass cites as evidence only the first line of the epigram "Conformity" (H-1040), "Conformity gives comelinesse to things." He does *not* cite, however, the second line, "And equall shares exclude all murmurings," a weighted omission.

11. Richard Lougy, "Herrick's 'The Hock-Cart, or Harvest Home,' 51–55," *Explicator* 23 (1964): item 13. Lougy's conclusion was disputed by Paul O. Clark,

Explicator 24 (1966): item 70, and, more polemically, by Roger B. Rollin, "Missing 'The Hock Cart': An Explication Re-explicated," *Seventeenth-Century News* 24 (1966): 39–40, and "The Decorum of Criticism and Two Poems by Robert Herrick," *CEA Critic* 31 (1969): 4–7. In "Missing 'The Hock Cart,'" Rollin concludes that "Robert Herrick is not, alas, a democrat, not a traitor to his class, but merely an ordinary (if outspoken) Royalist and Anglican—and an extraordinary pastoral poet."

"The Hock-cart" has been given simplistic readings in two Marxist considerations of pastoral poetry: Raymond Williams, "Pastoral and Counter-Pastoral," *Critical Quarterly* 10 (1968): 277–90 (reprinted in *The Country and the City* [New York: Oxford University Press, 1973]), and James Turner, *The Politics of Landscape* (Oxford: Basil Blackwell, 1979).

12. DeNeef, *"This Poetick Liturgie,"* p. 62.

13. Halli, "Robert Herrick's Epigrams on Commoners," pp. 37, 39.

14. For the influence of these two poems on "Upon Julia's Clothes," see Dale B. J. Randall, "The Roman Vibrations of Julia's Clothing," *English Language Notes* 21 (1984): 10–16.

For a much milder parody of Herrick's characteristic stance, compare a song in Davenant's *News from Plimouth* (performed 1635), a lower-class version of "Corinna's going a Maying":

> O Thou that sleep'st like *Pigg* in Straw,
>   Thou *Lady* dear, arise;
> Open (to keep the *Sun* in awe)
>   Thy pretty pinking eyes:
> And, having stretcht each Leg and Arme,
>   Put on your cleane white Smock,
> And then I pray, to keep you warme,
>   A *Petticote* on *Dock*.
> Arise, Arise! Why should you sleep,
>   When you have slept enough?
> Long since, French Boyes cry'd Chimney-sweep,
>   And Damsels Kitching-stuffe.
> The Shops were open'd long before,
>   And youngest Prentice goes
> To lay at's Mrs. Chamber-doore
>   His Masters shining Shooes.
> Arise, arise; your Breakfast stayes,
>   Good Water-grewell warme,
> Or Sugar-sops, which *Galen* sayes
>   With Mace, will doe no harme.
> Arise, arise; when you are up,

> You'l find more to your cost,
> For Mornings draught in Caudle-cup,
> Good Nutbrown-Ale, and Tost.

15. Gordon Braden, "Robert Herrick and Classical Lyric Poetry," in *The Classics and English Renaissance Poetry: Three Case Studies* (New Haven: Yale University Press, 1978), pp. 157, 161.

16. See also "Upon one who said she was always young" (H-462) and "Of Horne a Comb-maker" (H-595).

17. "To women, to hide their teeth" is immediately followed by an epigram "In praise of women" (H-739) that demonstrates again Herrick's self-mockery:

> O *Jupiter*, sho'd I speake ill
> Of woman-kind, first die I will;
> Since that I know, 'mong all the rest
> Of creatures, woman is the best.

18. See such poems as H-409, -428, -474, -648, -816, and -1079.

19. See Halli, "Robert Herrick's Epigrams on Commoners," p. 40. There are other instances where epigrams of praise are surrounded by compromising epigrams of mockery, such as the two poems on the marriage of Henry Northleigh to Lettice Yard (H-313, -314) offering them good wishes for a male heir. But the following poem (H-315) documents the murderous treachery of a greedy heir. After two poems to Bridget Lowman (H-354A, 355) praising her as the "Deity" of springtime and the emblem of rebirth, there follows "Upon Judith. Epigram":

> *Judith* has cast her old-skin, and got new;
> And walks fresh varnisht to the public view.
> Foule *Judith* was; and foule she will be known,
> For all this fair *Transfiguration*.

The Lowman, Northleigh, and Yard families were the leading families in Herrick's parish. Herrick's mockery is clearly not limited by class boundaries, but only made indirect.

20. See Alexander Wied, *Bruegel,* trans. Anthony Lloyd (London: Cassell; New York: Macmillan, 1980), p. 126.

21. Amy Richlin, *The Garden of Priapus: Sexuality and Aggression in Roman Humor* (New Haven: Yale University Press, 1983), pp. 30–31, 58–61.

22. Anthony Low, *The Georgic Revolution* (Princeton: Princeton University Press, 1985), pp. 263, 273. Low presents a great deal of evidence to substantiate his view of Herrick as a "subtle and imaginative" poet of the realistic countryside. Yet, finally, he backs away from his own interesting conclusion, returning to the conventional view of Herrick vigorously espoused by Raymond Williams and James Turner, critics who influence *The Georgic Revolution* throughout.

NINE The Epigrams of Advice

1. "To Dean-bourn" (H-86) seems to be a vehement rejection of Devonshire:

> Dean-Bourn, farewell; I never look to see
> Deane, or thy warty incivility.
> Thy rockie bottome, that doth teare thy streams,
> And makes them frantick, ev'n to all extreames;
> To my content, I never sho'd behold,
> Were thy streames silver, or thy rocks all gold.
> Rockie thou art; and rockie we discover
> Thy men; and rockie are thy wayes all over.
> O men, O manners; Now, and ever knowne
> To be *A Rockie Generation!*
> A people currish; churlish as the seas;
> And rude (almost) as rudest Salvages
> With whom I did, and may re-sojourne when
> Rockes turn to Rivers, Rivers turn to Men.

It is not, however, the complete renunciation that it may seem. The conclusion of the poem is a self-mocking joke, since he has just turned rivers into rocks and men into rivers in the imagery of his poem. He denounces Dean Prior, but, after exploding his frustration, he inverts his rejection with poetic irony. After all, "loathed" Devonshire and poetic inspiration remain cleverly linked in "To Dean-bourn." Roger Rollin suggests in his "prolegomenon" to further study of Herrick's poetry with which he prefaces *"Trust to Good Verses": Herrick Tercentenary Essays,* ed. Roger B. Rollin and J. Max Patrick (Pittsburgh: University of Pittsburgh Press, 1978), p. 9, that "no study of the psychological patterns of *Hesperides* should fail to take into account the tensions *within* his bucolic vision . . . and also the tensions *between* that vision and its alternative, which might loosely be termed Herrick's 'urban vision.'"

2. Lawrence Manley, "Proverbs, Epigrams, and Urbanity in Renaissance London," *English Literary Renaissance* 15 (1985): 247–76. Manley argues that the epigram became the voice of Renaissance London. Furthermore, "by the end of the sixteenth century, the Latin epigrams of Martial had become the nearest classical equivalent to what English poets regarded as their own sense of urbanity" (pp. 256–57).

3. Herrick, *The Poetical Works,* ed. L. C. Martin (Oxford: Clarendon Press, 1956), p. 536; *The Complete Poetry of Robert Herrick,* ed. J. Max Patrick (New York: New York University Press, 1963), p. 230.

4. Martin, p. 535.

5. The last line of the poem echoes Horace's First Ode, where Horace asks Maecenas for his favor.

6. Marchette Chute, *Two Gentle Men: The Lives of George Herbert and Robert Herrick* (New York: Dutton, 1959), p. 189; [P. J. Croft], "Robert Herrick's Poetical Commonplace Book (Lot 146)," *Bibliotheca Phillippica: Catalogue of the Celebrated Collection of Manuscripts Formed by Sir Thomas Phillipps, Bt. (1792–1872)* (London: Sotheby Sales Catalogue, 28–29 June 1965), p. 134.

7. "To the High and Noble Prince, GEORGE, Duke, Marquesse, and Earle of Buckingham" (H-245):

> Never my Book's perfection did appeare,
> Til I had got the name of VILLARS here.
> Now 'tis so full, that when therein I look,
> I see a Cloud of Glory fills my Book.
> Here stand it stil to dignifie our Muse,
> Your sober Hand-maid; who doth wisely chuse,
> Your Name to be a *Laureat Wreathe* to Hir,
> Who doth both love and feare you *Honour'd Sir.*

8. See Martin, pp. 526–27; Patrick (p. 173) raises a question about Martin's dating of the poem and suggests that such rumors were also current during the civil war. Sir Simeon Steward, however, was apparently dead by 1629 (see *DNB* and T. G. S. Cain, "Robert Herrick, Mildmay Fane, and Sir Simeon Steward," *English Literary Renaissance* 15 [1985]: 312–17).

9. Williams was imprisoned in the Tower from 1637 to 1640 and was charged with "betraying the king's secrets and with subornation of perjury." The case for revealing state secrets was weak, trumped up by Laud, Williams's enemy. Williams foolishly panicked, however, and tampered with a witness. As well as being imprisoned, Williams was slapped with an enormous fine of £10,000. There was a great deal of public sympathy for Williams: see Jonson's poem, *Under-wood*, 63. See B. Dew Roberts, *Mitre and Musket: John Williams, Lord Keeper, Archbishop of York, 1582–1650* (London: Oxford University Press, 1938).

10. Anthony à Wood is quoted in Martin, p. xiv.

11. Martin, p. xv.

12. Dell's private note was not dated and is conjecturally attributed to 1640 in *C.S.P. Dom* [1640?], vol. 474, no. 77.

13. "The suspition upon his over-much familiarity with a Gentlewoman" is followed by the epigram "Single life most secure":

> Suspicion, Discontent, and Strife,
> Come in for Dowrie with a Wife

and then by the song "The Curse," which begins "Goe perjur'd man . . ."

14. Herrick actually addresses his poem to Lady Mary Villiers, who was

Buckingham's daughter; he clearly meant Ann Villiers (Lady Dalkeith), since he calls Buckingham her "brave exalted Uncle." Herrick gets names and relationships wrong in other civil war poems to nobility as well, which may reflect his long absence from the court.

15. It is not possible here to duplicate the typography of *Hesperides*. Most of the Stuart poems and some of the epigrams of praise to high-ranking nobility are set in a variety of large types.

16. Eugene A. Andriette, *Devon and Exeter in the Civil War* (Newton Abbot, Devon: David & Charles, 1971), pp. 109–22. I am indebted throughout to Andriette's excellent study for the details of the Devonshire campaigns.

17. Andriette, *Devon and Exeter*, pp. 135–51.

18. Ibid., p. 144.

19. "Sylla's Fortune" is a reference to Lucius Cornelius Sulla (138–78 B.C.). During the Italian civil wars, Sulla soundly–and mercilessly–defeated his opposition, which relied upon freed slaves. Sulla, as dictator, reinstituted the aristocracy.

20. Edward Everett Hale, Jr., *Die Chronologische Anordnung der Dichtungen Robert Herricks* (Halle: C. A. Kaemmerer, 1892). See also John L. Kimmey, "Order and Form in Herrick's *Hesperides*," *JEGP* 70 (1971): 255–68.

21. See Martin, pp. xxvii–xxxi.

22. Herrick writes an *Hesperides* epigram "To his honoured friend, Sir John Mynts" (H-526):

> For civill, cleane, and circumcised wit,
> And for the comely carriage of it;
> Thou art The Man, the onely Man best known,
> Markt for the *True-wit* of a Million:
> From whom we'l reckon. Wit came in, but since
> The *Calculation* of thy Birth, *Brave Mince*.

23. Edmund W. Gosse, "Robert Herrick," *Cornhill Magazine* 32 (1875): 176–77.

24. A. Leigh DeNeef, *"This Poetick Liturgie": Robert Herrick's Ceremonial Mode* (Durham, N.C.: Duke University Press, 1974), pp. 125–41; Barbara Herrnstein Smith, *Poetic Closure: A Study of How Poems End* (Chicago: University of Chicago Press, 1968), pp. 196–97.

25. Martin, p. 563.

26. Ben Jonson, *Sejanus His Fall*, ed. W. F. Bolton, New Mermaids Series (London: Ernest Benn, 1966). All references to *Sejanus* will be to this edition.

27. Bibaculus's epigrams are not extant. He first wrote lampoons against Caesar, then an epic poem, the *Annales*, on Caesar's Gallic Wars, and finally returned to epigrams, this time attacking Octavian (Gordon Williams, "Political Patronage of Literature," in *Literary and Artistic Patronage in Rome*, ed.

Barbara K. Gold [Austin: University of Texas Press, 1982], p. 12).

28. Pecke's anthology includes six centuries of Owen's epigrams, Martial's *De Spectaculis,* and thirty-seven poems of Sir Thomas More, including the epigram that describes the good king as the watchdog of his flock and the bad king as the wolf.

29. See Samuel R. Gardiner, *History of the Great Civil War, 1642–1649,* 4 vols. (London: Longmans, Green, 1911), 2:234–53; and Charles Carlton, *Charles I: The Personal Monarch* (London: Routledge & Kegan Paul, 1983), pp. 287–90. See also Herrick's later epigram "Care a good keeper" (H-989):

> Care keepes the Conquest; 'tis no lesse renowne,
> To keepe a Citie, then to winne a Towne.

30. Clarendon, *Selections from "The History of the Rebellion" and "The Life by Himself,"* ed. G. Huehns (1955; reprint, Oxford: Oxford University Press, 1978), pp. 6–7.

31. There is a reference in "TO THE KING AND QUEENE" to the talking oak of Dodona, a reference that is also borrowed from *Hercules in Aetna* (ll. 1473–74) and that therefore points up Herrick's connection between the poems.

32. Patrick, p. 38.

33. The epigram following "Obedience," "Another on the same," is borrowed from a proverb of Erasmus:

> No man so well a Kingdome Rules, as He,
> Who hath himselfe obaid the Soveraignty

that offers a sardonic commentary on the epigram "Like Pattern, like People" at midvolume (H-614).

34. Gardiner, *Great Civil War,* 2:233; see also Carlton, *Charles I,* pp. 286–88.

35. Quoted by Graham Parry, *The Golden Age Restor'd: The Culture of the Stuart Court, 1603–1642* (Manchester: Manchester University Press, 1981), p. 241.

36. See also "Rules for our reach" (H-990):

> Men must have Bounds how farre to walke; for we
> Are made farre worse, by lawlesse liberty.

And see Leah Sinanoglou Marcus's discussion of Herrick's Laudianism, "Herrick's *Noble Numbers* and the Politics of Playfulness," *English Literary Renaissance* 7 (1977): 108–26.

37. See Andriette, *Devon and Exeter,* pp. 56–57.

38. Document 9 in J. S. Morrill, *The Revolt in the Provinces: Conservatives and Radicals in the English Civil War, 1630–1650* (London: Allen & Unwin; New York: Barnes & Noble, 1976), p. 162. It was to Shapcott that Herrick addressed two of his fairy court poems of the 1620s, "Oberons Feast" (H-293A) and "Oberons Palace" (H-443). See also "To his peculiar friend Master Thomas

Shapcott, Lawyer" (H-444), where Herrick praises the "Candid Actions" of this "Brave" man.

39. Andriette, *Devon and Exeter*, pp. 102–8, 137, 154.

40. See, for example, Carew's "In answer to an Elegiacall Letter upon the death of the King of Sweden" and Michael P. Parker, "Carew's Politic Pastoral: Virgilian Pretexts in the 'Answer to Aurelian Townsend,'" *John Donne Journal* 1 (1982): 101–16.

41. Sir Philip Warwick, quoted by Carlton, p. 277.

42. "A *Prince* is a Pastor of the people. Hee ought to seere, no[t] to flea his sheepe; to take their fleeces, not their fels. . . . He is an ill *Prince* . . . that makes his Exchequer a receipt for the spoyles of those hee governs" (Jonson, *Works*, ed. C. H. Herford and P. and E. Simpson [Oxford: Clarendon Press, 1947], 8: 602).

43. Herford and Simpson, 8:599.

44. See Andriette, *Devon and Exeter*, pp. 75–77, 104, 136, 142.

45. Jonson, in turn, is borrowing from Lucan, 8.484–95, a passage he also translated separately; see "A Speech out of Lucan," in *The Complete Poetry*, ed. William B. Hunter, Jr. (New York: Norton, 1963), p. 350.

46. DeNeef, *"This Poetick Liturgie,"* p. 136.

47. Seneca, *Thyestes*, in *The Complete Roman Drama*, ed. George B. Duckworth, 2 vols. (New York: Random House, 1942), 2:759.

48. See *Notes and Queries*, n.s. 25 (December 1978): 512–13. I am indebted to Nancy Klein Maguire for information on the significance of *A King and No King* during the civil war and the Protectorate.

CONCLUSION "With my Lines, my Life must full-stop here"

1. Claude J. Summers, "Herrick's Political Counterplots," *SEL* 25 (1985): 167–71.

2. I am indebted to Roger Rollin's suggestion in the introduction to *"Trust to Good Verses": Herrick Tercentenary Essays*, ed. Roger B. Rollin and J. Max Patrick (Pittsburgh: University of Pittsburgh Press, 1978), pp. 6–11, that a psychoanalytic approach to Herrick might prove fruitful and, in particular, that a "search for the father" might form a significant pattern in *Hesperides*.

3. Thomas Bastard, too, ends *Chrestoleros* with a haunting reference to death:

> Nature which headlong into life doth thring us,
> With our feet forward to our graue doth bring vs:
> What is lesse ours, then this our borrowed breath,
> We stumble into life, we goe to death.
> (7.47; "De Hominis Ortu & Sepultura")

(Spenser Society, 1888; reprint, New York: Burt Franklin, 1967.)

4. Erwin Panofsky, "'Et in Arcadia Ego': Poussin and the Elegiac Tradition," in *Meaning in the Visual Arts* (New York: Doubleday, 1955), pp. 295–320; originally published as "Et in Arcadia Ego: On the Conception of Transience in Poussin and Watteau," in *Philosophy and History, Essays Presented to Ernst Cassirer*, ed. R. Klibansky and H. J. Patton (Oxford: Oxford University Press, 1936), pp. 223–54.

5.   Farewell, thou child of my right hand, and joy;
      My sinne was too much hope of thee, lov'd boy,
    Seven yeeres tho'wert lent to me, and I thee pay,
      Exacted by thy fate, on the just day.
    O, could I loose all father now. For why
      Will man lament the state he should envie?
    To have so soone scap'd worlds, and fleshes rage,
      And, if no other miserie, yet age?
    Rest in soft peace, and, ask'd, say here doth lye
    Ben. Jonson his best piece of poetrie.
    For whose sake, hence-forth, all his vowes be such,
    As what he loves may never like too much.
                (*Epigrammes*, 45; italics added)

6. Herrick, *The Poetical Works*, ed. L. C. Martin (Oxford: Clarendon Press, 1956), p. 546, n. 225.

7. John L. Kimmey, "Robert Herrick's Persona," *Studies in Philology* 67 (1970): 221–36.

8. The closing words of Ben Jonson's *Epigrammes* announce the erection of a monument by the city of London. Perhaps Herrick means to recall at the end of *Hesperides* Jonson's gesture of closure. If he does, it is a disturbing memory. The last poem of *Epigrammes*, "On the Famous Voyage," tells of the adventures of two knights, one "for brawne, and braine, right able," the other "a squire, of faire degree" who wallow down into an excremental underworld, "Sans'helpe of *Sybil*, or a golden bough,/Or magick sacrifice." The poet, inspired by the Muse of Hercules, leads them through a moonlit place of farting witches and working-class drunkards and out the other side:

    In memorie of which most liquid deed,
    The citie since hath rais'd a Pyramide.
    And I could wish for their eterniz'd sakes,
    My *Muse* had plough'd with his, that sung *A-jax*.

Index to Herrick and His Works

Index to Herrick and His Works

General Index

Addison, Joseph, 48, 227n. 14
Adorno, Theodor W., 218n. 7
Ahl, Frederick, 56
Alabaster, William, 140
Alcaeus, 175
Anacreon, 60, 75; and More, 64–65. *See also* Greek Anthology; *Hesperides:* and Anacreon
Anagrammata Regia, 111–12
Andriette, Eugene A., 254n. 16
Ariosto, Ludovico, 239n. 4
Aristotle, 46, 195
Arundel, Thomas Howard, earl of, 244n. 12
Asals, Heather, 218n. 8
Ashburnham, John, 192
Ausonius, 61, 232n. 52

Bacon, Francis, 205, 226n. 3, 240n. 7
Bancroft, Thomas, 111
Bartly, Arthur, 136
Bastard, Thomas, 78, 81, 83, 86–88, 113, 235n. 2; *Chrestoleros,* 33–40, 86–88, 226n. 13, 256n. 3; "de subiecto," 33, 35, 36–40, 86, 92, 120, 225n. 11; and Elizabeth I, 34–36, 87, 189, 199; and Harington, 35–36, 87–88, 189, 237n. 31; and Martial, 86, 227n. 28; and structure of *Chrestoleros,* 86–88, 92. *See also Hesperides:* and Bastard
Baugh, Albert C., 227n. 16
Beal, Peter, 238n. 41
Beaumont, Francis, 204, 256n. 48

Bedford, Lucy, countess of, 103, 241n. 14
Berkeley, Sir John, 181, 202
Bibaculus, 187–88, 254n. 27
Bishops' Order (1599), 82, 86
Bloom, Harold, 241n. 15
Boileau-Despreaux, Nicolas, 47–48
Braden, Gordon, 19, 118–19, 122, 128–29, 166, 168, 229nn. 25, 27, 243n. 6, 244nn. 7, 9
Britanniae Natalis, 220n. 23
Brixius, Germanus, 72, 233n. 57
Brooks, Cleanth, 3
Browne, William, 41, 93
Brueghel, Pieter, the Elder, 170
Buckhurst, Lord (Sackville, Thomas, first earl of Dorset), 84
Buckingham, George Villiers, first duke of, 179–80, 181, 192, 253nn. 7, 14
Burton, Robert, 50

Caesar, Augustus, 187–88, 254n. 27
Caesar, Domitian, 49, 55–59, 98, 101, 118, 216, 230nn. 33, 37, 231n. 40, 245n. 13
Caesar, Julius, 49–50, 187–88, 229n. 24, 254n. 27
Caesar, Tiberius, 55, 187, 189, 190; in *Sejanus,* 203
Cain, T. G. S., 219n. 12, 253n. 8
Camden, William, 78
Campion, Thomas, 109–10, 221n. 31, 230n. 27, 242n. 21
Carew, Thomas, 3; *Coelum Britannicum,*

265

General Index

General Index

Lightbown, Ronald, 244n. 12
Lindley, David, 223n. 50
Loewenstein, Joseph, 241
Lougy, Richard, 158, 249n. 11
Low, Anthony, 172, 251n. 22
Lowman, Bridget, 251n. 19
Lowman family (Devonshire), 180,
  251n. 19
Lucan, 256n. 45
ludi Florales. *See* Saturnalia

McClure, Norman, 227n. 16, 238n. 38
Machiavelli, Niccolò, 201
McPeek, James, 50, 229n. 26
McPherson, David, 241n. 14
Maguire, Nancy Klein, 256n. 48
Maitland, Thomas, 156
Manley, Lawrence, 252n. 2
Marcus, Leah S., 24, 59, 136, 217n. 3,
  223n. 47, 255n. 36
Marius, Richard, 72
Marlborough, Helen, 134, 224n. 1
Marlowe, Christopher, 84
Marotti, Arthur, 239n. 47
Marshall, William, 222n. 34, 245n. 13
Marston, John, 81–82
Martial, 25, 48, 49–59, 60, 81, 83–86, 88–
  89, 109, 242n. 22, 255n. 28; Book 1:
  dedicatory epistle, 52–54, 124–25; Ep.
  1.3, 120–24; and Domitian Caesar, 55–
  59, 67, 73–74, 98, 100–104, 111, 118, 172,
  216, 230n. 37, 231n. 40; and Catullus,
  49–50, 52, 55, 61, 105; country poems,
  51–52, 58; "epigrammaton linguam,"
  49, 52–53, 57, 58, 101–2, 124, 231n. 41,
  239n. 4, 246n. 14; and Jonson, 98,
  100–104, 105–6, 108, 123, 125, 241nn. 8,
  14; persona, 51–59, 85, 120–25, 211;
  structure of centuries, 53–59, 78–79,
  83–84, 85–86, 104, 119, 139–40, 237n. 28,
  243n. 6. *See also Hesperides:* and
  Martial
Martin, L. C., 117, 139, 148, 174–75, 180,
  219n. 21, 243n. 2, 244n. 9, 245n. 13,
  248n. 15, 253n. 8
Marvell, Andrew, 19, 221n. 33

Mary Tudor (queen of England), 79,
  235n. 10
Mary Stuart (queen of Scotland), 90
Masefield, John, 224n. 1
May, Edward, 232n. 52
May, Thomas, 147, 236n. 25
May Day. *See* Saturnalia
Melville, Andrew, 112–13
Mercurius Aulicus, 204
Meres, Francis, 78, 234n. 2
Miller, R. H., 238n. 38
Milligan, Burton, 227n. 16, 234n. 2
Milton, John, 9, 22, 48, 82
Miner, Earl, 19, 246n. 17
Minturno, Antonio, 46, 49, 227n. 6
Mirror of New Reformation, 112, 242n. 27
Moorman, F. W., 248n. 15
More, Sir Thomas, 41, 61–77, 78, 89,
  233nn. 54–60, 236n. 21; *Epigrammata:*
  coronation epigram, 65–68, 72, 76,
  233nn. 58, 60; and Greek Anthology,
  61–65, 70, 233nn. 54, 59; and Henry
  VIII, 65–68, 72–75, 234nn. 62, 64; and
  Martial, 67, 73; in *The Metamorphosis
  of Ajax,* 74–75, 81, 234n. 64; publica-
  tion, 65, 72, 226n. 17; in Renaissance
  anthologies, 41, 60, 61–62, 75, 226n. 17,
  255n. 28; structural and political import of epigrams, 65–76, 233n. 60. *See
  also Hesperides:* and More
Morphirir, 83
Moseley, Humphrey, 226n. 17
Murphy, Avon Jack, 246n. 2
Musgrove, Sydney, 226n. 16
Mynts, Sir John, 184, 254n. 22

New Model Army, 183, 191–92, 202
Northleigh family (Devonshire), 180,
  251n. 19

Oldisworth, Michael, 141–43, 154
Oldys, William, 242n. 23
Orgel, Stephen, 23
Ovid, 126, 216, 246n. 15
Owen, John, 83–84, 255n. 28

Parkhurst, John, 232n. 52
Parliament, 131, 141–43, 179, 183, 196, 198, 199, 200, 221n. 31
Parrot, Henry, 82, 240n. 5
Parry, Graham, 244n. 12
Parsons, Thomasin, 181
Partridge, Edward, 103
Pasquill, 83
pastoral, 23–26, 30–31, 82, 121–24, 147–48, 170, 172, 174–77, 189, 199, 221n. 27, 239n. 4
Patrick, J. Max, 13, 15, 148, 174, 193, 245n. 13, 248n. 15, 253n. 8
Patterson, Annabel, 106, 221n. 27, 242n. 20, 248n. 14
Pecke, Thomas, 45, 47, 62, 75, 111, 188–89, 195, 227n. 10, 255n. 28
Pembroke, William Herbert, third earl of, 45, 96, 101–3, 142
Pembroke and Montgomery, Philip Herbert, earl of, 142, 248n. 12
Penkethman, John, 236n. 18
Peterson, Richard, 241n. 8
Pindar, 175
Planudes, Maximus, 39
Pollard, Alfred, 219n. 20
Porter, Endymion, 145, 147–52, 157, 179, 248n. 15
Post, Jonathan F. S., 238n. 42
Poussin, Nicholas, 211
Praz, Mario, 47, 224n. 3, 242n. 21
Propertius, 126
proverb, 61, 78–81, 88–89, 92, 218n. 8
Proverbs (Bible), 112, 235n. 9
Prynne, William, 136
Puttenham, George, 82–83, 102, 235n. 8

Quinn, Kenneth, 49
Quintilian, 56, 105

Rabinowitz, Peter J., 218n. 7
Ralegh, Sir Walter, 88
Randall, Dale B. J., 250n. 14
Randolph, Thomas, 220n. 23
Rastell, Elizabeth More, 78
Rastell, Joan, 78

Rastell, John, 78
Reed, Mark L., 219n. 21
Reid, Anthony, 231n. 41
Richlin, Amy, 172, 236n. 17
Riddell, James A., 233n. 54
Robortello, Francesco, 46, 49
Roberts, B. Dew, 253n. 9
Rogers, Lady Jane, 88, 90
Rollin, Roger, 134, 246n. 1, 249n. 11, 252n. 1, 256n. 2
Roper, William, 234n. 62
Ross, Alexander, 19–20
Ross, David O., 229n. 23
Ross, Richard J., 156, 219n. 20
Rowland, Samuel, 82
Rupert, Prince, 192

Salisbury, Robert Cecil, earl of, 98–100
Salmasius, Claudius, 60
satire, 81–82, 103, 113, 226n. 3, 242n. 27
Saturnalia, 53, 59, 100, 124
Scaliger, Julius Caesar, 46, 49
Schleiner, Louise, 110
Sébillet, Thomas, 32
Selden, John, 135, 179, 244n. 12
Seneca, 193, 204, 255n. 31
Shakespeare, William, 8, 31, 32, 55, 84, 101, 145
Shapcott, Thomas, 198, 255n. 38
Sheppard, Samuel, 37–38, 40, 225n. 13
Shirley, Sir Charles, 111
Sidney, Sir Philip, 21, 32, 101
Simpson, Evelyn and Percy, 101
Smith, Barbara Herrnstein, 185
Smith, James, 184
Soame, Stephen, 136
Soame, Sir Thomas, 195–96
Soames, Sir William, 47–48
Solomon, 112, 137, 218n. 8
Somerset, Robert Carr, earl of, 221n. 31
sonnet. *See* epigram: and sonnet
Soter, Joannes, 59–60
Southey, Robert, 156, 165, 172
Southwell, Sir Thomas, 179
Spectator, 48
Spenser, Edmund, 8, 9

General Index